Platt Brothers and Company

Matthew W. Roth

Platt Brothers and Company

Small Business in American Manufacturing

UNIVERSITY OF CONNECTICUT

Published by University Press of New England/Hanover & London

University of Connecticut
Published by University Press of New England,
Hanover, NH 03755
© 1994 by the Trustees of the University of Connecticut
All rights reserved
Printed in the United States of America
5 4 3 2 1
CIP *data appear at the end of the book*

Contents

Illustrations

Acknowledgments

THE ERRORS are mine. The following people did their best to minimize them.

My greatest debt is to Bruce Clouette, now the sole owner of and formerly my partner in Historic Resource Consultants, Inc. In twelve years of working together he was my most insightful critic and warmest friend, and he laughed at my jokes (most of the time). His knowledge of primary sources and his skill as a social historian guided the research design, and his perceptive commentary kept the writing on track. I miss him every day.

There might be more helpful and congenial institutions than the Mattatuck Museum in Waterbury, Connecticut, but I doubt it. Its archive is conveniently housed and exhaustively cataloged. Deborah Grazier orchestrated my access with other researchers' needs and a staggering list of other uses for the space without ever letting me think that this one small project was any less important than the other demands on her time. Marie Galbraith and Dorothy Cantor directed me to many sources and, along with Jeanette Malick, were good company during coffee breaks and lunches. The magnificent Ann Smith directs this pleasant and productive crew. Her support, criticism, and friendship can never be repaid, but I do hope to chip away at my debt for copies.

Platt Brothers subsidized the research on which this book is based. On behalf of Platt Brothers, Richard Miller, retired vice president, contracted with Historic Resource Consultants to look into the history of his company. When I realized the larger significance of that history, Platt Brothers gave me the rights to the work so that I could write this book. The chairman, Orton Camp, Jr., and the president, Milton Grele, granted access to records, sat for interviews, and welcomed the most forthright approach to their history. Miller and retired treasurer Curtiss Hart also consented to interviews. The idea for this study originated with Richard Miller. From the day we met more than five years ago, he has not wavered in his interest or encouragement.

Fred Carstensen, of the University of Connecticut, and Laurence Gross, of the University of Massachusetts, Lowell, read drafts of the entire work. Both recommended research strategies and methods of interpretation, offered detailed criticism of the manuscript, and kept me abreast of appropriate works in their fields—business history from Carstensen, labor history from Gross, and the history of technology from both.

Thanks also to the staff at University Press of New England for all of their work and kindness; Professor Joel Kupperman, the University of Connecticut campus representative for University Press of New England, for shepherding the manuscript through review; the anonymous referees for the publisher, for broadening the arguments and sharpening the text; Kevin Seymour, for schooling me in family-firm literature; Dean Nelson, Museum of Connecticut History, for sharing his definitive knowledge of Civil War soldiers' gear and help with illustrations; Mark Tveskov, Department of Anthropology, University of Connecticut, for x-ray fluorescence testing of early buttons; and my new colleagues in Los Angeles, Janet Fireman, Don Chaput, Errol Stevens, Tom Sitton, Louise Coffey-Webb, and Dick Meier, for their help in seeing it through.

Patricia St. Clair never objected when this project took over a room in our house, and she rescued half a chapter after the computer ate it. Our daughters, Rebecca and Teresa, learned how to stay quiet so that I could write at home, and never asked me for refills of hot chocolate more frequently than once every half hour or so.

February 1993   M.R.
Los Angeles, California

Platt Brothers and Company

Introduction

THIS BOOK is a case study of one manufacturer, Platt Brothers and Co., that spans the industrial era in the United States. By following a single firm (and its direct predecessors) through the long history of industrialization, this story can address not only the causes and characteristics of manufacturing growth, maturity, and decline but also the relationships among those stages. Beyond establishing such causal connections over time, the story of this firm can illuminate aspects of business history that have only recently been understood as significant in the scope of America's manufacturing past: small business, family business, and the role of industrial regions. By placing this firm within its evolving contexts, this narrative also presents a long-term view of non-ferrous metalworking in the United States and the industrial history of Waterbury and Connecticut's Naugatuck Valley, the city and region that dominated the nation's non-ferrous metal production for three generations.

Focus on a single firm offers the chance to comprehend economic change in its human dimension. The story of these people, their ambitions, the difficulties they faced, and the solutions they devised provides modulation to the broader views of industrial history. If those generalizations require amendment to encompass businesses such as Platt Brothers, that change will only strengthen them.

Small Business in Manufacturing

Sixty years ago a leading historian of business could state that "the story of the New England cotton industry is the story of industrialization in America." Since then, as synthetic overviews and single-sector monographs have begun to deepen our understanding of the more common industrial experience of the nineteenth century, the capital-intensive production of staple goods that propelled industrialization in Waltham and Lowell have been recognized as unusual rather than typical. In her work on the paper manufacturers of western Massachusetts, Judith A. McGaw summarized the more representative productive enterprises of last century: "Most American factories were small concerns, owned by proprietorships and partnerships, located in small towns or rural areas, and operated by relatively modest work forces and locally resident entrepreneurs." To McGaw, the Industrial Revolution was "a story of small men and women making small decisions, accumulating capital, acquiring machines, and reordering work incrementally." That description precisely fits Platt Brothers and its early competitors and allies.[1]

In Waterbury's first generation of metal-goods production, lasting almost to the middle of the nineteenth century, limited investment capital caused a slow pace of growth. Capital for early manufactures came from the small margins of country storekeepers, mortgages of a few hundred dollars on farms and shops, and reinvestment of the meager revenues from initial operation. Even when banks and wealthy individuals started financing the Naugatuck Valley metals industries, they loaned or invested one or two thousand dollars at a time, not the hundreds of thousands marshaled by textile magnates. The career of Alfred Platt, who founded the firm that preceded Platt Brothers, offers an especially vivid example of bootstrap financing. He exercised every possible means to fund his ventures, from triple mortgages on his real property to loans against his household furniture.

This case study further provides a rare opportunity to examine the development of the commercial practices that were pivotal to the rise of fabricated metal-goods production. Particularly for Connecticut enterprises, the role of marketing has been obscured by the tenacious mythology of the smooth-talking, fast-dealing Yankee peddler, which ignores the system of commerce in which the peddlers' work was embedded. The trinket peddlers did not work independently but as employees of storekeepers in the producing towns. The storekeepers told the small "dooryard" shops what goods to produce and in what quantities. The romance of the peddler also slights the role of the commission merchants in the nation's major cities, who completely supplanted the peddler system by the 1830s. Effective commission merchants predicted changing styles, anticipated levels of demand, and coordinated the production schedule. They set prices by gauging customer needs and producer costs and by assessing general economic conditions. They suggested new products, evaluated prototypes, and acted as clearinghouses for information on materials and production methods. They designed packaging and labeling and monitored freight rates and insurance. Manufacturers who continued to rely on peddlers quickly perished.[2]

The commercial systems initiated by rural merchants and peddlers, and expanded by commission merchants, encouraged small manufacturing enterprise. By undertaking all of the sales and distribution tasks, they minimized the range of expertise and extent of investment required to start a manufacturing business and thereby stimulated the proliferation of small shops throughout Connecticut's metalworking region. A distinguishing trait among the handful of oligopolistic large firms that achieved dominance of the brass-products sector later in the nineteenth century was that they brought the marketing functions into the firm and bypassed the commission merchants. But the commission system did not simply represent a transitional phase through which successful manufacturers passed on the way to becoming big. It persisted into the middle of the twentieth century, connecting markets to producers and helping small metalworking shops. In the early 1930s, for instance, a hardware jobber from New York persuaded a near-dormant knitting needle manufacturer in Connecticut to adapt its tiny shop to make nutcrackers and nut picks, which sustained the business until the proprietor retired in 1975.[3]

Platt Brothers and its predecessors offer a superb illustration of how marketing influenced small producers. Alfred Platt disdained commercial manipulation, a sentiment reinforced by the setbacks he suffered at the hands of merchants. Consequently, although Platt and his sons achieved proficiency in production, they toiled at metalworking for almost twenty years before they profited consistently. That came only when they placed their trust in their selling agents, who then devised and implemented an astute marketing strategy, instituted long-range planning, and schooled the Platts in the ways of commerce.

Alfred Chandler, the leading historian of big business, recognized that all firms were small before 1850, but in effect he contended that only those that outgrew small size deserved description as "modern businesses." Chandler's powerful synthesis of the history of industrial capitalism depended on his definition of modern businesses as multiunit, hierarchically managed enterprises; it confined attention to areas in which mass marketing opportunities were accompanied by huge throughput increases, and omitted sectors that served more specialized markets and thrived without adopting mass production. Central to the experience of the sectors and enterprises that demonstrated Chandler's general propositions was the expectation of continued economy-wide and sectoral growth and the development of a managerial class and managerial strategies to capture growing markets. Chandler described the basic strategy as "productive expansion."[4]

Platt Brothers instead fits into the story of small business in manufacturing, which has only recently begun to take shape. Part of the difficulty and delay in addressing small business lies in its definition: what is small? Government agencies have adopted different numerical measures, but eligibility for Small Business Administration programs or General Service Administration set-asides circumscribe the subject too narrowly for the purposes of history. The absolute numbers vary dramatically and inconsistently over time; contextual figures necessary for constructing relative analyses are not always available; and it is far from certain that quantitative data alone provide sufficient means to track the performance of small, specialized firms.[5]

Functional characteristics offer favorable steps toward a definition. Mansel Blackford, in a recent survey of the historiography of small business, suggested that an approach directly opposite to Chandler's would provide the necessary delineation: small business is single-unit and nonhierarchical. This useful observation does not constitute a definition, however, because it describes small business in terms of what it is not—it does not fit the Chandler paradigm—rather than what it is.[6]

The ephemeral nature of many small businesses has contributed to the difficulty of strong characterization. In one small New England industrial city, thirty-four manufacturing firms with fewer than fifty employees opened between 1954 and 1961. In 1980 only eight of them survived, although another two dozen had begun since 1961.[7] Such firm-by-firm discontinuity poses special challenges in the effort to analyze any change over time in small business, and historians have attempted by several means to overcome this difficulty. Statistical overviews have demonstrated that the high closure rate of individual firms is roughly balanced by constant renewal in the form of start-ups, and that small business as a whole has consistently accounted for at least a third of the nation's manufacturing jobs during the industrial era.[8] In the aforementioned New England city, small shops as a group employed more people in 1961 than did the largest corporate-owned factories, which included a General Motors plant and the home facility of the nation's largest spring producer. But such statistical approaches, even at the level of a single community, offer no insight into the specific challenges faced by small producers, the tactics they developed to meet them, the motivations and rewards that drove the effort, or how the technology and labor of the production processes might have differed from those of large throughput enterprises.

Another method used to overcome the lack of candidates for long-term small-business case studies has drawn from cultural history to assert the importance of small-scale entrepreneurship in the American character, and to trace the political impact of ideology favoring small-scale proprietorship.[9] These efforts ultimately devolve into analyses of irrationality as the attempt to construct a significant cultural role for small business encounters the high closure rate of small firms. Cultural studies that do not examine business operations also overlook the paradox that large firms offered genuine efficiencies in many of the sectors attacked by small-business proponents (notably retail). Even when the "neorepublican dream" of virtuous proprietorship forced government action, the results often ran counter to the intent and benefited large enterprises at the expense of small ones. The Sherman Antitrust Act did not so much discourage the formation of large businesses as determine the legal form they would take, and the interpretation of the law arguably accelerated industrial combinations.[10]

The most cogent insights into small-business history first came from studies with a tight focus on a particular region. Geographic limits allowed the delineation of specific experiences at the level of the community, the firm, and even the household, and subsequent scholarly enterprise has begun to piece these contributions into broader patterns of small-business behavior. Such a lurching progression toward synthesis comes with the danger of provincialism; but that peril is worth contending with if the alternative is insipid generalization, and positive examples of regional inquiry demonstrate the magnitude of the reward. McGaw's work on Berkshire County paper production traced not only the course of regional industrialization but the role of this regional complex of modestly scaled firms in the creation of the larger industrial economy and society, including the relations between papermakers and the commercial hub of New York, regional competition for plant location in the nineteenth century, the interplay of managerial and proprietary concerns that conditioned technological change, and the creation of male and female spheres of work. Anthony F. C. Lewis's *Rockdale* offered a detailed examination of the technology, labor, and management of small-scale textile production in the early industrial period, embedded in the social and cultural history of a community in southeastern Pennsylvania. Multiple layers of interfirm relations, innovation through borrowing, depth of community involvement by proprietors, and the ability of personality and morality to influence business are aspects of small-scale manufacturing that emerged from this narrative.[11]

James Soltow addressed more directly the purpose of characterizing small-scale production in his study based on the experience of eighty machine builders and metal fabricators in eastern Massachusetts. Soltow did not view small firms as miscarried attempts to build large ones but identified critical attributes of small manufacturers based on their own experience. Thus, the measures of success were not growth but survival, a modest return on investment beyond the wages of owner-managers, and the exercise of some degree of independence. The overlay of sectoral focus provided

Soltow with a viewpoint sufficiently concentrated to discern the strategies critical to that success: capturing market niches, minimizing facility costs, and above all, maintaining a flexible and responsive approach to technology, markets, and organization.[12]

Though Soltow concluded that the contributions of small firms helped to distinguish the industrial economy of the United States, he saw small-scale manufacturing as symptomatic rather than causative. Just as the extent of a market determines the division of labor to serve that market, he argued that the large size of the American economy explained the emergence and tenacity of small shops as a group. In this view, small businesses represented simple differentiation of production, based on an increase in the diversification of intermediate and final products associated with economic growth. The promising qualitative distinction of small shops thus faded from significance in favor of statistical analysis, with all of the limitations noted above. This conclusion also failed to account for the prevalence of small firms in the early industrial period, before the scale and differentiation of the economy that, by Soltow's reasoning, would have fostered small business.

The experience of Alfred Platt can help to refine these views of small business by elucidating the goals he sought to achieve and the strategies he conceived to fulfill them. Alfred Platt sought and gained the economic rewards of manufacturing while resisting the massive increase in scale of operations that most often serves as the gauge of business success. He kept his metalworking company small because he preferred to continue his other occupations of farming and gristmilling alongside his manufacturing ventures, instead of pursuing industry with relentless single-mindedness. He also valued independence and self-determination, which to him meant retaining the family-based partnership, rather than the corporation, as the organizational structure of his enterprise. In these choices Platt did not merely seek nostalgically to preserve the attributes of his eighteenth-century boyhood. Although a certain stubborn simplicity is evident in what we know of Platt's personality, his goals reflected his times, not his father's. He did not stumble along to accidental success but made pointed selections among up-to-date technical and commercial practices.

Alfred Platt worked for fifteen years as a partner of Aaron Benedict, who built the Naugatuck Valley's largest nineteenth-century manufacturing corporation. Benedict's firm, Benedict and Burnham, started making buttons before 1820, then began making the brass used for buttons, and then produced an array of other goods from brass and other alloys. Platt's firm differed sharply from Benedict's. Platt always insisted on close control over the machinery and processes employed in his business, instead of withdrawing into a less-involved managerial role as Benedict did. Benedict led

Naugatuck Valley manufacturers in the sophistication of his marketing effort, the extent of investment he was able to attract, and his frequent reorganizations to take advantage of every change in the laws governing business. Platt shunned all of these tactics.

Platt, however, did copy Benedict's strategy of integrated production. Platt recognized that making the primary metal stock as well as fabricating the end products protected Benedict from cyclical downturns in either field, gave him some control over the material consumed in his fabricating operations, and permitted him and a handful of cohorts who headed similar enterprises to limit competition. To create such an integrated enterprise on a smaller scale, Platt and his sons built their firm around zinc, a cheaper, less widely used metal than brass.

Specialization in zinc was fortunate but not accidental; it was a positive decision that fulfilled Platt's basic purposes. Thus the story of Platt Brothers presents a view of industrial capitalism that is more complex than commonly recognized. Alfred Platt and his successors never pursued growth for its own sake. They examined how an opportunity for expansion helped or hindered their basic goal of self-determination based on family ownership and management, and on several occasions they rejected the rapid expansion that would have been necessary to respond to a specific market opportunity.

Before following this purposefully small firm into successive generations, it is first necessary to conclude as far as possible the functional definition of small manufacturing enterprise. Regional and sectoral focus on textile manufacture in Philadelphia provided the proving ground for the work of Philip Scranton, in which a new synthesis of American business history has begun to emerge.[13] Covering the years up to 1885, *Proprietary Capitalism* presented an alternative to the large-scale textile-based corporate industrialism that developed in eastern New England. Agility in response to market conditions, highly skilled adaptation of technology, and a pervasive ideology that favored proprietorship over purely numerical growth combined to shape a durable regional network of specialty goods producers and intermediate-process jobbers. In *Figured Tapestry*, which continued the Philadelphia textile story through 1941, Scranton charted the decline of flexible production under the stresses of evolving market relations; but he also raised a larger challenge: if the story of Philadelphia's proprietary capitalists cannot be told within the existing framework of business history, then the framework must change. In subsequent work incorporating case studies in different branches of metalworking (machinery and jewelry), Scranton formulated an inclusive approach to the history of American manufacturing enterprise.[14] Offered with a work-in-progress caveat, this effort deserves the thorough testing that Scranton himself prescribed.

Central to Scranton's argument is the balance of economic significance imputed between bulk and mass production versus batch and specialty production. Though the contributions of batch firms have been recognized before, Scranton placed them alongside bulk producers at the core of American industrial experience during the Second Industrial Revolution, the years between 1880 and 1930 that also witnessed the rise of big business. The study began with a survey of United States manufactures in the closing years of the nineteenth century, in which Scranton found numerous sectors in every class of production (infrastructure, producers' goods, intermediate goods, consumer goods) that did not adopt the techniques of standardized design, repetitive manufacture, and mass marketing. The example of furniture affords a simple comparison between batch and mass production. Making a chair consumed standard-size boards and standard nuts, bolts, and screws, but the chair itself differed according to fashion or seasonal market variations. The lumber mill and the screw maker could produce for inventory with relatively low risk, whereas the furniture maker much preferred to produce after confirmation of sale to prevent the stockpiling of goods that a volatile market could render worthless.

Far from peripheral, batch producers included the "Second Industrial Revolution's hallmark sectors" of specialty metals, machinery, and electrical goods, along with an array of other products with technological and cultural significance, as well as economic:

From locomotives to turret lathes, batch work helped define American technical prowess. From carpets to collar buttons, it shaped the image of American consumption. In a sense, batch capacities lay behind the aspects of national culture that resonated with constant change, suspected standardization and uniformity, and sustained the ideal of individualism expressed through purchase and display.

Beyond even the goal of an inclusive approach to manufacturing, in this view batch production demands recognition as crucial in American history.[15]

Platt Brothers offers a case study highly pertinent to Scranton's thesis because its products included two of those hallmark sectors. The Platts began primary processing of zinc, a specialty metal, in 1847, and the firm's renewal in the early twentieth century was based on electrical fuses. The Platts also contributed to the fashion-sensitive consumer goods sector by producing buttons and other apparel hardware for some 150 years.

In response to the narrow and ephemeral demand for their goods, specialty producers employed the strategies that Scranton identified as profusion, pricing, and proximity. The example of Platt Brothers supports and extends Scranton's observations based on these strategies, though not uniformly. Proximity of producers and the development of industrial regions will be examined first, then profusion and pricing will be considered together.

The strategy of proximity that Scranton ascribes to batch producers refers to the phenomenon of industrial regions that featured multiple linkages among firms engaged in the same sector. Concentrations of specialty manufacturers spread the risk of innovation among numerous participants and offered to each the chance to capture "external economies" in production through subcontracting. In all of these regions, groups of firms established systems of joint governance, such as manufacturers associations, to manage their contacts and to provide a mechanism for solidarity in crisis.[16] The case of Platt Brothers supports these observations for the period after 1880 that is covered by Scranton, but it also suggests a more formative role for regional complexes in the process of industrialization. Interfirm relations among nominal competitors were not just a survival tactic among batch producers extant after 1880 but an indispensable condition for the initial growth of industry in the Naugatuck Valley.

The community, not the firm, was the basic unit of industrialization in Connecticut's metalworking region. Limited capital dictated a structure of enterprise that could utilize resources and expertise beyond what was available in any single firm, even to Aaron Benedict in his early ventures. The early history of Platt Brothers cannot be understood except as part of a community-wide process distinguished by shared services and facilities, shared commodity supplies, the wide use of interfirm credit, and extreme fluidity in the ownership and structure of enterprises.

Profusion is the "capacity to create a wide range of intermediate or final goods and . . . [the] amassing [of] sufficient lumps of diverse demand to keep the works going." Building such capacity ran counter to maximum subdivision and simplification of labor, in favor of multipurpose equipment and diverse skills. In pricing, bulk producers developed techniques, notably collusion, to inhibit competition, thus assuring some level of profit on steady output of standard goods. Batch firms, however, negotiated at the point of sale, often through agents, and faced the vicissitudes of "visible market power relations, in which influence over prices was situational, shifting erratically from buyer to seller and back." Many firms that built diverse production capability and experienced the ups and downs of competitive market pricing grew in size to rival mass producers, especially "bridge firms" that pursued both mass and batch techniques. But if all batch producers were not small, certainly the great preponderance of small manufacturing firms were batch producers.[17] Examination of these strategies is indispensable in formulating effective evaluation of small business in American manufacturing.

The strategies of profusion and pricing most profitably coincided when a batch producer could "hit the market" with a novel item and reap the lavish, if transient, rewards of the sole-source provider. The marketing, product development, and production efforts of many small manufacturers constituted the search for this precise situation, although operations did not always resemble the organized program that statement implies. Just as often, the chance came from crisis, war, or other short-term market dislocations, and capitalizing on an unexpected opportunity meant scrambling to get the goods out faster than one's competitors could. Though Scranton mentions the concurrent implementation of profusion and pricing, the history of Platt Brothers indicates that this tactic was especially salient for small batch producers and that they applied it across a broad range of markets, including producers' goods, intermediate goods, and consumer goods.

This approach to productive enterprise fortifies the functional definition of small business in manufacturing that began with observations drawn from Blackford and Soltow: profitability for small producers depended on temporary price advantage in a market niche instead of multiplying standard outputs. Small firms also strived to maximize the life span of a fruitful niche and to produce as much as possible during that interval.

Platt Brothers and its predecessor firms demonstrate that this distinguishing trait shaded every aspect of small manufacturing enterprise. Long-term survival required constant, or at least periodic, product development work; as a niche advantage faded, others had to replace it. Unlike the research and development programs undertaken by large mass producers, small companies like Platt Brothers rushed samples or prototypes to market for rapid feedback so that promising articles could beat the trade and losers could be abandoned without further expense. The difficulty of sustaining that effort goes far toward explaining the high closure rate among small manufacturers, rather than any disadvantage inherent in the small size of a firm.

The search for profitable niches further provides positive meaning to Blackford's definition of small business as nonhierarchical: niche producers required close connection among market awareness, technical decision making in production, and the authority to commit financial resources to favorable opportunities. Bureaucratized management could not rapidly cross those functional boundaries. The close control of all aspects of their firm by Alfred Platt and his successors did not spring from longing for a simpler time but from the agility demanded by competitive markets for their products.

Platt Brothers also manifested another strategy in batch production that warrants insertion into Scranton's triad of proximity, profusion, and pricing. Near the end of the nineteenth century, some family members and their allies sought to begin production of buckles and other apparel items, in competition with the integrated brass companies that dwarfed their firm. The family owner-managers eventually decided not to undertake that production, despite the prospect of immediate, if not long-term, gain. In this strategy of avoidance, the Platts refrained from competition against much larger firms that could sustain loss pricing to gain or defend market share.

Counter to Chandler's model of "productive expansion," the strategy of avoidance reveals that growth was not the only path to long-term success in manufacturing; Chandler himself has recently recognized the need to explain the success of enterprises that do not fit his earlier view.[18] In pulling back from a growth opportunity, the Platts displayed sophisticated analysis of their markets, capabilities, and resources. Whether or not they belong in Chandler's category of "modern," their performance can certainly be described as managerial. The survival of the firm and the family's ability to retain control equated to success for its owners.

The Platts' experience, and that of thousands of other small manufacturers, points to a more central role for small business in American industry than previously accorded. The statistically high rate of closure among small manufacturers, which has obscured that central role, should not be mistaken for failure. Many who capitalized on a fertile niche financed expansion with the proceeds and outgrew the classification of small. The large, integrated brass firms of the Naugatuck Valley offer prime examples.[19] Other proprietors never reproduced the bounty of manufacturing for an exclusive demand, and closed operations after earning considerable wealth.[20] Platt Brothers' long-term survival as a small manufacturer reflected a middle course between expansion and closure—continued renewal of niche production at a modest scale.

Family Business

Since data have been available to chart the course of family firms, some two-thirds of them did not survive into the second generation of family ownership and only a tenth reached a third generation. The percentage that continued into a fifth generation, such as Platt Brothers, was infinitesimal. Despite this lack of endurance by individual firms, family-owned firms in aggregate presently account for about 40 percent of gross national product, half of national employment, and more than 90 percent of all businesses. It is not surprising that the long-term statistical significance of family business and the high rate of closure by family firms is similar to these patterns for small businesses: most small businesses were family-owned, and most family businesses were small.[21]

Chandler associated the "family business world" with the traditional forms of enterprise made obsolete by the rise of big business.[22] Other disciplinary viewpoints have also dismissed family business as an archaic or inconsequential survival, when it is found to exist at all.[23] Historical profiles of individual firms or families offer accounts of issues such as generational transition, successor training, the often difficult overlap of family and business relations, and the relationship between family owners or owner-managers and nonfamily managers. While most such works do not seek to characterize broader experience through their case studies,[24] occasional examples consider their subject firms within the larger spectrum of family-business history.[25]

Social scientists have devoted increasing attention to family business over the past twenty-five years. *Family Business Review,* a multidisciplinary journal that began publication in 1988, is devoted entirely to the subject.[26] Social science analyses of family businesses tend to seek prescription for active firms and those who would counsel them. Though limited, for the most part, to data from the second half of the twentieth century, these studies have established broad approaches that offer perspective on family business and some useful context for the history of Platt Brothers.

Social science interpretations fall into two general areas, the rational approach and the systems approach. They hold in common the premises that family businesses have distinctive characteristics and that both the business and the family must be studied in order to comprehend these firms. They differ in the value accorded to family participation. The earlier-developed rational approach has tended to view family ownership and management as an obstacle to long-term success, while the systems approach takes a less partial view.

The rational approach originally contrasted the emotion-laden nature of family life with the dispassionate judgment considered necessary for sound business management. The unrealistic view that the family should be partitioned from the business has been tempered by recognition that the loyalty and commitment of family members provide an uncommon advantage to such firms, and that family businesses hold no monopoly on poor judgment or decisions contaminated by irrationality. The most significant contribution of this approach was to focus attention on succession in management and ownership as the most obdurate barriers to family-business survival.[27]

The founder's role has accounted for a substantial part of the works within the rational approach, an appropriate concentration in light of the difficulty family firms encounter in surviving into a second generation. However, the chronological bias of this emerging field of study has tended to limit attention to men who came of age during the Depression, and the attempt to develop normative insight has relied on psychoanalytic concepts to explain the character of the entrepreneur. These concepts run the risk of extreme attenuation when applied to Alfred Platt, who belonged to a time and place in which entrepreneurship was more common in manufacturing enterprise, not a rare exception to the corporate industrial order. The principal contribution of this approach to understanding Platt Brothers is the observation that a strong founder can establish in a company fundamental characteristics that survive as long as the company does. The principal limitation in focusing on the personality of the founder is that it overlooks the many contingencies that shape the later embodiments of his vision.[28]

The application of systems theory to family business has produced an encompassing view that attempts to trace the interaction among all possible elements—the individuals, the family, the firm itself, and the "environment," which can include locality, markets, competitors, and technology, among other factors. Change in any of these elements can require response in any of the others. In the rational approach, this high degree of mutual influence causes the weakness of family firms, but the systems approach focuses instead, and more subtly, on how family firms respond to episodes of change in internal or external variables. Most of these findings have been applied, with reported success, in the diagnosis and counseling of family firms.[29]

Presentist bias tends to limit the variation in external variables. Extreme caution must therefore be exercised when applying these observations to the industrial experiences of earlier generations. Adding production equipment, for example, was not a straight-line decision based on measurable factors of cost and schedule, and the options for a manufacturer varied considerably across time. Does anyone make the needed machine? Is the capability of building machinery in-house available? Is it worth developing that capability to increase flexibility, to maintain the secrecy of a process, or to substitute in-kind expenditures for cash? The answers and the questions differ for diverse sectors and periods. A textile manufacturer could readily buy whole production machines in the 1830s, a buttonmaker not until the 1860s, and a garment maker in the 1870s. Systems-theory explanations of family business have not been tested in the complex arena of industrial history in its full chronological scope.

The most persuasive observations proceed from the view that the combination of task and kinship considerations create a larger system that is the family business itself. The systems approach is joined with organizational life-cycle theory to produce models in which overlapping spheres of family membership, business ownership, and business management account for the "phases and stages" of experience within the firm. Change or growth in the organization is recognized as discontinuous and can arise when accustomed patterns break down or respond poorly to a new situation, such as rapid expansion or contraction of the firm or the family, the aging or demise of a key participant, or even a natural disaster. A host of hypotheses offer different numbers of intervals to encompass the life cycle of enterprises (five and seven stages are the most popular),[30] but more important than these exercises in periodicity has been the provisional delineation of the distinctive structural and emotional attributes of family business.

Participants in family businesses fulfill simultaneous responsibilities in both spheres, each with the potential for benefit or harm to the business. Shared identity and lifelong common history that includes both family and firm can imbue a sense of common loyalty or have a stifling effect. Emotional involvement, the shared private language of the family, and mutual awareness among family members can improve communication, foster trust, and nurture a strong sense of mission; or they can trigger painful memories, create mixed feelings when the business appears to threaten family unity, leave some family members feeling trapped, and deny nonfamily managers access to critical information.[31]

When family and business goals coincide, the family firm can provide a most hospitable setting for the slow-growth or no-growth strategy noted above in the discussion of small business. Continuation of family ownership directs decision making toward long-term viability of the business rather than short-term profit considerations. Family ownership can therefore allow a business to remain static in size without viewing that condition as failure.[32] When success equates to survival and a modest financial return, the goals of the family firm overlap with the small manufacturer's strategies of seeking a series of market niches and avoiding competition against larger or oligopolistic foes. Beyond the statistical correlation between small business and family business, these operational similarities suggest that family ownership has a place in the functional definition of small business in manufacturing.

The issues of succession, successor training, and transition to nonfamily management address the critical episodes of change that determine continuance or closure for a family business. For family and nonfamily successors alike, the prescriptive literature identifies the same indicators for effective transition: clear designation of successors, training sufficiently long to inculcate in the successors the values and procedural complexities of the business, and latitude for the successors to adapt the firm to changing circumstances.[33]

Historical studies examining training and succession tactics extend these observations by demonstrating the range of responses conditioned by changing markets and technology. Scranton found in Philadelphia's textile concerns at the turn of the century a blend of "technical schooling and shop-based learning" that prepared proprietors' sons to assume superintendency and prolong family ownership for another generation. Among the midnineteenth-century cordwainers of Lynn, Massachusetts, William Mulligan related how new shoemaking machinery disrupted the transmission of skill within the family and helped to displace the family proprietorship from its role in shoe assembly despite the extensive training of clearly identified successors. The flexible production learned and later exercised by the young textile proprietors contrasts with the shoemakers' less elastic response to external changes.[34]

The history of Platt Brothers and its direct predecessor firms supports many of these efforts to explain family business. The influence of the founder emerges readily in the case of such a forceful and idiosyncratic personality as Alfred Platt. Beyond the distinctive approach to manufacturing that he imparted, the circumstances of the founding offer intriguing suggestion as to the connection between personal character and business strategy. He started the firm that became Platt Brothers when debt from his subsidy of a church-building project placed him in the worst financial condition of his life. He may have begun the company specifically to discharge those obligations. Though he later pursued the business for more worldly goals, a compelling, if necessarily speculative, relationship exists between long-term survival of the firm and its founding for reasons other than immediate economic reward.

The transition to his sons, Clark and William, revealed both the potency of his vision and the value of their long apprenticeship in translating that vision to a new economic and industrial order. Though Alfred built for future productive capacity, he did not provide a suitable institutional structure. Alfred had equated self-determination with the family-based partnership, but in resolving his estate the sons confronted its crippling effects. They had to extract from Alfred's vision the fundamental goal of autonomy and discard the organization he had contrived to achieve it, which they did by choosing the protection of incorporation. This transition also required the sons to revitalize the firm's ability to pursue the basic strategy of developing unique offerings with advantageous pricing in noncompetitive markets, by isolating their batch capacity from the products that had achieved regular demand. To do so they borrowed an organizational tactic from the brassmakers by splitting their firm into two: Patent Button Company for goods that had won steady business at high production volume, and Platt Brothers for primary metals and specialty goods. As their father had adopted the brassmakers' earlier strategy of vertical integration at a smaller scale, Clark and William Platt copied the brass firms' post–Civil War multiunit strategy that produced captive fabricators.

The next transition also required careful redefinition of manufacturing proprietorship. Corporate structure considerably eased the passing of ownership to the sons, daughters, and sons-in-law of Clark and William Platt, but the untimely death of their most technically proficient heir demanded novel approaches to managerial leadership. At Patent Button, the absence of capable new-product innovation, as well as a dulled appetite for the fray, relegated leadership to the selling agent, who preferred to buy out competing lines than to undertake aggressive new sales tactics. When this policy threatened autonomy by pitting the firm against the brass giants, the family hired a new manager for marketing (the function at which the Platts had never excelled), and his innovative strategies sustained the firm for another generation. Family members continued to serve as operating officers and to run various production and staff functions, but only by extending managerial leadership outside the family did they achieve their goal of continued ownership.

Platt Brothers in the early twentieth century suffered weakening in its long-term prospects. The goal of self-determined manufacture did not change, but the firm lacked the insightful blend of technical prowess and market awareness needed to sustain that goal. The owners resorted to financial and organizational tactics—the creation of a voting trust and the maintenance of a sequestered cash reserve—to erect obstacles to selling out. These methods carried the company into the 1920s, when two members of the next generation—Clark's and William's grandchildren—revitalized the strategy of seeking price advantage in specialized niches. The new owner-managers prepared for their roles by working in the plant since boyhood, attending elite universities for engineering training, and, for one of them, serving as a salaried manager at another firm. The range of responsibilities in specialty production and the rapid authority to carry them out required a close identification between ownership and management. To survive as a family firm in the early twentieth century, Platt Brothers required family management as well. A generation later, when the firm did turn to nonfamily management, the successful chief operating officer took office only after fifteen years of experience, including ten as manufacturing superintendent.

Family ownership provided the structure for and authority within Platt Brothers during its entire history but does not by itself account for survival into the late twentieth century. Because family ownership generally predicts extinction rather than endurance, the company's history can best reward our attention by identifying its differences from other small, family-based manufacturers. In that regard, the unshakable dedication to survival and the extensive range of adaptations to constantly changing circumstances are the most significant characteristics.

Starting with Alfred, the Platts accorded the highest priority to long-term survival under family ownership and based their policies on this elemental goal. Family members served long apprenticeships in the business, usually starting with arduous and low-paid tasks. When these younger members reached positions of responsibility, they were equipped with well-honed knowledge of the operations, and they were indoctrinated with the fundamental goal of long-term survival without being bound to specific products or policies. Upon assuming control, new family managers changed the business by reorganization; the introduction of different products, processes, or sales methods; the application of technical education; and the judicious placement of outsiders in critical areas of management.

The Naugatuck Valley

Connecticut's metalworking region merits study in its own right for its contributions to the nation's industrial economy. In 1860 the Naugatuck Valley produced 90 percent of the nation's basic brass products (sheet, tube, and wire that were fabricated into finished goods). A generation later, in 1890, the valley still produced almost three-quarters of the nation's output. The ready availability of basic brass products and other non-ferrous alloys stimulated an array of fabricating enterprises in west-central Connecticut, making buttons and other clothing hardware, pins and needles, builders' hardware, clocks, tableware, and ordnance. In the early twentieth century, the state's factories produced 77 percent of all the plated ware made in the United States and 39 percent of all the buttons, buckles, and other clothing hardware. Mere statistical recitations, however, can diminish appreciation of the larger impact wrought by the Naugatuck valley's metalworking sector. In their high-volume production and innovative marketing of light metal goods, the valley industries helped to usher in the consumer age.[35]

The region's industrial history, particularly its early history, has never been subjected to careful study. Henry Bronson's 1858 history of Waterbury is the departure point for virtually every examination of that era.[36] It was based on the notes of Henry's father, Bennet Bronson, a lawyer, merchant, and investor who reaped a fortune from his ties with Aaron Benedict and his associates. This participation gave an eyewitness quality to the Bronson history but also shortened its perspective. The transformation of the region to a vast industrial complex was not yet complete, and Bronson overlooked the everyday operations of the enterprises that caused that transformation. To him they were commonplace, not revolutionary, and the intricacies of ministerial succession in colonial churches received more attention than the work going on down the street. Overreliance on Bronson has misled subsequent chroniclers into minimizing the enormous effort and innovation that lay behind the region's industrial growth and contributed to a false sense of inevitability regarding the process.

Nearly fifty years after Bronson, Joseph Anderson, a Waterbury minister, compiled a massive history of Waterbury and nearby towns.[37] The Anderson work belongs to the genre of commemorative institutional histories that flourished in the late nineteenth and early twentieth centuries. Though it offers a wealth of biographical data and details of corporate ownership and management succession, manufacturing appears as monolithic as well as inevitable. In Anderson, the only differences among the region's manufacturing firms are the identities of the owners, the size of investment, and the list of products.

Waterbury and the Naugatuck Valley had to wait only a little more than twenty years before William J. Pape, publisher of the city's largest newspaper, issued the next commemorative history.[38] Similar in structure and approach to Anderson, Pape's work provided much additional detail, particularly on the World War I period. The short interval between the two histories emphasized the increasing pace of change in the region and suggested that the populace, or at least one of its more careful observers, felt the need to explain fast-moving events. In common with Bronson and Anderson, Pape offered scant data on non-Yankee residents beyond brief accounts of parish churches and clergy.

Theodore Marburg's 1956 case study of Smith and Griggs Manufacturing Company, a fabricator that officially began operation in 1865, was the first account of a Waterbury metalworking firm based on systematic examination of primary records.[39] It offered an authoritative view of the interlocking relationships among the region's metals firms but suffered from two significant blind spots in its interpretations. Despite the title of the book, *Small Business in Brass Fabricating*, Smith and Griggs originated as a captive fabricator to two of the "Big Five" brassmakers of the post–Civil War period; Marburg told more about this one aspect of large multiunit brass enterprises than about small business. Marburg also slighted the context that could have illuminated the multiunit strategy, failing to recognize that Smith and Griggs's nominally independent corporate origin reflected an organizational response to post–Civil War consolidation in the brass industry.

In the immediate aftermath of the Civil War, fabricators with abundant wartime earnings pushed more precarious firms to failure by means of sacrificial pricing. The shrinking number of participants put an end to the feverish competition in many fabricated goods. The five major brass firms effectively divided up the markets for consistently remunerative items. They all established subsidiaries to offer limited product lines that enjoyed regular demand and therefore could utilize routinized production processes. Not all of the captive fabricators were founded as direct subsidiaries. Some represented outright acquisitions (both friendly and hostile) by the integrated brass firms, and others were controlled through interlocking ownership or directorship. The parent brass firms retained production of primary metals and those fabricated goods with irregular demand (thus becoming the archetypal "bridge firms" that combined mass and batch production).[40]

The presidents of two large brass firms controlled the stock of Smith and Griggs, and the differences between its management and that of Platt Brothers owed much to that dependent relationship. From the start, a majority of Smith and Griggs's work came from customers passed along by a buckle-making company controlled by the large brass firms. Rather than seeking new offerings to sustain profits, Smith and Griggs relied on pool agreements among the buckle makers. When garment makers or hardware jobbers solicited help in developing new products, Smith and Griggs referred them to others. In the twentieth century, Smith and Griggs passed up opportunities to gain customers in the newly important automotive and electrical fields in favor of increased reliance on long-term regular customers. When orders fell in the early 1930s, Smith and Griggs cut its prices to maintain production volume, which served only to drain assets before the company ceased operation in 1936. Far from the obituary of small manufacturing that Marburg implied, his work instead documented the loss of vitality in captive enterprises that sprang from market manipulation on the part of larger firms.

More recently, two social historians have produced illuminating works on Naugatuck Valley industrial history.[41] Bucki's *Metal, Minds and Machines* contributed the first analyses of immigration and ethnicity, the everyday lives of working people, and the processes and environments of labor in the brass industry. Though it ended in the 1920s, it is a sturdy accomplishment to which every subsequent study of the region owes a debt (including this one). Brecher's *Brass Valley* addressed workers' lives in the twentieth century. It is a rich and reliable chronicle of ethnic neighborhoods and institutions, labor unions and strikes, and selected technological changes in the brass industry. Though eloquent on the impact of industrial decline and disinvestment in the region, it attributed that decline to callous, greedy, absentee corporate ownership. Without contending that the corporate managers who presided over the closing of the brass plants were any more virtuous than the general run of humanity, or that the distress they endured compared to that of the displaced workers, the abrupt loss of industry in the Naugatuck Valley cannot be understood without considering its markets. Since World War II, demand has fallen for the high value-added fabricated goods on which the region thrived, as plastics have replaced nonferrous alloys in many uses, such as apparel hardware, builders' hardware, cosmetic cases and jewelry, cameras, and wiring devices. *Brass Valley* brackets Bronson's history in unintentional and ironic fashion: together, the two works provide invaluable direct witness to the beginning and end of the region's industrial history, while overlooking the larger forces that shaped those eras.

The history of Platt Brothers traces a long trajectory from the typical to the unique. Embedded initially in the local experience of industrial growth based on non-ferrous metal goods, for two generations the company thrived by complementing the offerings of the larger firms in its region and its sector and selectively borrowing some of their organizational schemes. At the same time, its founder charted a course apart from his peers, distinct in its goals and the means to achieve them, and adaptations of the vision he transmitted sustained the firm to the present. Though representative in many ways of family business, Platt Brothers' five-generations-long record of family ownership is highly unusual, especially in manufacturing. That prolonged record also distinguishes the firm among small businesses and batch manufacturers although, again, there is much in its history that characterizes most such enterprises. The most striking divergence between Platt Brothers and its setting is the company's continuing prosperity, when the Naugatuck Valley's once-dominant metals firms have closed or left.

The history of Platt Brothers offers a means of understanding that industrial decline and flight, not a prescription that could have changed it. Its long-term survival as a small, family-owned, Naugatuck Valley metals firm represents one polar extreme of performance in all of those categories. There are scant lessons in it, though, because the conditions of that performance cannot be reproduced. History instead offers perspective on the shifting relationships between intention and situation that underpinned this successful enterprise. Recent proposals to renew industrial production by imposing flexibility and innovation[42] would gain credibility (and lose emotional impact) by considering more fully the layers of circumstance from which successful examples emerge, rather than isolating the hoped-for prototypes outside of history.

"A Sett of Rolls for Hard Metal"

ALFRED PLATT (1789–1872) presided over the transition of his family's livelihood from farming to manufacturing. His father, Nathan Platt (1761–1845), had initiated the family's involvement with the entrepreneurial mechanics of the Naugatuck Valley. Before them, the first five generations of Platts in Connecticut all worked the land. The four generations that followed all headed manufacturing firms. Long after Alfred Platt had passed from the scene, the firm he founded remained small while those of his early peers reached massive scale. Later still, the company continued to prosper when much of the region's industrial capacity had closed or fled. These atypical qualities of the family business can be attributed to the distinctive character Alfred Platt imparted to his enterprises.

Most of what we know of Alfred Platt comes from his transactions: deeds, loans and other financial obligations, account books and ledgers from the last third of his life, and business agreements. Most striking among those transactions are the difficulties he encountered from the depth of his devotion to his Baptist faith. His legacy differs from that of other early industrial proprietors because of the long-term survival of the family enterprises, but in his day Alfred Platt was most distinctive among his peers for risking all he owned in support of his parish.

Platt also differed from his fellow industrialists in the high priority he placed on land ownership throughout his life. In common with his contemporaries, Platt established manufacturing enterprises within the social and economic structure of small-scale farming, in which real property was the only significant asset for many. The early entrepreneurs all relied on land and the value it held as a means to finance industrial ventures. But while others sold or traded away land, Platt used his to secure mortgages that allowed his continued use of the property. He held resolutely to a family economic base that included farming and traditional processing enterprises, notably a gristmill. Metalworking production had a place in his vision, but it never eclipsed his other pursuits to become the sole focus of his economic ambition.

Tracing to their origins the distinctive nature of Alfred Platt's industrial ventures requires a collateral examination of the regional, and ultimately national, economic transformation in which he took part. This chapter examines that regional experience of incremental production growth, small-scale manufacturing interwoven with farming, and reliance upon the skills and resources of a community of nascent manufactures. It also sketches in the youth and middle years of this unusual participant and his role in the larger picture of the transition from an agricultural to an industrial economy. That story begins in the waning years of the eighteenth century, with a young boy's arrival on the banks of the Naugatuck River in Waterbury.

The first of the Connecticut Platts, Richard and his wife, Mary, arrived on these shores in the 1630s with the small band of English Puritans who first settled the New Haven Colony. In 1639, following a typical pattern among the people of colonial Connecticut, the Platts joined with sixty-five other families to settle the new town of Milford, seeking more and cheaper land than was available in New Haven. Their son Josiah (1645–1725) and his son, Josiah II (1679–1759), spent their lives farming in Milford. Josiah III (1707–1795), responding to the same land pressure and economic ambition that drove his forebears to Milford, sought property beyond that town. In 1729 he obtained a small land grant in Waterbury, but the best farmsteads had already been staked out. Josiah III spent a decade cultivating the steep, rocky hillsides of the Naugatuck Valley, then moved further west to Newtown, in upper Fairfield County. He donated his Waterbury land to the town's Congregational Church, reserving five acres for the pastor, Mark Leavenworth. Josiah III spent his life farming in Newtown and subdivided his holdings there for his children to farm.

Josiah III's grandson, Nathan Platt, reached maturity during the Revolution, and he served in the Continental army. By the late 1790s, when Nathan and his wife, Ruby, had two sons and needed land, the Platt holdings in Newtown could not be subdivided any further without creating farmsteads too small to support a family. Just as the third generation in Milford had to look elsewhere for land, so did the third generation in Newtown need to move if they hoped to prosper. Nathan and Ruby, however, came from that generation of Connecticut people who encountered a fully settled state. Tens of thousands of their contemporaries left Connecticut, settling entire new towns in New Hampshire, Vermont, western New York and Pennsylvania, and the Western Reserve (Ohio). Nathan Platt belonged to a smaller group who sought to overcome the limitations of the state's agricultural land by processing commodities rather than raising them. In 1797 he did not follow his family's history of looking north or west but instead looked east, to the more thickly populated Naugatuck Valley.[1]

Nathan Platt probably came to Waterbury with the help of Mark Leavenworth, the grandson of the minister who had received the land from Nathan's grandfather. This younger Leavenworth, an innovative merchant-industrialist, established buckle-making and clock shops that were direct precursors of the large, integrated metals firms that would later dominate the Waterbury economy. Leavenworth began his career as an apprentice to Joseph Hopkins, who made silver-plated trouser buckles and other clothing hardware. In 1797, after a long career in numerous small manufacturing enterprises, Hopkins sought to sell his property, and Nathan Platt came along to buy it. The sale included thirty acres with a house, barn, gristmill, and sawmill, plus half the rights to a dam and water privilege on the "Great River," near the southern end of Waterbury. The dam was the only developed waterpower site on the Naugatuck in Waterbury and would remain so for some fifty years. This property, especially the waterpower, was the central asset in the manufacturing ventures that Nathan's son and grandsons would develop.[2]

For more than twenty-five years prior to the Platts' arrival, Hopkins and other mechanics had attempted to capitalize on the waterpower. Though their success was mixed, their experience did offer some benefit to the Platts, and their use of the site makes clear that when Nathan Platt moved to Waterbury, he had something different in mind from his contemporaries who sought land for a growing family.

The industrial use of the Naugatuck mill site began in 1772, when Lemuel Hoadley bought the property and built the first dam and races. Hoadley sold half of the water rights to Joseph Hopkins. These two men and various members of their families, notably Hoadley's brother Calvin and Hopkins's son Jesse, began several processing enterprises on the site—a sawmill, a gristmill, a flax-breaking mill, and a nailworks. A different partnership ran each of these enterprises, and ownership of the facilities grew very complex through mortgages and distributions among partners. The buildings probably had multiple uses, at least for short periods, and it is unlikely that all of the processes ever operated simultaneously. The sawmill and gristmill exemplified the typical applications of waterpower in the agricultural economy. By substantially reducing the human labor necessary in the basic functions of grinding grain and sawing lumber, such mills allowed the nearby farm families to devote their labor to agriculture. The flax-breaking mill altered somewhat the traditional distribution of labor by mechanizing a task previously performed in the household. The nailworks, headed by Jesse Hopkins, represented a significant departure from these other ventures: instead of providing a product for local consumption, Hopkins wanted to sell nails throughout the nation. This ambitious project demanded more power than did the other enterprises. By 1796 the Hopkins family had gained control of the entire water privilege, and Jesse Hopkins had erected a separate building for his nailworks.[3]

Jesse Hopkins, a metalworking artisan like his father, was also a visionary industrial promoter whose plans resembled those of several others in Waterbury. With his partner, Jared Byington, Hopkins learned or created what amounted to high-technology metalworking of his day: slitting rolls for cutting iron. Petitioning the state legislature in 1795 for a $5,000, no-interest loan to develop the nail business, Hopkins and Byington claimed "that they have invented a machine for the manufacture of cut nails which promises great advantage in the expediency of making, as well as in the quality of the nails. Their machine is so constructed that they can cut their nails lengthwise." Accompanying the Hopkins petition was an affidavit from a man who used the nails: the machine was not just a scheme but an actuality. Nathan Platt moved next to one of the few mechanized metalworking operations in the state.[4]

The petition of Hopkins and Byington reveals a great deal more about these country mechanics of central Connecticut, the men whom Nathan Platt joined when he came to Waterbury. They believed that mechanized production offered many advantages beyond the specific attributes of their nail-making process. (On that score they argued that the slitting process, by cutting with the grain of the iron, offered stronger nails than the traditional blacksmith method of cutting them "crosswise of the iron.") They claimed speed and adaptability: "This machine enables the manufacturer to cut nails about four or five times as fast as they are cut in the common method and also to cut all sizes in use." They offered fuller use of scarce material and suggested some economy to the customer, although, as careful Yankees, they hedged the latter claim: "[The nails] will count more to the pound and will probably be afforded at a lower price." The petition demonstrated an intent to sell the nails beyond the local market through merchants in distant cities, as well as an astute commercial sense that saw not only the opportunity afforded by elevated production but the problem of creating a glut: "By encouragement from Merchants in Philadelphia and New York we find there is no danger of overstocking the market in that article."[5]

Hopkins and Byington were also keenly aware of the implications for material supply that came with the dramatic rise in volume they claimed for their machine. They hoped to develop primary production of the metal they consumed—a large rolling mill to make the bar iron to slit—exhibiting the same impulse toward vertical integration into material supply that led neighboring entrepreneurs fifteen and twenty years later to pioneer America's primary production of brass in Waterbury: "Your petitioners find that to establish the business on a respectable and profitable basis we must have a rolling mill annexed to our manufactory, as depending on foreign mills for supplies will subject us to frequent disappointment and much greater expense."[6]

Their concept of manufacturing enterprise was recognizably modern. It embraced market potential and access, technical expertise including innovation based on powered operations, the full range of production needs, and finance. This last need thwarted their ambition and brought them before the legislature: "[The rolling] Mill, the necessary buildings & machinery, and stock sufficient to introduce and prosecute the business requires a Capital larger than is at present in our power to raise." It was larger than anyone but a handful of the urban mercantile elite could have raised. In a society where real property was the basis of wealth, where money was extremely scarce, and where goods and services were bought and sold through the device of account book entries among the parties to a transaction, liquidity of the scale required simply did not exist. More than anything else, this lack of capital limited the growth of central Connecticut's early metalworking industries.[7]

After the General Assembly denied the loan request in October 1795, the Hopkinses raised capital by selling some of their property, which brought the Platts onto the scene. Joseph Hopkins's 1797 sale to Nathan Platt specifically excluded Jesse's nailworks and half of the water rights. Platt paid about $1,700, less than the Hopkinses needed, and offered only a portion in cash; Hopkins held a mortgage for the balance. Struggling to hang on six months later, Jesse Hopkins raised a little under $300 more by mortgaging his shop and his half of the water privilege to Aaron Benedict, Sr., a Waterbury merchant.[8]

A similar lack of cash afflicted Nathan Platt, who raised money several ways to pay off the mortgage and consolidate control of the property and water privilege. In 1801 he sold half of the gristmill and part of the water privilege to his cousin Gideon Platt for a little under $600. A year later he mortgaged his remaining interest in the property to the First Congregational Society, the same parish to which his grandfather had donated land in 1740, and paid off his mortgage to Hopkins. Jesse Hopkins defaulted on his mortgage to Aaron Benedict, Sr., and the Hopkins family left the area without ever building the rolling mill. In 1804, Nathan Platt received some money from Newtown after prevailing upon his mother to release her interest in his father's estate. Soon afterward Platt paid Benedict the balance of $150 on the Hopkins mortgage and thereby acquired the abutting nail-works property and full control of the water rights. Nathan's only obligation was to the church, a benign note-holder that had little interest in running a gristmill or nail shop and that in any case might have felt kindly disposed toward the grandson of a beneficent donor. He paid off the church note slowly and was free to grow his crops, run his mills, and raise his family.[9]

Nathan's son Alfred, born in 1789, eventually brought industrial development to the old Hoadley and Hopkins mill site. A brother, Levi, preceded him, and six more siblings followed: Eli, Almon, Anner (or Annah), Leonard, Sarah, and Martha. All of them spent at least part of their childhood in Waterbury, and Alfred, Almon, Anner, Leonard, and Martha stayed nearby. Levi settled in Danbury, leaving Alfred first in succession to the Waterbury property. Eli moved to Norwich, Connecticut, and Sarah to Wisconsin. Nathan's family retained close ties to their Newtown branch (Nathan had five siblings) and to the family of cousin Gideon, who lived in Middlebury.[10]

The Platts valued education and intellectual pursuits. Like every Connecticut child, Alfred learned to read, write, and calculate in local schools, probably in both Newtown and Waterbury, where he moved at the age of eight. Unlike most of his contemporaries, Alfred's education continued beyond that level, at James Morris's private school in Litchfield. He was sufficiently accomplished to qualify as a district schoolteacher in 1808, at the age of nineteen. Alfred's business pursuits would depend on his literacy, as manufacturing for remote markets required clear communication through the mail. Younger brother Leonard also maintained an interest in learning. In the 1830s, Leonard worked for a nearby industrial firm and, like his co-workers, took a substantial part of his wages in goods from the employers' store. Most of these in-kind payments were food, cloth, shoes, and household articles. Uniquely among his co-workers, Leonard also received payment in books, including a "philosophy."[11]

Besides education and helping at farmwork along with his brothers and sisters, Alfred's early life included two other activities that shaped his adulthood. Working in his father's mills, he learned the work of the mechanic and the millwright. No one in the family wrote down an account of Alfred dressing a millstone, setting a lantern gear, or starting the waterwheel, but his career showed him to be adept at mechanical work, to an extent that could only be grounded in long experience. To judge from his later accomplishments, from the age of eight Alfred must have spent many hours a week observing the work of the mills and learning about waterpower, power transmission, and the use of tools and machinery.

The other distinctive aspect of Alfred's youth was his family's Baptist faith. The Baptists dissented from the state-sanctioned Congregational religion at a time when distinctions among Protestant sects exerted profound influence on both religious and secular affairs. Membership in the Baptist church made Alfred something of an outsider from an early age and helped to make him comfortable with nonconformity. Later in life, Alfred did not hesitate to diverge from the path followed by others. Alfred Platt's faith was one of the cornerstones of his world, and his complete devotion to his church would also help to shape his industrial career.

Alfred Platt, Young Mechanic and Miller

The Platts bought a developed water privilege but maintained it themselves, and they rebuilt the facilities after floods in 1801 and 1803. They applied the practicality and broad aptitude of the New England farmer, but their work carried beyond experience with a range of tools and tasks: they became millwrights. They might have read one of the few treatises on milling available around 1800, but mostly they learned by doing. For a few years the Platts shared the dam with the experienced Hopkins family, and no doubt absorbed some lessons from those more seasoned mechanics. Millwrighting encompassed dams, races, buildings, waterwheels, power transmission, and the construction of working equipment such as saws, grindstones, and slitting rolls. It demanded familiarity with the crafts of the carpenter, stonemason, blacksmith, and wheelwright, and with the developing craft of the machinist. The millwright knew surveying in order to locate structures and watercourses, mastered arithmetic and basic geometry, could calculate the speed and power of machinery, and had to draw plan and section views. He was the "key technician of the preindustrial and early industrial age, the craftsman predecessor of the civil and mechanical engineer."[12]

Nathan, Alfred, Leonard, and probably Almon also acquired the millwright's skills. Nathan and Leonard apparently applied their skills to metalworking and machine-building ventures before 1820, making bent-wire eyes for button manufacturers who had by then solidly established production in Waterbury. A family reminiscence from more than one hundred years later claimed that before 1820 Nathan and Leonard had a foundry and machine shop to make their wire-forming equipment. Another unsubstantiated recollection held that two neighbors, David Wooster and Lucian Judd, innovated brass-casting and wire-drawing techniques enabling them to supplant imported English wire, and that the Platts acquired this process. These stories accorded improperly early credit for subsequent events and probably attributed more, and more diverse, production than actually occurred by 1820. It is certain, however, that by 1820 the Platts had joined

Nathan Platt House (center), c. 1805; photograph taken in the 1890s. Built in the traditional center-chimney style, with a stylish Georgian doorway, this type of house was typical for well-to-do farmers of the early national period. It was later Alfred Platt's house and then was divided into three apartments for factory employees. It was destroyed in 1955. The small brick building in the left foreground served as an office. The two-story house in the right background was the Platt boardinghouse. (Mattatuck Museum)

Waterbury's dynamic metalworking sector geared to consumer metal goods; the 1820 manufacturing census recorded a button shop at this location, operating under the name of Platt and Wooster, probably the wire-eye shop of Nathan and Leonard.[13]

Alfred would later turn to metalworking, but in his late teens and twenties he did almost everything else. He may have taught school for a time in Brookfield (next to Newtown), the town that issued him a teaching certificate in 1808. He courted Irene Blackman of Brookfield, but lack of funds forestalled their marriage. District schoolteachers earned very low pay, and Irene did not come from a wealthy family. In 1814, Irene received a windfall from her father's estate, land valued at $250. A year later Alfred bought his first property—a third of his father's house and a small piece of adjacent land—for $300. The year after that Irene and Alfred married and began their life together under the same roof with Alfred's parents and siblings.[14]

Along with his marriage and property purchase in 1816, Alfred built a wool-carding mill on the family water privilege. He also worked in the saw-mill and gristmill. Nathan, pressed for money, had again mortgaged his property to the First Congregational Society in March of that year. Discouraged by the low income available from his father's encumbered assets, Alfred spent two or three years exploring the potential of mercantile pursuits. Around 1819 he traveled south, peddling Mark Leavenworth's wooden-movement clocks. In 1821 he joined neighbor Jesse Wooster in a short-lived partnership running a general store.[15]

Alfred kept working at saw- and gristmilling while he tried commerce. He soon realized that his uncommon mechanical skills offered his best opportunity and that productive rather than mercantile work best satisfied him. In subsequent years he would express some disdain for gain through manipulation, for those who profited by buying and selling the results of his work. A later advertisement[16] for the gristmill announced: "Notice is hereby given that I will grind Buckwheat for Customers as far as they want for their own use, but do not expect to grind for them to sell." Platt's simultaneous pursuit of sawmilling, gristmilling, and commerce showed his inclination and capacity for multiple occupations, a characteristic of pre-industrial work that Alfred would continue throughout his life. To succeed at many jobs, he had to set the pace of his own work and the distribution of his time among numerous pursuits. A wholesale merchant took the same amount of time to order one barrel of flour as twenty. For Alfred though, the larger order would occupy his mill for a whole day rather than one or two hours. When other demands pressed for his attention or in times of low water, when only one process could run, the larger order could hamper his attention to other obligations. To the end of his days, Alfred Platt jealously guarded the ability to set his own priorities and schedule.

Alfred's resistance against attempts to turn his work or his time into a commodity also derived from his sense of pride and accomplishment in productive work, particularly the craft of grinding grain. Late in life, after decades of diverse experience, including the operation of a successful button and metalworking firm, Alfred could offer many possible answers to a query about his occupation. He responded "Master Miller," the work he valued most highly. Alfred would deal with merchants and businessmen to serve his family's best interest, but he would not concentrate his own efforts on those functions. Alfred was a producer.[17]

Directed then both by need and preference, Alfred devoted himself to the family's small industrial base. He rebuilt the sawmill and by 1822, at the age of thirty-three, had started the venture that would have the most lasting impact on his family and his city: working on buttons in the old Hopkins nail works, near the house. It soon paid off. In June 1822 he bought another small piece of land from his father and started building a barn.[18]

In his earliest button shop Alfred probably worked alone or with the intermittent help of a few relatives or neighbors, using the power of the

Naugatuck River for some of the operations. He might have made complete buttons or performed some of the manufacturing steps for other button-makers. In either case, he did not market his buttons or buttonmaking operations directly to their ultimate consumers. Unlike flour and lumber sold to local people, the mechanized, volume production of buttons targeted a national market and brought Alfred Platt into close business relations with the most ambitious industrial capitalists of his day, notably the younger Aaron Benedict.[19]

Benedict, Platt, and their contemporaries led west-central Connecticut from a rural, agricultural economy to a market-oriented, industrial economy. When Nathan Platt took his family to Waterbury, artisans and mechanics had begun producing tinware, clocks, and buttons for out-of-state sales. The early producers worked in dooryard shops and depended on farming as much as manufacturing to feed their families. In Alfred Platt's time, manufactures emerged as distinct from the preexisting agricultural society, and for most people in Waterbury industrial work replaced the farm-based way of life. Primary production of brass and other alloys drove Waterbury's industrialization. In the early nineteenth century, manufacture of metal buttons brought Waterbury entrepreneurs both the need and the opportunity to move into primary metal production. Once they established a steady supply of metal for their button shops, they developed other markets for their metal and new products to make from it.

Alfred Platt might have started his button shop in the old Hopkins nail-making building specifically to supply Benedict. He would soon join Benedict's partnership (though not pursuing it full-time), providing Platt with the proprietary role he cherished. By July 1824, Platt had supplied products, labor, or facility rental to Benedict's firm worth over $500, more than he had ever realized from any of his other pursuits. The relationship with Benedict also provided Platt the chance to work with the most accomplished buttonmakers. James Croft, another of Benedict's partners, was the leading button artisan in Waterbury. Born in the English Midlands in 1774 and trained as a gilt-button maker under the craft tradition in Birmingham, Croft arrived in Waterbury around 1817, worked a year for the Scovills, and then joined Benedict.[20]

For Platt, the knowledge and skills from millwrighting and his other mechanical ventures provided the perfect background to learn buttonmaking from Croft. Button techniques included finish-rolling metal to a smooth surface; making dies and machines to impart figured patterns to metal button fronts, to form the cup-shaped fronts, to finish the edges, and to press together the fronts and backs; the use of edging dies and machines to finish the circumference; and a range of finishing skills such as recipes for the mercury and gold mixture used in gilding, the heating methods used to apply the gilding, and burnishing and polishing. This interaction between the Waterbury millwright and the English artisan was the type of episode repeated throughout the United States in the early national period. New World resources and pragmatic technical facility blended with Old World craft skills to create the American version of the Industrial Revolution.[21]

Alfred Platt: The Young Baptist

In the eighteenth and early nineteenth centuries, Baptist beliefs and practices differed significantly from those of the Congregational church, which functioned as an arm of the colonial and state government of Connecticut. The Congregationalists believed that God selected the holy, and they baptized infants so that any potential saint would be raised in God's way. Baptists believed that the conscious acceptance of God offered the means to salvation and practiced adult baptism, in which individuals by their own free will accepted God as the savior. For the early Puritans and their Congregational successors, religion also carried civic import. Holiness resided in the church or the assembled people, and they felt a duty to enforce strict adherence in order to preserve the sanctity of the whole community; one sinner contaminated all. Church and state served the same goals, and to separate them was to risk damnation. The Puritans saw no contradiction in having taxes support the church in each town, nor in preserving the sanctity of their community by declaring other faiths illegal. Even after the Great Awakening of the 1740s, when charismatic preachers led powerful opposition to the established church, the political-religious leadership only grudgingly accepted the existence of dissenting faiths, and then only to preserve order.[22]

That acceptance allowed the Baptists to gain a foothold in Connecticut, and by 1760 some nine churches claimed about 450 members. Spread by itinerant evangelists, the faith grew to thirty churches with 1,800 members in 1784, and fifty-five churches with 3,200 members in 1795. This last surge included the establishment in 1791 of the Second Baptist Church of Wallingford. The earliest Baptists in Waterbury belonged to this parish. They traveled the twelve miles to church every month or so; the rest of the time they worshipped in a member's home. In 1803 the Waterbury Baptists claimed thirty members, including Nathan and Ruby Platt, and they joined with brethren to the south and west to establish their own congregation.[23]

The small group met in the homes of members, rotating among five locations that included the Platt homestead. Though the faith was based on adult acceptance of God, as a child Alfred certainly attended worship with his parents, listening to the sermons of lay preachers or traveling exhorters and participating in Bible reading and hymn singing. Starting around 1800, Connecticut Baptists adopted the practice of public baptism by full immersion. The Waterbury congregation used the Naugatuck River for this rite, at a location, immediately downstream from a tannery, that must surely have tested the rigor of the faithful. Sometime around 1810, clad in the white raiment of the newly born Baptist, Alfred Platt submitted to ritual dunking in the Naugatuck.[24]

Platt joined the church during a period of growing fervor, when membership increased many times over. His congregation reached one hundred members before splitting into two groups in 1817. Alfred's parish, the northern group, soon built their first church, two and one-half miles east of the center of Waterbury. A crude affair "with benches only for seats and no means of warming in winter," its opening nonetheless brought forth a joyous festival among the congregants. Deacon Timothy Porter, a pillar of the congregation, took part in games and races with the children, scandalizing the "excellent old ladies." Though devout in their beliefs and devoted to their church, these Baptists were not dour.[25]

Alfred Platt's religion had important political implications in his early adult life. Baptists had to arrange special dispensation from taxes that supported the official church. They believed that Connecticut law violated their freedom of conscience, an opinion supported by the First Amendment to the United States Constitution. (Connecticut had refused to ratify the Bill of Rights largely because of this provision.) While the Congregationalists considered state support of religion fundamental to maintaining moral order and social control, the Baptist alternative to an established church was "evangelical voluntarism," a political expression of their individualist approach to holiness. Both groups feared secularism, and the Baptists had to walk a careful middle course. Their petition-writing campaigns favored disestablishment but did not oppose devotion to the Protestant God. And their evangelical efforts intertwined with their political program: every conversion represented not just a soul for God's kingdom but also a vote. The rise in the Waterbury congregation from thirty members in 1803 to one hundred in 1817 occurred against this background.[26]

In 1816 the Baptists formed an important part of the state political reform movement that named itself the Toleration Party. Their candidate for governor, Oliver Wolcott, Jr., won office in 1817. After reelection in 1818, with a ticket that won a majority in the legislature, Wolcott called for a new state constitution that would establish freedom of conscience. It was drafted over the summer and ratified in the fall. For the first time since English settlement, church and state were separated in Connecticut.[27]

As a dedicated Baptist, Alfred Platt took part in this political revolution, and the struggle influenced him in several ways that would be apparent throughout his life. Membership in a minority church that was officially disapproved (until 1818) required a certain self-confidence in his own actions and opinions, which was reinforced by the individualist basis of Baptist beliefs and confirmed by eventual political success. Platt favored voluntarism over coercion, again following the Baptist approach to holiness combined with reaction to the established church. Alfred Platt did not even coerce his own family in religious matters, and his son Clark later joined the Congregational church. Alfred also tolerated his wife's lack of religious dedication; one of their sons once observed that "Mother has been to meeting two sabbaths in succession: a very uncommon thing for her."[28]

Platt's Baptist congregation upheld a liberal viewpoint on other matters too. Timothy Porter was Waterbury's leading abolitionist. In 1840 he organized the local Liberty party, which was based on opposition to slavery, and Baptists were a major portion of its members. In public forums Porter debated the issue against Green Kendrick, a southern merchant who had moved to Waterbury after marrying into a local family.[29]

Out of naturally greater comfort with those of like beliefs, and their banding together in the face of official disapproval, the Waterbury Baptists became a tightly knit group whose mutual regard extended into business affairs. When Timothy Porter started a small carding and spinning mill on his Mad River property around 1813, he took as partner his fellow Baptist Benjamin Farrel. Alfred Platt's partner in the short-lived general store, Jesse Wooster, was also a Baptist. The Baptists did not confine themselves strictly to dealing with their brethren, and after the Constitution of 1818 the Protestant sects generally grew closer together. Nonetheless, shared faith would later play a critical role in Alfred Platt's business. When he needed to place his trust in a marketing agent for his metal goods, he would turn to the sons of his best friend, Timothy Porter.[30]

Alfred Platt: The Middle Years

The Platt homestead must have been a lively place between 1818 and 1828, when Irene Platt bore six sons in quick succession: Nirom in 1818, Charles in 1820, William in 1822, Clark in 1824, Legrand in 1825, and Seabury in 1828.[31] As the family grew, Alfred Platt acquired more property from his father and other relatives and eventually gained control of the water privilege and surrounding land. While his sons were growing up, Alfred continued to run the sawmill, gristmill, and button shop. Working with Aaron Benedict exposed Alfred Platt to a scale of enterprise that ranked among the largest in American metal fabricating, as well as to Benedict's shrewd conduct of business.

Alfred Platt approached the button business from the viewpoint of the shop, but Aaron Benedict took a very different route. Born in 1785, his father, Aaron Benedict, Sr., was a prosperous farmer and merchant who lived in the upland section of Waterbury that was set off in 1807 as the town of Middlebury. Both Aaron Benedict and his older brother studied at Yale, but ill health forced Aaron to drop out before graduating. Unlike Alfred Platt, who grew up working in field and mill, for Benedict manual labor came as therapy: after a sea voyage and a season spent at farmwork he regained good health. In 1804, at age nineteen, he opened a general store in Waterbury, financed by his father.[32]

General-store merchants were the only people in rural Connecticut who could finance small manufactures. Like farmers they operated on credit, but unlike farmers they accrued credit from a larger portion of the community. Farmers dealt with each other for help in plowing and other labor, or for produce one did not raise. Each farmer traded with only a limited number of neighbors, but they all patronized the storekeeper for cloth, shoes, paper, and the like. Farmers settled up with surplus produce that the storekeeper either resold for further credit or marketed to wholesale merchants in Hartford or New Haven in return for cash or the goods that the storekeeper sold in his home area. The storekeepers' small accumulations of cash and credit represented the only investment capital in a country town like early-nineteenth-century Waterbury. It was probably cash raised in this manner that Aaron Benedict, Sr., had paid Jesse Hopkins for the nailworks mortgage in 1798.[33]

These small general merchants also bought the metal goods produced in local shops, which they resold in the cities or marketed through peddlers traveling out of state. In this way Benedict came into contact with small manufacturers in the area. The contact deepened in 1808 when he married Charlotte Porter, daughter of Abel Porter, who headed the town's largest buttonmaking firm. In 1812 Benedict started his own company, making bone and ivory buttons while continuing to run the store; Benedict never performed production work but hired others to do it. After obtaining a water privilege on the Mad River, Benedict began using some powered operations. With Croft's production expertise, Benedict entered production of gold-plated brass, or gilt-metal, buttons, the business that brought Alfred Platt into the firm.[34]

Benedict was a sophisticated businessman and a convincing promoter. While Platt chose to remain a country mechanic, Benedict innovated or adopted far-reaching strategies in finance, marketing, functional integration, and organization. Rather than mortgaging his assets to obtain manufacturing capital, as Platt later did, Benedict sold equity. Chief among his early investors was Bennet Bronson, a Yale graduate from Woodbury who had been appointed judge of the New Haven County Court in 1812. Bronson had profited from his investments in Leavenworth's clock business, and in 1823 he devoted $2,000—at the time an enormous sum—to Benedict's button venture. Bronson also persuaded three associates from New Haven to invest $1,000 each. With the help of his New Haven cohorts, Benedict raised further capital in the form of a loan from that city's Eagle Bank. Though Benedict's button shop property was valued at $1,500, the bank lent him $3,000; unlike most of the small manufacturers of the time, Benedict received funds on the basis of his prospects, not just his collateral.[35]

Benedict's marketing efforts set the pattern for Waterbury's entire nineteenth-century consumer metal-goods sector. He began soliciting advice from those who sold for him on how best to package and present his buttons. In 1817 commission merchant Garret Smith advised:

Have them [i.e., the buttons] accurately sized & stuck in the common unglazed pasteboard instead of the glazed Bonnet paper & have the pasteboard cut all of an exact size as well as to have the holes in the paper for the eye of the button punched out at equal distances & at right angles—these little things want attending to promote the sale of the buttons—should not object to have some of the buttons one size and some of another size—only let the small ones be packaged by themselves.

Smith and Benedict were grappling with a new situation. Appearance gained paramount importance for impersonal sales in remote markets. Smith wanted the buttons to be grouped by size and the dimensions within each size to be consistent, but the appearance of regularity given by the method of packaging demanded greater care than the selection of pasteboard: quality of materials did not matter as long as the holes were spaced evenly.[36]

The central Connecticut consumer-hardware producers based their trade on making cheap, showy merchandise. The early Waterbury gilt buttons were often reproached as being plated with "dandelion water," and Benedict's shop must have contributed to that observation: in 1824 the inventory of materials included $25 worth of gold, along with $16 worth of what the bookkeeper called "Counterfeit gold."[37] How easy it must have been for a peddler to gain a reputation for cunning with goods like that.

Benedict's market awareness helped him lead the way in market access. His gilt-button business of the early 1820s completely superseded the legendary system of the Yankee peddler. Benedict sent goods to New York and Boston wholesale merchants, who earned commissions on the sales of buttons to garment makers. Garret Smith belonged to Smith & Curtis, commission merchants from Waterbury with an office and a small warehouse in New York. When merchants began to offer the products of many manufacturers and to pit manufacturers against one another to obtain lower wholesale prices, Benedict responded by bringing the wholesale marketing function into his own firm. In 1834 he engaged the full-time services of the accomplished salesman Gordon W. Burnham by making him a partner in the firm. Two years later Burnham established a New York office for the firm, and in 1837 he moved there permanently. In 1844, Burnham set up a subsidiary commission house in Boston, managed by Arad W. Welton of Cheshire, one of Waterbury's neighboring towns. Through Burnham's efforts Benedict gained thorough access to the principal markets.[38]

Benedict also integrated his firm's activities backward from button production into material supply. Around the time Alfred Platt joined the firm, James Croft traveled home to England for rolling equipment that would allow Benedict's shop to produce the sheet brass and copper from which buttons were cut. The rolls he returned with, some eleven inches in diameter by thirty inches long, "were regarded as of wonderful size." Croft also provided the skills necessary to make the alloy of brass by the carefully controlled mixing of molten copper and zinc. By mid-1824 the company had a "casting shop" to make brass, where the stock on hand included the bulk raw materials to make the alloy: 1,500 pounds of copper and 100 pounds of "spelter," as raw zinc was commonly referred to in the nineteenth century.[39]

Aaron Benedict reorganized his company frequently to take advantage of changes in the laws governing business structure, to lock up expertise in production and marketing by making key people partners, and to bring in more capital. In 1827 he renewed the original partnership of 1823. Bronson, who had kept the books for the firm, turned the accounting over to new partner Israel Coe, who became Benedict's full-time bookkeeper. Alfred Platt continued as a partner. At the same time he was paying into Benedict's partnerships, Platt was also buying more of his family's property and water privilege. It is doubtful that Platt had enough money to pay cash for all of these obligations; the use of his button shop must have been assigned a value that accounted for at least part of Platt's membership in Benedict's firm.[40]

In 1829 Benedict reorganized under a new state law that encouraged commercial investment in "Special Partnerships" by limiting the liability of investors. The New Haven investors dropped out, but Bronson's increased interest of $3,000, another $3,000 invested by Benjamin DeForest of Naugatuck, and Benedict's own reinvested profit more than made up for the New Haven shares. Platt and Croft received ownership interest of $1,000 each in the total capitalization of $15,000. Benedict and Coe served as "general partners and agents . . . alone authorized to bind the company by contract or otherwise." The others were "special partners," not liable for any obligation beyond the value of their shares. All of the partners would receive 6 percent interest on their shares before distribution of dividends, which were paid in rough proportion to investment: five-sixteenths to Benedict, one-sixteenth each to Platt and Croft, and three-sixteenths to each of the others.[41]

The business fared extremely well over the next five years, and when the partnership came up for renewal in 1834, the price of entry rose. Alfred Platt's $2,500 was the smallest share in the total of $40,000. Croft could no longer meet the cost of proprietorship, lost his partner status, and spent the rest of his career as Benedict's salaried employee. The difference between Platt and Croft was that Platt controlled his own shop and water-power that he devoted to Benedict's production. Rent or use fees for the facilities boosted Platt's income from Benedict beyond the money Platt received from interest, dividends, and compensation for work he performed. Platt did not have $2,500 in cash; he probably received advance credit on use of the shop to help make up his contribution. Bronson and DeForest continued to invest with Benedict, bringing their sons in as well. General partners Aaron Benedict and Gordon Burnham each received one-quarter ownership of the firm without contributing cash; the others were "Special Partners" and had to pay in.[42]

When Benedict renewed this same structure in 1838, the capitalization rose to $70,000, the smallest share to $5,000, and Platt dropped out. He could not participate at that level, particularly because his personal holdings were by then securing church obligations. Benedict renewed the partnership in 1840 at $100,000, reserving 51 percent for himself and Burnham without cash contribution. Arad W. Welton, who would run the Boston sales office, became a partner. In 1843, Benedict and Burnham became the first Waterbury firm to organize as a joint-stock corporation under Connecticut's Hinsdale Act, which strengthened the protection for investors.[43]

Benedict kept his general store and remained very active in buying, selling, and mortgaging local real estate, but he viewed these activities as subsidiary to his central business of making metal and buttons. The store provided a means to pay wages and other obligations in goods rather than money, an advantage that Benedict exploited at least into the 1850s. His land transactions demonstrate that manufactures stood first and other activities were simply a means to finance or stabilize the industrial ventures. While Alfred Platt would risk bankruptcy in the effort to buy more real estate and keep control of it, Benedict sold land to finance manufacturing. Benedict sold the Mad River factory property to his partners for less than it was worth, substituting real estate for dividends. He thus conserved cash for operations and bound his partners more fully into the firm.[44]

In the late 1840s Benedict's reorganizational strategy reflected the company's expanded primary-production capacity and diverse product lines. Primary production of brass and other metals had grown to outweigh the fabrication of any single finished product such as buttons. In 1835 the firm had begun alloying and rolling German silver, an amalgam of copper, nickel, zinc, and iron that was the principal material consumed in the production of tableware. Fabricating operations expanded into new products, notably pins, and button output also rose. Concentrating primary production in his original firm, Benedict spun off the secondary production into separate joint-stock companies that he controlled: American Pin Company in 1846 and Waterbury Button Company in 1849. At midcentury, after thirty years in metalworking that began with gilt buttons, Aaron Benedict stood at the center of a far-flung industrial empire based on his primary-metals production.[45]

For some fifteen years Alfred Platt filled an important production role within Benedict's growing enterprises. The income from Benedict helped Platt support his family and acquire more property. Platt also gained the expertise in primary-metal production and buttonmaking that allowed him to fit up and operate his own small button business after leaving Benedict. Platt had no exposure to the marketing side of the business nor, based on his earlier choice of productive over mercantile pursuits, did he wish to develop expertise in that aspect of the trade. He brought buttons, button parts, or rolled metal to Benedict or shipped finished buttons directly to Benedict's out-of-state agents. Platt was certainly acquainted with the people who shaped Benedict's market awareness and established Benedict's market access, but he had little direct dealing with them and was not part of the pricing, packaging, and competitive strategic marketing plans they helped to devise.

Platt deployed his assets not toward creating an industrial empire but toward the more limited and traditional goal of building financial security for his family. To Alfred Platt, that security lay in land as much as in enterprise. Platt followed a very different scheme as well in organizing his diverse business activities. Instead of a corporate structure like Benedict's, Platt organized his business life around the family, setting up partnerships with his sons, cousins, and nephews. Platt never distanced himself from daily shop operations by creating a management structure, as Benedict did by delegating marketing, production, and bookkeeping functions to separate employees or partners. Platt's metalworking ventures were smaller and relied on his close involvement. He was a proprietor and a businessman but, unlike Aaron Benedict, Platt did not set policy for others to execute. He made deals and fulfilled them by his own labor and the labor of those who worked beside him.

The Family Enclave: Platts Mills

The money Alfred Platt made with Benedict enabled him to buy his relatives' property around the Naugatuck River water privilege and to expand the family's holdings. In February 1823 his brother Almon sold Alfred a house adjacent to their father's dwelling. The deed stated that "said land lies near Platts Mills, so called," the first time the family name appeared in a document to describe the area. Alfred, Irene, and their sons finally moved to their own house.[46]

Over the next eight years Alfred devoted any surplus income to securing waterpower rights and the manufacturing facilities he had developed on the family property. In December 1823, for the nominal sum of $50, his father, Nathan, and second cousin Gideon sold Alfred the carding shop he had built, along with its water privileges and the right to install a new water-wheel. Alfred's share of the water rights was estimated to be one-twelfth of the total. A little over a year later, they sold him the button shop for $75. It occupied the building they called the "Old Nail Works" and came with further water rights that brought Alfred's share to about one-fifth of the total.[47]

The addition of Alfred's carding mill and button shop had already caused concern over the capacity of the water privilege and, more important, over the distribution of available power among the various processes. The location of the dam across the Naugatuck (probably a timber cribwork structure with stone fill) had been established by Hoadley, along with the headrace that conducted water from the dam to the mills. The race ran parallel to the river, perhaps five or ten yards from the east bank, leaving only limited land between the river and the race for erecting shops that needed waterpower. Alfred's carding mill, the fourth building on the channel after the gristmill, sawmill, and nailworks/button shop, had to be built directly over the downstream end of the race.[48]

The button works upset the balance of waterpower distribution along the race and increased the overall power required from the water privilege. The Platts expanded the system in 1824 by building another race parallel to the older one, to the east. When the flow from the Naugatuck kept both races filled, the available power approximately doubled. Coordinating power usage among the different shops was also considerably eased. On the new ditch they installed another gristmill, which was "at all times to have the preference of drawing water." They also built what they called "Breastwork Gates," a bulkhead with gates that controlled water flow to the respective races.[49]

Alfred's next purchase, in 1831, also concerned the waterpower. He paid his father $300 for the ten acres between the race and the river—the land occupied by the power system. Nathan Platt continued to control the mills he had owned since arriving in Waterbury, but Alfred gained the ability to alter the channels as his power needs required. He probably widened the old race at this time to increase the flow volume, thereby increasing the power yield. Raising the raceway walls could have yielded even more flow, but it would also have required raising the height of the dam.[50]

By the early 1830s, Alfred Platt had charge of the day-to-day activities at Platts Mills, but the real estate, the gristmill and sawmill, and four-fifths of the water rights remained in the hands of his father and Gideon, his father's cousin. Gideon had moved to a farm in Middlebury more than twenty years earlier. Nathan remarried after the death of Alfred's mother in 1829 and moved to Wallingford with his second wife. After Nathan moved away, he probably ceased relying on the agricultural produce from the Waterbury property for his table. He did, however, continue to share in any cash gains from the shops. Gideon too may have received some income from his Platts Mills holdings.[51]

Alfred's gradual assumption of ownership culminated in 1835, when he bought all of his father's remaining property for $3,200: twenty-seven acres, the sawmill, Nathan's half of the gristmill, the remaining two-thirds of Nathan's house (Alfred already owned one-third), and all of Nathan's share in the water rights. Alfred paid $1,000 in cash, and his father took a note for the balance. The note was open-ended as long as Alfred made annual interest payments. Alfred gained complete control of the property in 1836 by buying Gideon's last portion from his heirs. This included Gideon's family's half of the gristmill and water rights, the "millers house" attached to the gristmill, and some additional land.[52]

The long and gradual process of succession, as the younger generation represented by Alfred gained property over several decades, established a pattern for the Platt family businesses that would persist for generations to come. Alfred began his career at Platts Mills as a boy, helping his father and learning millwrighting; shared work was a defining characteristic of the relationship between the generations and the transition to ownership and management by the younger generation. From that base Alfred acquired an increasing portion of responsibility and ownership, and with it some latitude to implement his own plans. The small initial purchases gave Alfred a stake in the family holdings. As his efforts increased the value of the property, he stood to share in the gain, and as Alfred profited from buttons and metalworking, the older generation would receive some benefit too. By charging Alfred nominal sums for the carding shop and nailworks/button shop, Nathan and Gideon encouraged Alfred's ambition by providing him with the resources to pursue it. He also remained dependent on his elders because they controlled the property. Dependency worked the other way too: Alfred helped to support his father by working in his mills.

The 1830s transactions readjusted the balance between dependence and responsibility. When Alfred gained effective control of the waterpower system in 1831 to allow further development of mechanized production, Nathan still kept his hold on most of the property. Nathan's ownership was not an obstacle to his son's career: Alfred was able to implement his ideas about using the power even though they might have exceeded his father's more modest ambition. Alfred eventually gained full responsibility by obtaining the entire property. Nathan cashed in his life's work by selling the property to Alfred, and his old-age income depended on loan payments from Alfred. Father and son obviously trusted each other and seem to have tolerated each other's point of view. Alfred honored his father's concern for security and was willing to move slowly. Nathan understood Alfred's desire to elevate production and was willing to help advance it. They achieved the transition to the younger generation in increments of gradually increasing ownership and responsibility.

This gradual process of succession is remarkable in light of Alfred's apparent desire to push ahead. Just two months after establishing full ownership of the water privilege in 1836, he started raising the dam in order to boost the available waterpower. Since the heightened dam would raise the water level in the river upstream, and consequently widen the river's channel, Platt had to pay for the right to flood his upstream neighbor's land.[53]

Alfred Platt then reconfigured the entire site. He removed the carding mill, the old nailworks building, and the old gristmill. He continued the system of two parallel "ditches," with the sawmill on the older race that was closer to the river and the gristmill on the newer race to the east, and installed the buttonmaking machinery in the gristmill. His forty-two acres included cultivated fields, pasture, woodlot, and meadow, and he owned three houses and at least two barns. Alfred, Irene, and their sons lived in one house, and a changing cast of relatives occupied the other houses.[54]

Alfred and Irene Platt brought up their sons much the same way that Alfred had been raised. The boys all worked at farming and in the family mills. They all became proficient enough mechanics to run buttonmaking shops or gristmills as adults, and four of them would make their careers in these fields. The family was well-off, if not wealthy. They ate a great deal of pork raised on the farm and were never short of grain. The boys slept on feather beds, their parents on a "French Bedstead." Around the table stood eight "Fancy Chairs" with cane seats, and each family member had a silver spoon. After a hearty dinner of smoked shoulder, fresh bread, turnips from their fields, and raspberries from their orchards, Alfred and Irene could retire to their "two best Rocking Chairs" to reflect upon the good fortune of the Waterbury mechanic.[55]

The Platts raised their sons in the Baptist church, and William and Charles would later become deacons. If all of the boys did not observe the faith with the same devotion, religious activity nonetheless provided the most consistent opportunity, except work, for the family to gather together in common purpose. It helped the Platts to become a close and affectionate family, if by no means blind to each other's faults; Clark would write of a cousin that "having concluded to labor with his hands [I] hope he will be able now to get a living (and earn it too)." Nor was mutual affection completely unqualified, as when Legrand later wrote of a visit from Charles: "I have had 3 Tons of him this Fall." But the letters that contained these pointed remarks were also replete with fond references to family members and long lists of salutations that the recipient was asked to transmit. Though the sons later argued bitterly over money, the bickering did not harden into hate. They found ways to accommodate each other and to work with each other.[56]

All six boys achieved basic literacy in the district public school. Even in times of financial duress, Alfred and Irene found the means to pay tuition for their four youngest sons' continued education at private schools beyond the district level. William attended the Waterbury Academy, a private secondary school, before going on to study physics and chemistry under Amos Smith in New Haven. Legrand also studied in New Haven. Clark spent a year at the Connecticut Literary Institute in Suffield before joining the family button business. Only the youngest son, Seabury, attended university, entering Yale in 1848. He later read law under a Waterbury attorney and was admitted to the bar. Seabury moved to Derby to open a law practice and served as a District Court judge. He was the only brother who had no active role in the family enterprises as an adult.[57]

Alfred's younger brothers Leonard and Almon followed manufacturing careers mostly independent from the family in Platts Mills. By the early 1830s both worked at the Scovill button shop on Waterbury's Mad River. This firm, J. M. L. and W. H. Scovill, or Scovill Manufacturing, was Aaron Benedict's largest competitor in primary-metal production and button-making. In the 1830s, Scovill innovated mechanized button assembly based on a sequence of presses operated by unskilled female workers. Leonard, an expert in wireworking machinery, probably made the wire eyes (or the equipment that made the wire eyes) that these presses attached to the backs of the buttons. Almon, also a skilled mechanic, supervised a half-dozen employees, among them his sister Anner.[58]

By 1835, Leonard Platt had put aside enough money to set up his own shop immediately upstream from the Scovill factory. For $225 he obtained two and a half acres "on both sides of the Mad River . . . also all the water or mill privilege on or attached to the land." The prior owner had developed the privilege, but Leonard built a new, longer headrace to increase the power. His tailrace emptied directly into the pond behind the Scovill dam. According to a later reminiscence of one of his boarders, Leonard's factory was, by 1836, turning out wire eyes on an "automatic machine" of Leonard's devising that supplanted the hand-cranked bending apparatus used previously. Leonard soon spent $800 to buy a house and barn on two acres abutting his factory property. Button eyes provided a good income, but Leonard's shop had more significant financial implications for him and his family. It stood in the way of the Scovills' expansion, and they would pay to remove it.[59]

The New Baptist Church and Alfred Platt's Financial Crisis

During the years that Alfred Platt worked with Aaron Benedict and bought the Platts Mills property, his church was "verily the house of God and gate of heaven," enjoying a period of harmony and growth. The Waterbury Baptists did not have a full-time pastor, but a series of deacons obtained preaching licenses and ministered to the flock. Timothy Porter brought outstanding vigor to this role from 1827 to 1835, baptizing dozens of new converts, including twenty-three in 1828 alone. By 1835 the parish had more than doubled its initial membership of 1817 and undertook to build a new church on South Main Street, in the center of town.[60]

The Baptists hired David and Cyrus Silliman, builders from the town of Weston in Fairfield County, to erect the new church. A handsome brick edifice in the Greek Revival style, it presented an institutional appearance of formality and solidity that was far removed from the crude wooden building of twenty years earlier. Construction cost $6,500, and the land purchase added almost another $1,000. Once the building was complete, the parish hired the Reverend Russell Jennings to serve as their full-time minister.[61]

To guarantee the Silliman contract, in 1836 four of the most well-to-do parishioners pledged their personal assets: Enoch Frost, Jared Hall, Alfred Platt, and Timothy Porter. The full membership contributed to pay the debt, though progress was slow and payments fell behind. Then the Panic of 1837 brought a severe economic contraction,, accompanied by an extreme shortage of cash. Many parishioners failed to meet their assessments. The parish could no longer afford to maintain a minister and again fell back on the services of elders and deacons.[62]

The Baptists who could afford to pay were charged with three assessments, amounting to one-quarter the value of each parishioner's property. Alfred Platt was assessed the enormous sum of $900 under this plan. With local resources drained, the parish tried to protect the four guarantors by raising donations from other Connecticut Baptist churches. Still awaiting final payment, the Sillimans placed a lien on the church and would not allow midweek services and Bible classes or other uses of the building until the debt was settled. Instead of serving its hoped-for role as the center of Baptist community life, the grand new church was closed except for worship on the Sabbath.[63]

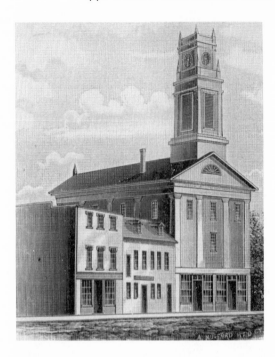

The New Baptist Church of 1835, South Main Street, Waterbury. (Mattatuck Museum)

The financial problems of the new church caused some difficulty but not immediate crisis for Alfred Platt. He was already indebted to his father for the purchase of Platts Mills, and his principal source of cash income, the button shop, was of little benefit in the aftermath of the Panic, when collapse of the banking system broke the line of payment from out-of-state markets to manufacturers in Waterbury. In 1837 he could not even pay his local taxes without borrowing $100 from a neighbor, Stephan Cowell. He raised more cash that year by borrowing $200 from a New Haven merchant after his brother Levi agreed to countersign the note. Nonetheless, when the button shop started making money again in 1838, Platt did not pay off his notes but instead bought additional land to the north of Platts Mills and to the west, across the river, including twenty-six acres from the neighboring Nettleton family.[64]

When the Benedict & Burnham partnership came up for renewal in 1838, the parish debt was a source of worry to Platt, but he did not fear losing everything. Moreover, the nationwide financial panic had subsided, business had picked up, and there was money to be made in buttons. Though perhaps not the most propitious time to strike out on his own, Platt chose this moment to begin his own button business independent of Benedict. Platt used the payout from the prior partnership to capitalize expansion of metalworking at Platts Mills. A little more than a year later, in January 1840, his money was gone and he had to borrow $714 from yet another New Haven merchant. Platt then turned to the experienced investor Bennet Bronson, who in April 1840 lent $2,000 secured by the gristmill, sawmill, button factory, all of the machinery, and the four acres occupied by the mill complex. That same day Alfred mortgaged all of his property to his brother Leonard for $2,500, plus Leonard's promise to repay the $714 to the New Haven lender. The land and waterpower, shops, and equipment that Alfred had slowly acquired over twenty years was completely mortgaged to both his father and his brother, and the factories had an additional mortgage held by Bronson. Alfred Platt's total debt came to some $6,500. His assets were worth about half that much.[65]

Leonard Platt could help because the Scovills had bought his Mad River property. They too were eager to expand after the economic crisis relented, but Leonard's water privilege prevented the Scovills from raising their dam and increasing their waterpower. In a series of transactions with Scovill Manufacturing in late February 1839, Leonard Platt established a financial base that helped to stabilize the enterprises of his brother and nephews. He sold his shop for the fabulous sum of $10,000, including $4,000 in cash. For another $3,000 he sold just one acre on the Mad River, which must have been the land adjacent to his mill dam. Then he received an additional $500 for the narrow strip of land "that my ditch runs through." Leonard's mechanical skill in developing wireworking machinery and building up his waterpower, his eye for a good water privilege, and his foresight or luck in buying immediately upstream from one of the town's largest manufacturers yielded the money that kept Platts Mills in the family. Besides fraternal affection, he was probably motivated by concern for his aged father, whose income depended on Alfred's continuing to make payments on the purchase of Platts Mills.[66]

Even Leonard's good fortune could not rescue Alfred from his financial difficulties, with payments for the church on one side and the capital needs of the button shop on the other. Several thousand dollars of debt remained on the church, and one of the guarantors, Jared Hall, placed his own lien on the building to protect himself in the event of default. If the Sillimans or Hall gained title to the church, sold it, and still did not receive the amount owed them, Platt's property would be forfeit. In the spring of 1841, facing financial collapse, Alfred Platt once more found leverage in his landholdings by using the Nettleton property as collateral for a loan from Aaron Benedict. Later in June, Platt issued yet another mortgage on the factory property to Bennet Bronson, as payment for the accrued interest on Bronson's loan. Bronson then agreed to consolidate his claims on Platts Mills with a new mortgage issued to Benedict and Burnham, which loaned Platt a little over $1,000, secured by the full forty-two acres with all buildings, machinery, and water rights. The Bronson note had covered only the mill property, but now Alfred's former partners held a note on his farm and dwelling too.[67]

These arrangements bought Platt a few months of security to continue his search for cash to pay for the church, without sacrificing the use of the water privilege. In November 1841 he borrowed $200 from a neighbor, Samuel Potter, by pledging his household furnishings as collateral. As earlier obligations came due in the spring of 1842, for the first time Alfred Platt lost some of his land. Stephan Cowell took title to the acreage that had secured his 1837 loan to Platt. Platt sold the former Nettleton property to another neighbor, Hial Bristol, yielding a little cash after retiring the mortgage on that parcel. Platt's son Nirom co-signed some $900 worth of notes, secured by Alfred's metal-rolling, toolmaking, and button-fabricating equipment. Nathan helped him raise $500 in June by co-signing another note. On July 8, 1842, Alfred leased the casting shop and more machinery to his son Charles. The lease gave Alfred the last part of the church payment, and three days later he paid the Sillimans $1,250.[68]

Retiring his church debt alleviated Platt's financial pressure only temporarily, and his fortunes hit bottom in November. He sold "Two Button Stamps [stamping machines] which I have recently built" to son Charles but still failed to satisfy Samuel Potter's demand note of a year earlier. Potter then took possession of Platt's household furnishings—beds, silver spoons, chairs, a bureau, and a stove. Debt had posed abstract problems before, a matter of obligations with the potential for causing hardship. After the Potter foreclosure, however, Alfred Platt and his family had to sleep on straw mattresses rather than feather beds and sit on wooden benches rather than fancy chairs. In December 1842, Alfred resorted to subterfuge by deeding all of his holdings to his sons Nirom and Charles. Alfred still owed the three mortgages on Platts Mills, but any creditor seeking to foreclose would at least encounter some delay in untangling the title.[69]

Alfred Platt held no animosity over the worldly trials he had undergone on behalf of his parish and continued to support the church any way he could. Upon discharging his personal obligation for the construction debt in July 1842, Platt gained title to one-quarter of the meetinghouse. In early 1844, after his own and the parish finances reached a stable, if still debt-ridden, condition, Platt donated his share of the church to the parish. Later that year the church hired a minister, the Reverend Ally Darrow. Platt provided the Reverend Mr. Darrow with vegetables and pork, and his gristmill ground the flour for the minister's bread. Platt duly recorded every transaction, but when it came time to settle the account with Darrow, Platt offered "Cr[edit] in full to balance."[70]

The Next Generation Comes of Age

Alfred Platt could feed his family with produce from the farm, and the gristmill and sawmill provided a small income, but metalworking and buttonmaking offered Platt his best opportunity to earn the money he needed to get out of debt. By 1842 he had established a smaller version of the integrated manufacturing facilities of Benedict. In 1841 or 1842 he built a casting shop about one hundred yards east of the gristmill, with "Bellows, anvill [and] metal moulds," where he could alloy brass or make ingots of other metals. The rest of the metalworking equipment he fit into odd spaces and corners of the gristmill. In the north end of the basement were "a sett or pair of Rolls for rolling hard metal . . . likewise rolling shears for slitting metal [slitting rolls]." The south end of the basement held "a Scalping machine" used for imparting precise thickness to rolled metal. The main floor of the gristmill was divided into three rooms. The north room contained an "Edging machine" for buttons plus the toolmaking equipment: general-purpose machine tools, including three lathes and a "press drill machine," with fixtures and implements for building his own production machinery and tooling. The rest of the buttonmaking machinery stood in the center room: machinery for "forming and stamping buttons," including the "Two Button Stamps" that he built in 1842, and finishing equipment consisting of "polishing and Burnishing machines." In the loft was a "die lathe." Far from emerging as an industry distinct from the complex of family enterprises, button production was spatially dispersed and operationally entwined among the gristmill equipment.[71]

Nirom, twenty-four years old in 1842, had begun his career as a general merchant, providing the family with a connection to the mercantile sector that his father avoided in his own affairs. For most of his adult life Nirom ran a grocery store in partnership with his cousin Merrit Platt. Of most immediate importance for Alfred Platt in the early 1840s, Nirom had access to credit. When Nirom received the rights to the metalworking equipment in May 1842 in return for countersigning Alfred's loans, the ultimate source of the money was the New Haven Bank, which at that time judged Nirom a better risk than his father.[72]

Charles, twenty-two years old in 1842, leased the buttonmaking operation from 1842 to 1844. To judge from later agreements with other sons, Alfred continued to work at buttonmaking and was compensated for his time, as well as sharing the profits, in return for leasing the facility to Charles. The next son, William, began his experiments with rolling and stamping zinc during Charles's tenure in the button shop. In the early 1840s, the button shop employed no workers apart from Alfred Platt's sons and perhaps his nephews, the sons of Asahel Judd. The button business made money during the two years that Charles and Nirom held title to it, enabling Alfred to keep up interest payments on his major obligations. The sons shared Alfred's concern over servicing the mortgage debt and clearing the title to Platts Mills. Unable to reduce the principal from the more recent mortgages, in 1843 Charles and Nirom at least paid off their grandfather Nathan's forty-year-old mortgage to the Congregational church.[73]

The promise of the button business attracted Alfred Platt's nephews Lorin, D. Baldwin, and William, the sons of Levi. In 1844 Alfred, probably with the help of Leonard, provided them with button-eye machinery and other equipment to set up a shop in Newtown. Known as L. L. Platt and Company, the Newtown cousins made buttons of animal horn and bone, with wire eyes for attachment to garments. While not a diversification scheme on the scale of Benedict, L. L. Platt at least provided the Waterbury clan with some income in the form of payment for the machinery.[74]

In early 1843, Leonard Platt sold his mortgage on Platts Mills to Benedict and Burnham. It was worth over $3,500 counting the accrued interest, bringing Alfred Platt's debt to Benedict and Burnham to more than $6,000. Platt applied all of his capacities to keep up interest payments to Benedict. Besides rolling metal for Benedict, Platt supplied merchandise to the store that Benedict used to pay his employees' wages. Platt's abundant turnip harvests went to the store, fifty bushels, worth $8, in one 1846 delivery. The gristmill paid interest to Benedict in the form of grain orders, no less than one hundred pounds at a time for buckwheat flour, rye flour, and sifted meal. Platt's multifaceted asset base—farm, gristmill, sawmill, and metal-working—gave him many ways to maintain his economic independence.[75]

In 1845, Nirom paid back enough of the Benedict & Burnham mortgage to clear title to a half-acre, a barn, and one of the houses. Alfred then sold that property to Nirom, who already lived in the house with his wife, Eliza Kirtland of Waterbury. This small purchase began the transition to the third generation of Platts who would occupy the Naugatuck River property.[76]

When Nathan Platt died in 1845, Alfred still owed him over $2,000 for the purchase of Platts Mills. In his will Nathan divided his estate more or less equally among eight heirs. Alfred's share was contingent on paying off the $500 note that Nathan had co-signed in 1845. By retiring that note and gaining his share of Nathan's legacy, Alfred also reduced his debt to Nathan's estate by one-eighth. Alfred paid off one or two of his siblings with land in Platts Mills, reducing the property he controlled from forty-two acres to thirty-seven. His other siblings were content to wait for Alfred to pay them.[77]

In 1845, at the age of fifty-six, Alfred Platt had achieved a measure of security after years of risk and trials. The farm and gristmill meant that his family would never lack for food. Though indebted to Waterbury's largest manufacturer, he had the means to pay the interest. The button and metalworking trade had recovered from the Panic of 1837, and Platt had every reason to hope that local customers would eagerly buy the output from his shops.

Over the next two decades, in his years as the patriarch of the Waterbury Platts, Alfred endeavored to assure that his sons and their families would continue to benefit from the family's ownership of a superior waterpower site in one of the nation's most industrialized regions. Having secured the property, however, Platt still encountered a host of trying issues that would occupy him for the rest of his life and some that would not be resolved until after his life had ended.

Throughout his financial crisis Alfred Platt displayed extraordinary tenacity, which would become a defining trait of the metalworking business. He accorded the utmost priority to retaining his land, waterpower, and shops, however highly leveraged. Personal hardship and the loss of possessions meant little to him compared with these central assets of his working life. Nor did he succumb to bitterness toward the faith that had contributed to his difficulties. During subsequent crises in the metalworking business, Platt's heirs and descendants persevered as well. His sons may have drawn strength from Alfred's direct example, out of honor for what he had endured in their behalf or perhaps as a lesson that hard times could be weathered. But their followers did not witness Alfred's exploits; they inherited along with the business the commitment to survival that he inspired.

CHAPTER TWO

"You Are Now Lucrative in Business"

B E T W E E N the early 1840s and the late 1850s, Alfred Platt managed an intricate and idiosyncratic process of industrialization. He had to increase his power supply and further mechanize production, tasks that were common to the growth of all manufactures but no less challenging for being typical. Long-established economic relationships with neighboring Yankee farmers and tradesmen evolved from their traditional character, and an entirely new labor force of wage-earning Irish immigrants came onto the scene. Platt's distrust of the mercantile sector made market access particularly difficult, resulting in several false starts and only marginally profitable operations. By establishing a link with the local bank he gained access to credit other than private mortgages secured by his property. In all of these aspects—technology, labor, marketing, finance—the new tactics did not suddenly replace the old but coexisted with them.

As his sons reached adulthood, Platt tried to anticipate succession in the family enterprises. He helped two of his sons establish themselves far away from the family homestead, and he pursued the metalworking business with William and Clark. Alfred seized on William's experiments with zinc as the basis for the primary-production component of a small, integrated manufacturing firm.

The accelerating pace of production and employment growth in the region's non-ferrous metals sector created an environment laden with both opportunity and danger for small fabricating shops. Convenient material supply, production expertise, and markets for intermediate goods helped small producers, but they also were vulnerable to manipulation of the material supply and the economic clout the large firms exercised in market relations. The small producers' role as allies, or foils, in the pricing tactics of commission merchants assured some level of sales. But Alfred Platt preferred a production-based complementarity with the region's dominant firms, not one based purely on the merchants' promotion of competition among manufacturers.

In 1840 all of Alfred and Irene's six sons, except Nirom, lived in the same house with them. Nirom, newly married to Eliza Kirtland, lived next door in the house he would buy from Alfred. Abijah Crofut, who worked in the gristmill, probably occupied Platt's third house. While all eight males in the enclave likely spent time working in both fields and shops, only one (probably Alfred or one of the sons) listed his occupation with the census taker as "agriculture." The other seven answered "manufacturing."[1]

Irene and Eliza spent their days working too, though the census taker recorded no occupations for them. Irene tended the garden, picked apples, and fed the livestock. She probably churned the butter and helped to pack the salt pork and smoke the pork shoulders that the family ate and that Alfred traded for labor and supplies. Though Alfred never recorded in his account books the farm and household labor of female relatives, the family's finances and life-style depended on their contributions.[2]

The farm could feed everyone, but the enclave could not support manufacturing careers for all of the sons if they wanted to run their own businesses. Nirom chose a career in storekeeping, and Seabury chose the law, but the other four sons could not all achieve proprietorship based on the family resources as they stood in the mid-1840s. Alfred selected which of his sons would stay and work with him and helped the others get established elsewhere.

Between 1844 and 1848 three of Alfred's sons—Charles, William, and Legrand—spent time in Newtown with their cousin Lorin, helping him with his horn-button shop, L. L. Platt and Company. William went first, in 1844. Only twenty-two at the time and less experienced than Charles, he had mastered many buttonmaking and metalworking operations, and Charles was still occupied with his lease of the Platts Mills button shop. William helped set up the machinery, which came from Waterbury, to make metal-backed buttons with fronts of horn or bone.[3]

In 1847 Platt chose William and Clark to join him in the metalworking business at Platts Mills, which they named A. Platt and Company. (A. Platt and Company is the direct antecedent of the present firm of The Platt Brothers and Company.) The second son, Charles, went to Newtown to assume William's role at L. L. Platt and Company. With Seabury entering Yale in 1848, only Legrand remained without a prospective career. Legrand aspired to proprietorship, but his father kept the gristmill and sawmill to himself and had already selected William and Clark to join him in metalworking. Trusting Charles more than Legrand to start up a new business, in 1848 Alfred Platt sent Charles to western Massachusetts in search of a partner to help establish a gristmill in that region. Legrand then replaced Charles at L. L. Platt in Newtown. Legrand did not want to leave Platts Mills, jealously describing those who stayed as his "rich relatives." Perhaps to ease the transition, Alfred bought Legrand a complete set of "Blue Armory" dishes and crockery to help set up the kitchen in his new home.[4]

Charles formed a partnership in West Stockbridge, Massachusetts, with Thomas Barnes, a merchant and miller. Barnes provided a mill and a local outlet for the flour. The Platts equipped the mill, and Charles ran it. As with the Newtown button shop, providing, setting up, and maintaining the machinery was no small contribution: it gave Platt and Barnes Company a link with Waterbury's superior machine-making capability. Each year Alfred Platt's dozens of purchases from local machine-builders included materials for the shops in Newtown and West Stockbridge, as well as those in Platts Mills. The principal basis for the West Stockbridge expansion was Alfred Platt's method of sorting the hulls from the kernels of buckwheat. The process first cracked the buckwheat to loosen the hulls, then removed the hulls by shaking the grain under an air current made by wooden fans. Platt's buckwheat flour was much finer than that of other millers because it lacked the gritty particles of ground-up hull.[5]

Taking advantage of his own mechanical talent and that of his sons, Alfred Platt solved for a time the problem of succession at Platts Mills by sending Charles and Legrand to those two shops remote from Waterbury. Charles settled in West Stockbridge to run his gristmill, married a local woman, and raised a family there. Over the next decade, Legrand suffered financially, and his resentment against the rest of the Platts grew. In the late 1840s, however, the affairs of the clan were settled sufficiently so that the sons who remained at the homestead could devote themselves to raising their own families and expanding their metalworking pursuits.

In 1844 William married Caroline Orton, the grandniece of Deacon Timothy Porter. Five years later, when she gave birth to their first child, Helen, Alfred sold William an acre of land to build a house. Clark's experience was similar: after he married Amelia Lewis in 1846 the couple rented from Alfred, then bought property in the enclave when their first child, Bertha, came along in 1851. Clark bought his land from Nirom, who then moved to West Main Street, closer to his store in Waterbury center. Clark's house must have been the fanciest in Platts Mills. Though he hired neighboring tradesmen to build it, he bought the "glazed sash" in New York and the "thin [clap]boards" in Bridgeport.[6]

Industrial Waterbury

Fifty years after the Platts arrived in Waterbury, the vision of Jesse Hopkins, Mark Leavenworth, and the other late-eighteenth-century promoters—economic growth based on manufacturing—was fulfilled. The size and composition of the population reflected the decline of agriculture and the expansion of industry. As those seeking better farmland began to move elsewhere in the first decade of the nineteenth century, Waterbury's population had declined some 11 percent, to about 2,900 people. Not until the mid-1830s would Waterbury again surpass three thousand inhabitants. By 1850 population had grown to slightly over five thousand, including one thousand Irish people who had fled the famine in their homeland. Continuing Irish immigration contributed to Waterbury's population doubling again between 1850 and 1860.[7]

Primary production of non-ferrous metals and the manufacture of buttons, pins, and other consumer products from those metals were the two pillars of the local economy. In primary production, which involved making brass (and other copper alloys) and rolling it into sheet or drawing it into tube or wire, both the high cost of entry and monopolistic practices limited the number of competitors. Benedict and Burnham, capitalized at $100,000 in 1840, represented an investment of $400,000 by 1856. Waterbury Brass began with $40,000 in 1846, and increased to $300,000 in ten years. In this period the average brassworks capitalization was more than ten times the average investment for Connecticut firms in other industries. The American Brass Association, established in 1853, further limited competition by setting production quotas, penalties for overproduction, and uniform prices for its members, guaranteeing each company a share of the market. As a result, a handful of men controlled the primary-brass industry of the Naugatuck Valley and the nation's brass supply. Chief among them was Benedict, joined by James and William Scovill, Benedict's erstwhile partner Israel Coe, and the energetic Israel Holmes, who had a hand in the establishment of five brass mills. In 1850 four primary-production firms operated in Waterbury, the smallest employing 45 people and the largest 107; they made brass as well as the German silver and silver-plated brass consumed by tableware makers.[8]

The primary producers also made buttons, builders' hardware, lamps, costume jewelry, and harness hardware, as well as supplying other shops with the metal to make such products. In 1850 eleven shops engaged principally in button production. The largest was Benedict's Waterbury Button Company, with eighty workers and an output of 110,000 gross of buttons. Platt ranked smallest in number of workers, with six, although its production of 12,000 gross exceeded that of three other makers. Together, the

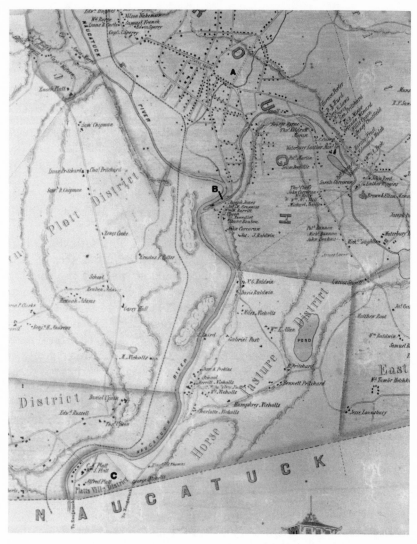

The southern half of Waterbury in 1852. Downtown is designated as A, the Benedict and Burnham factory as B, and the Platt enclave as C. From A. Budington and R. Whiteford, *Map of the County of New Haven, Connecticut* (New Haven, 1852). (Mattatuck Museum)

primary producers and the buttonmakers employed over six hundred workers, an eighth of all residents and a fifth to a quarter of the employed people.[9]

Alfred Platt's metalworking ventures were integrally connected with this larger industrial scene. His skill base was the metal rolling and buttonmaking he had learned while working with Benedict, and his perception of the opportunity in metalworking was based on the experiences of many other local firms. One of Platt's closest and longest-standing links with the wider industrial community of Waterbury involved the purchase of parts for his machinery and power-transmission system. Machinery for metal goods production had achieved a degree of sophistication beyond the abilities of a country millwright. Platt could perhaps have developed his skills further in order to perform all of the iron casting, forging, and machining necessary to build equipment capable of fine adjustment and even delivery of power. By the middle of the nineteenth century, however, machine-building expertise was available because growth in metalworking had stimulated the establishment of such firms in the local area. The Foundry Company (later known as Farrel Foundry and Machine Company and later still as Waterbury-Farrel) would rival in size some of the brass mills it supplied, employing hundreds of molders, pattern makers, forge hands, machinists, and laborers. The Platts relied on Farrel and other local firms for machine-body castings and specialized parts such as gears and large screws to control machine movements ("lead screws"). Not until the 1860s would they buy entire machines from outside suppliers.[10]

Midnineteenth-century Waterbury was largely but not completely transformed from its rural character of the late eighteenth century. Manufacture of primary metals and fabricated metal goods was firmly established. The population included a shrinking number of farmers and a growing number of industrial workers, many of them Irish immigrants. The metals industries supported one of the nation's largest concentrations of machine builders. An expanding retail and commercial sector, including stores, carting companies, builders, and hotels, served the needs of manufacturers and their workers. Between 1850 and 1853 more than 450 new houses went up, and the first bank opened.[11]

Spurred by Green Kendrick, the owners of the largest factories invested their own money and obtained legislative approval for bond financing to build the Naugatuck Railroad, which opened in 1849. Following the banks of the Naugatuck and Housatonic rivers, it connected Waterbury with the New York and New Haven Railroad that paralleled the coast of Long Island Sound. Spurs entered directly into the yards of the major brass mills. At Platts Mills the tracks ran along the west bank of the river, across the stream from the homes and shops of the Platts. The Platts had access to rail service at Union City Depot, a mile's wagon ride to the south. Before the Naugatuck Railroad opened, they had received freight by sending a wagon to meet steamboats twelve miles away at Derby (where the Naugatuck joined the Housatonic) or twenty miles away at New Haven.[12]

Alfred Platt. (Mattatuck Museum)

A. Platt and Company: A Business in Zinc

While capitalizing on opportunities afforded in the Naugatuck Valley's dynamic metalworking sector, Alfred Platt continued to follow his own distinctive view of industry and industrial society. The family-based orientation dictated a scale of operation much smaller than the integrated metals firms, and to complement this approach the Platts sought product lines that would not put them in competition with the Benedicts and Scovills. Alfred Platt also differed from other Waterbury industrial proprietors in his wariness of marketing. This wariness did not come from any sense of ideological purity regarding money or business but apparently from just a simple distaste for, and probably distrust of, the practices of commission merchants. Platt undertook every kind of financing tactic to retain control of his real estate, but for as long as he could he avoided full participation in the commercial machinations connected with the metal-goods trade.

By the mid-1840s the Platts had begun building up expertise in processing zinc, which for over a century would provide a fruitful market niche for the family businesses. The opportunity presented itself because raw zinc (or "spelter"), one of the main components in making brass, was available in Waterbury through ties with wholesale merchants in New York and Philadelphia. But the large primary-production firms did not roll zinc, concentrating instead on brass and other copper alloys of wider application and marketability. The Platts could specialize in zinc without competition from the giants.[13]

The large firms probably declined to process zinc because it was worked differently from brass, it offered a small market, and brass sufficed for many applications that would take zinc. Zinc has a crystalline structure when cold and requires heating to malleable temperature (annealing) before it can be rolled without breaking. Impurities in the spelter, such as lead, cadmium, iron, and copper, cause zinc to harden during rolling. As late as 1904, a leading metals journal called zinc a "peculiar metal" and confessed to having no advice that would yield consistent results in rolling. Brassmaking also employed a combination of rolling and annealing, but the rhythm was different; brass roller hands lacked the experience to know when and how to anneal zinc, how many passes to take through the rolls before annealing, or how much thickness to reduce in a pass. The markets for zinc did not attract the major metals firms strongly enough for them to fund the experimentation and development necessary to work it. And if they needed some rolled zinc, by 1850 they could buy it from the Platts and save themselves the cost of establishing a capability that promised only limited payoff.[14]

That payoff meant a substantial income for a small business, or at least enough potential for Alfred to indulge his son William's interest in rolling zinc. William had begun experimenting with zinc rolling by the mid-1840s. His techniques did not involve fundamental innovations in rolling mill technology but rather the experience-based knowledge of the adjustments and timing necessary to adapt the widely known (in Waterbury) processes to a different metal. A contemporary of William's asserted that "before the age of twenty-one [i.e., by 1843] he had acquired the art of rolling sheet zinc, and was the first to produce it successfully in Waterbury."[15]

William's success with rolling zinc provided the central product base for the firm of A. Platt and Company, the partnership formed in January 1847 by Alfred, William and Clark. Intending from the start to build the business around zinc, that same January the Platts received a large order of spelter from Phelps, Dodge of New York. Some 2,800 pounds, it came in "49 [and] 1/2 slabs," whole slabs averaging about 56 pounds. Another 100 slabs, some 5,500 pounds, came in August. The equipment present in 1843 allowed the Platts to melt and recast the slabs into billets for their rolling mill, roll the billets into sheets, scalp the sheets to the proper thickness, and slit them into three- to five-inch widths for the button press. It took more than one machine to bring the billets of several inches' thickness down close to a button's thickness of less than one-sixteenth inch, and the Platts probably built at least one more rolling mill for either the "breakdown" roll (the coarsest process), the "rundown" roll (the intermediate process), or "finish" roll on the strip.[16]

By 1850 the shop consumed twenty thousand pounds of zinc in a year, the greatest part of that going into the Platts' own buttons. They sold the rest to other buttonmakers in the form of rolled strip. A typical order came in 1850 from Warren, Wheeler and Woodruff, a button firm in nearby Watertown: "500# zinc 3-7/8 wide [and] 500# 4-1/8 wide." Another frequent customer was William R. Hitchcock and Company, a Waterbury button factory in which Scovill invested heavily. Hitchcock stamped out zinc blanks from the strip supplied by the Platts and used them as the base for cloth-covered buttons.[17]

The buttons the Platts made from their zinc strip, known as "whites" or "hard whites," had the dull finish of zinc. They were more appropriate for work clothing than for formal wear, which used brighter brass buttons. In the late 1840s the Platts made two kinds of buttons: "straps," which went onto the shoulder straps of overalls, and "suspenders," which went onto the waistband of men's pants to secure suspenders. They would soon produce trouser-fly buttons too, known as "fronts." In these uses the whites did not compete with brass but with buttons made from tin-plated sheet iron, and they offered some advantage over tinplate because zinc would not rust. Covering all of the possibilities in the field of utilitarian buttons, the Platts also made them from tinplate and from the tin-copper alloy known as Britannia, though not in the quantities they offered in zinc.[18]

The button machinery present in 1842 continued as the basis of the manufacturing process into the mid-1850s. A. Platt and Company made one-piece buttons with a wire eye for attachment. Alfred's "Button Stamp" punched the buttons out of rolled strip. Smaller presses imparted the figuring or other design onto the fronts and finished the edges. The earliest known example of an A. Platt and Company button has a concentric raised section in the center of the back, slit to receive the wire eye that was soldered in place. One of the presses, or another forming machine, made the raised section. The slit was probably made in a separate operation; it may have been formed at the same time as the raised section or perhaps cut by touching the raised section to a small saw. Later Platt buttons feature two or four punched holes for attachment, rather than a wire eye.[19]

A. Platt and Company sold buttons unfinished or "japanned." Japanning imparted a hard, lustrous black surface in imitation of Asian lacquerware. The actual Japanese product used a vegetable varnish, but the Connecticut metal-goods shops based what they called japan on a coal tar distillate known as asphaltum. Alfred Platt made up numerous recipes for japan, including special versions for other manufacturers. The recipe for his own buttons used "4 lbs. Gum Asfaltum, 1 quart Linseed Oil, 1/4 lb. Rosin, 1 Gal. Turpentine." After this gooey substance was applied to the buttons, they were baked and polished. Platt bought most of the materials locally at Apothecaries Hall, a supplier of chemicals and other industrial supplies. As production volume increased in the 1850s, he began sending to New York for barrels of japanning supplies.[20]

With casting and rolling, fabricating and finishing, the Platts in the late 1840s established an integrated metalworking firm on their own terms. Long experience in Waterbury industry had shown Alfred that integrated operation provided a market mix that tended to smooth out fluctuations in the business: if the firm's own consumer-oriented products fell out of favor, the Platts could still sell metal or button parts to industrial customers. Alfred Platt could not finance that range of production in brass, nor did the large scale of operation then necessary in brass appeal to him. With just the three Platts and fewer than a half-dozen employees, A. Platt and Company was small enough that the family members could oversee the entire operation without anyone serving principally as a manager.

By specializing in zinc, the Platts created a company that could reap some of the benefits of integrated operation without competing against the highly capitalized metals firms. The move to zinc was fortuitous but not serendipitous. It reflected Alfred Platt's selective ambition and resulted from his and his sons' ability to discern an opportunity and develop a strategy that borrowed from the experience of the largest Waterbury metals firms without duplicating their scale, methods, and markets.

Perceiving and capturing this market niche in zinc was the most important episode in the formation of the family business. The basic goal of the firm was to remain an independent family business, and zinc provided the means to fulfill that ambition. While many shrewd decisions, much hard work, and some good luck went into sustaining the Platts' role in this market and in broadening the uses for zinc, two early and pivotal characteristics would endure: zinc would remain one of the smallest metal markets, and specialized technology and expertise would be required to work it. The family's ability to adapt these basic features of the zinc business to subsequent changes in the broader economy was a fundamental reason why the Platts' business would outlive so many other Waterbury industrial enterprises.

Selling Zinc and Buttons

The Platts continued the type of relationship Alfred had long enjoyed with the community's larger metalworking firms, and eased their start-up, by minimizing their marketing function: they sold rolled zinc and some zinc buttons directly to other manufacturers. By not competing with brass buttons the Platts avoided an encounter they could not win and provided a product that complemented the offerings of the larger firms. Some of the Platts' zinc buttons, or buttons made by others from the Platts' rolled strip, simply joined the stream of goods already flowing through the marketing apparatus of the large firms. Other buttonmakers valued Platt's japanning skills too, and in its first three years A. Platt and Company sold this service to local manufacturers.[21]

To sell the majority of its buttons, however, A. Platt and Company had to negotiate with commission merchants. No one in the family had much exposure to the business practices that were common among the whole-salers by midcentury, such as gauging high sales periods (and scheduling production) according to the seasonal variations in garment production or setting prices months in advance of deliveries. A. Platt and Company had no experience in managing the delicate relationship between manufacturers and merchants.

That relationship was the product of two opposing impulses: manufacturers tried to maintain minimum price levels, and merchants tried to lower the prices they paid by pitting manufacturers against one another. Manufacturers could not control competition in buttons and other formed-metal goods as thoroughly as they did in primary metals. Since a button shop had lower capital needs than an alloying foundry or a rolling mill, a prospective competitor could set up a shop more easily. And as part of the fashion-sensitive garment trade, the markets for buttons were far more diverse, volatile, and difficult to control than the markets for brass sheet or wire. The merchants could always find a buttonmaker willing to cut prices, as Legrand Platt recounted in 1856:

Last spring the Connecticut buttonmakers held a meeting and agreed among themselves to put the price of Buttons at $1.25 per [great] gross and have been at work all summer trying to get them up. But late in the Fall . . . a Mr. Hall has kicked the dish all over by giving in to the market and selling his goods for what he could get and then going home and telling the rest that he should not stick to the agreement any longer. . . . He got rid of his goods and left the rest with a stock on hand and Buttons have fell off to about $1.00 per [great] gross.[22]

Many of the leading New York button merchants were Waterbury men who had originally sold the products of a single firm. By the mid-1840s the more successful wholesalers had developed such large markets for such a diverse array of buttons that no single firm could fill every order for them. Aggressive selling thus brought an end to the exclusive arrangements between makers and merchants, and each merchant sold the output of numerous producers. Gordon Burnham, who had established Aaron Benedict's sales operation in 1834, set up an independent commission house just ten years later to offer products beyond what Benedict produced. A branch of Burnham's independent merchant business was the Boston sales office that Arad Welton joined in 1844. Welton repeated his mentor's pattern, leaving Burnham in 1853 to sell buttons in New York for Cheshire Manufacturing Company, and soon offered the goods of other Naugatuck Valley makers too. His cousin, J. C. Welton, set up William R. Hitchcock Company's New York wholesale office around 1840, and by the end of the decade he also was selling the output of other shops. In a similar manner, Eli Curtis did not let Scovill's initial sponsorship of his button wholesaling business deter him from offering the buttons of other Waterbury shops if he saw a profit in it. These men and others like them comprised "the market" that Legrand referred to in his letter. When two producers made closely similar items, the merchants pushed the less costly alternative, offering lower prices to their customers and sometimes increasing their own wholesale markup.[23]

This situation made the Platts very uncomfortable. When A. Platt and Company began operations, the principals had no direct experience with the commission merchants and no means of assessing the merchants' claims. The Platts sold a limited amount through Eli Curtis, 81 great gross in 1847 and 105 great gross in 1849, no more than 10 percent of their button output. Curtis probably appealed to the Platts as a more sympathetic figure than the other merchants. While most of the merchants took up residence in New York and adopted the habits of that cosmopolitan city, Curtis kept his home in nearby Watertown and continued to run a general store while he sold buttons for Scovill. Not only would Curtis have been closer in manners and appearance to the determinedly rural Alfred Platt, but by supplying store goods in return for buttons he offered immediate and tangible payment instead of notes due six to eight months after delivery, the common payment method among the other merchants. In 1847 the Platts received from Curtis a dozen ax heads, gingham and calico yard goods, and books. A. Platt and Company also minimized cash obligations in the first three years of operation by trading buttons for Curtis's manufacturing supplies, such as japanning chemicals, tissue paper and cardboard for boxes to pack the buttons in, and a wagon priced at $65 (the most expensive item). Despite such advantages Curtis could not provide the Platts with the same market access as merchants based in New York.[24]

Wary of the price squeeze, the Platts wanted to arrange with a single merchant to sell the majority of their buttons. In choosing this agent Alfred Platt placed his hopes on his relationship with Timothy Porter. As guarantors of the construction debt for the new church, abiding affection and trust had grown between the two deacons while they struggled to assure the survival of their parish. When Alfred Platt wrote his first will in 1858, it was "put into Timothy Porters hands for Safe Keeping." William Platt's marriage to Porter's grandniece made Alfred Platt and Timothy Porter distant in-laws of each other, extending their relationship beyond the already strong ties of shared religion and high personal regard. This multifaceted friendship influenced Platt's selection of Porter's son-in-law, J. C. Welton, as the principal commission merchant for Platt buttons. Welton had ceased selling exclusively for William R. Hitchcock Company and had opened his independent sales office in New York. As the son-in-law of Alfred's most trusted friend, and a distant relation by marriage, J. C. Welton was an obvious choice among successful sales agents as the Platts ventured into the sharp-dealing arena of metal-goods wholesaling.[25]

The Platts nonetheless did not escape the typical relationship between maker and wholesaler. The two parties first agreed on the range of prices offered to the garment makers. Japanned buttons sold a little higher than whites, but the major factor in price variations was the size of the order. In one month, the Platts charged $1.375 per great gross for a shipment of forty-seven great gross of straps and $1.75 for an order of a single great gross. Following the standard arrangements for commission sales, Welton received payment from the garment makers, then deducted his 10 percent commission, the cost of shipment from Waterbury to New York, the cost of insuring the goods in his storeroom, and the cost of delivery to the customer to arrive at the net amount owed the Platts. In one six-month period in 1849, the Platts netted $691.68 on gross sales of $779.09 after deductions of $77.90 commission, $5.01 freight, and $4.50 insurance and delivery.[26]

By September 1847, Welton had cultivated customers for the strap and suspender buttons, both white and japanned, and urged the Platts to produce more and to do it faster: "We are entirely out of your white strap and suspender buttons and wish you to hurry them on as fast as possible as we have now orders for the suspenders which we are unable to fill. We need a case of Jap'd straps and suspenders this morning." Not a year into the business, Alfred Platt already found himself under pressure to quicken the pace.[27]

Welton's plea showed him to be a normal commission merchant, making a sale and then pestering the manufacturer to fulfill the promised delivery schedule. But Welton worked for his 10 percent. He helped to get zinc buttons accepted by the garment makers in the first place, and in the early years of A. Platt and Company he sold over 80 percent of the buttons not marketed directly to other manufacturers (perhaps 60 percent of the Platts' total button output). The urgent tone of Welton's September letter reflected his attempt to capitalize on the busy season for garment makers. In the second half of 1849, two-thirds of his sales came in August and September, when clothing houses were building up inventory for the busy fall trade. The largest single order, ninety-three great gross of straps, came in August. The other critical sales period ran from late January through the end of March, corresponding to the garment makers' accustomed sales surge in the spring. Quick delivery in the busy seasons would increase sales volume, Welton advised, as his customers liked to buy in bulk if they could get the buttons soon enough. "An early trade is always much the larger," he wrote in January 1850.[28]

Like other merchants, Welton absorbed inventory by taking deliveries and storing the buttons himself, and he accepted some of the risk by crediting the Platts' account for buttons shipped to him but not yet resold. He much preferred to pass the goods on immediately, and constantly attempted to coordinate the Platts' production schedule with the anticipated demand and his own mix of goods on hand. On January 10, 1850, Welton expected demand to rise and ordered one hundred great gross of white straps and fifty of white suspenders, noting that "we shall soon be out of them," and the following week implored the Platts for more japanned buttons of both types. He usually wanted the opposite of what he had just received so that he could fill any order quickly. And some customers ordered both, as Welton wrote with some urgency in late February, requesting more whites, adding that "many of our customers will not buy the Jap^d unless they can [also] have the white ones."[29]

Through Welton's efforts the Platts gained unprecedented (for them) sensitivity to the button market, but this access had its cost. In the first three years of A. Platt and Company, rare was the letter from Welton that did not express an emergency in getting some type of button. Welton usually needed the buttons on the day he wrote. Alfred Platt's hard-won control over his own labors became subject to Welton's chance to profit on the goods.

Welton paid the factory in the notes of obligation that came due six to eight months from date of issue, usually adding 5 percent interest. He carefully monitored the account so that he did not get too far ahead on payments. In June 1850 he wrote that a recent note "falls due 3 months before the account averages due, and we have dated this [enclosed] note for the same amount forward to make up for the difference in time." The Platts frequently asked for expedited payment, and Welton was "very happy to accommodate you if we could do so without great inconvenience to ourselves." In return for early payment, the Platts let Welton deduct the interest on the notes.[30]

The Platts did not relish the mercurial and often urgent demands that Welton's keen market timing placed on their work nor the irregular income stream that resulted. They also realized that if they worked steadily, rather than intermittently to meet weekly (and sometimes even daily) market variations, they could make many more buttons. Late in 1849, Clark Platt offered to supply Welton five thousand great gross during 1850, some five times more than the prior annual production. Welton accepted, reserving the right to specify product mix and delivery schedule and on condition that the Platts sell only through him. The Platts hesitated to offer exclusive agency, and Welton agreed to let one hundred great gross go to other merchants. Welton proposed to sell the buttons at $1 per great gross regardless of finish or type, but the Platts replied, "After much close figuring we have come to the conclusion that we cannot afford to sell you the Jap[nd] Suspender buttons for less than $1.15." Welton's response demonstrated the aggressive tactics of a successful commission merchant: "We should be very glad to pay you the price . . . but we find it an impossibility to get a proffit [sic] on them at that, *B. Platt's* being sold so *very much lower.*" Since B. Platt was a Newtown cousin who worked with Lorin and Legrand, Welton was playing producers against each other even when they came from the same family.[31]

After some further dickering to agree on prices, the arrangement worked as the Platts had hoped. Welton ordered larger lots with longer delivery schedules than previously. "You can send us what buttons you have finished," said one order. Welton's market timing took a longer view, at least a month and sometimes a season ahead, rather than a week or a day. In early June he wrote, "Send 1000 Gr gross straps . . . after 1 July" and assured the Platts that "we shall give you notice of our wants in time for you to get them up." Welton adopted a more proprietary attitude toward the Platts, advising them of customer complaints rather than selling another maker's goods to preserve his own standing: "Some of our customers complain that the suspenders are not so heavy as formerly." But he still kept a close eye on prices and competitors and several times enforced the agreement in less than tender fashion. When the supply of white suspenders dropped, he again mentioned the alternative source, though not without some obligatory regret: "We . . . hope you will be able to furnish us with fifty or 100 Gr. Gr. or so of them soon or we shall have to get some of them of B. Platts which we should be very sorry to do." The Platts tried to sell through L. B. Horton and Company, a Boston commission house, at higher prices than Welton paid. But Welton found out about the proposal and, acting quickly to preserve his position, offered Horton the same goods at a profit for himself yet far below what the Platts had asked. Horton did not appreciate the squeeze: "We were offered your strap buttons by Messrs. J. C. Welton and Co. of N.Y. at 1.25 [due in] 8 mos. and they sold them at that price in this market to any who would purchase of them. We cannot, of course, sell them at 1.62 1/2 when others are selling them so much less. Will you advise us what we are to do with them?" Besides the 10 percent commission Welton earned, he made an additional $.15 to $.20 per great gross on these Boston sales. No wonder Welton saw fit to encourage the Platts at midyear, writing that "You are now Lucrative in business."[32]

Alfred, William, and Clark made the first distribution of profits in April 1849, more than two years after starting A. Platt and Company. The firm paid Alfred for the time and materials he had put in and $.04 per great gross for rent on the shop and equipment. After Clark and William also received compensation for labor (at about $1.50 a day) and materials, the net stood at $2,417.62, or slightly less than $1,200 a year. Alfred received half, for a dividend of just under $600 per year, and his sons divided the rest for an annual share of some $300 each. To accord with the greater proportion of their time that the sons spent in the metalworking business, in December 1849 the dividend changed to three equal shares. The Platts divided $1,404.67 in April 1850, each receiving $468 for the prior twelve months. The following April, a year after striking the large-volume deal with Welton, the payout reached $529 apiece, and Welton still owed a hefty balance in unpaid notes. In January 1852, when the proceeds from the agreement for five thousand great gross were all in, the three Platts split up $1,844, each getting over $600.[33]

While profit dollars rose, however, the margin fell. Clark and William saw their dividend double between the payouts in 1849 and 1852, aided by the change to an equal three-way distribution. Despite his reduction from a half to a third of the profit, Alfred's dollar share also increased slightly over the same term. But production had multiplied five times over, the Platts (particularly the sons) spent far more time at buttonmaking, and the number of employees had probably doubled. Beyond increased labor costs, the major reason for the proportionately slow rise in profits was falling prices. In March 1849 the month's production brought the Platts an average of $1.99 per great gross, and in May 1849 they received an average of $1.59. The large-volume agreement of 1850 set prices considerably lower, averaging a few cents over $1.00. In January 1851, Clark Platt tried to renew the agreement at the higher rates of $1.60 for suspenders and $1.25 for straps, but had to settle for "last year's prices." Financially, the Platts found themselves running in place. Alfred continued to pay interest on his long-standing mortgage debt but did not reduce the principal he owed. Meanwhile Welton made more and more money in wholesale markups and commissions on the Platts' rising output.[34]

Welton's orders fell off in 1852, as he began reducing his selling activities to look for opportunities in manufacturing. For that year each of the Platts' dividends declined to $272.56. Then, in early 1853, Welton invested his merchant profits in two of the integrated brass firms and returned to Waterbury to participate in managing them. Alfred could not have appreciated the sardonic tone of Welton's final decision to leave the commission trade: "I have however at last concluded to allow those already engaged in that lucrative business to remain for the present unmolested by me and to turn my attention to some other golden channel."[35] His feelings toward Welton could not have improved when Welton assured the Platts that "should I embark in that business again I shall be very glad to make an arrangement for your buttons and am confident that I can sell more of them than all the other Yankees in New York put together."[36]

Welton had certainly helped A. Platt and Company, but the relationship proved more "lucrative" for him than for the Platts. The Platts had invested more time and money in metalworking to meet the volume generated by Welton. From May through July 1852, Alfred built one or more "slitters" for zinc strip and a "Press" for buttons, buying the body castings and gears from local production goods suppliers, machining other parts himself, and assembling the new equipment on site.[37] But when the Platts had built up their manufacturing capacity, Welton abandoned them. The relationship could not have changed Alfred's low opinion of commerce.

Alfred still had his debts on the property, and the business had increased its obligations to equipment suppliers and workers, but the market access of the Welton agreement had vanished. Rather than follow the example of Waterbury's more prominent industrialists and establish an in-house marketing capacity, Alfred Platt spent the next few years trying to redefine the metalworking company. He reconfigured the waterpower system, refinanced his debt, and with his sons' help attempted to deemphasize buttons by introducing new uses for zinc.

Living and Working in Platts Mills

Metalworking occupied about half of Alfred Platt's work time during the first six years of the business. In 1850 he had forty-six acres under cultivation or in pasture and another nine as a woodlot. He grew corn, rye, oats, and hay and tended apple trees and raspberry bushes. Livestock included two oxen for draft work, three swine, and one milk cow. Platt took pride in his farm, reporting prize hogs to the local newspaper's "Speaking of Pigs" column. "Mr. Alfred Platt," read one 1848 notice, "Has handed us weight of a 9-1/2 months Spring pig, which when dressed weighed 424 pounds! This however, he thinks little of—having killed one last season weighing 500!"[38]

Most Connecticut farmers relied on neighbors to help plant, cultivate, and harvest their crops. Platt needed more help than most because his shops took time away from farming, and the shops also had labor demands that neighbors helped to fulfill. The sawmill and gristmill in turn provided the means to compensate his neighbors for their efforts. In the 1840s, members of more than thirty families worked intermittently for Platt while running their own farms or businesses. Generally, they traded labor for the output of Platt's sawmill and gristmill, but Platt struck individual deals with each of his neighbors that often included some specialized equipment or skill beyond simple labor. Alfred Platt's accounts with Bennett Pritchard, George Roberts, Hial Bristol, and Thomas Upson demonstrate the multifaceted economic relationships he maintained with his neighbors.[39]

Bennett Pritchard offered particular expertise with oxen. Platt usually hired Pritchard and his team for plowing the fields, mowing hay, "sledding" logs to Platt's sawmill, and hauling earth and rocks during repair of the dam after a flood in 1852. In some fifteen years of dealings with Platt, through the late 1850s, Pritchard received cash only once every few years. He usually took meal, provender, and buckwheat from the gristmill, or fence posts, planks, and slabs from the sawmill.[40]

Farmer George Roberts hired out for farm and maintenance chores. He earned $1 per day, the nearly universal day rate for male common labor, for such jobs as "Diging [*sic*] potatoes," "pulling turnips," "haying," and "work at Mill Ditch." Roberts offered particular skill with livestock. For winter butchering, Platt at first paid the standard rate but raised it to $1.20 in 1854. Platt also hired Roberts for "Doctoring Cow" and "fixing Ox foot." They made individual bargains for specialized tasks, such as "Grading oats" for animal feed. Because a day of this earned Roberts double the usual compensation, Platt wrote the special notation "agreed" next to the daybook entry to remind himself at settling-up time that the high rate was no mistake. Once, in August 1853, Platt bargained Roberts down to $1.25 for grading the oats because, he noted, it was a "shortish day." Payment only rarely took the form of cash, once or twice a year in small amounts between $.50 and $3.00. Starting in 1849, when Platt hired a full-time hand for common labor, he occasionally compensated Roberts and other farmers by the work of this helper. Normally though, Roberts received processed grain in the form of meal, rye flour, or buckwheat flour and meat such as a "leg of veal."[41]

Hial Bristol, a neighboring blacksmith, spent most of his time working iron and relied on Platt's hired hands and other neighbors to get his farm-work done. He also depended on Platt for a great deal of the food consumed in his household, receiving produce more frequently than other neighbors and in smaller amounts intended for immediate consumption, such as half a bushel of turnips. Except for occasional notes to settle accounts, the only thing Platt took from Bristol was smith work. Bristol forged and repaired farm tools—"sharpning [*sic*] pick"—but mostly he helped Platt keep his shops going. Platt must have worn a path to the next-door forge in 1846 and early 1847, when Bristol performed almost $100 worth of blacksmithing for the fledgling zinc business. But Bristol was a country blacksmith, not a machine builder, and as the zinc business grew in technological sophistication, its demand for his services declined. Between 1847 and 1857, Bristol's work for Platt averaged under $30 a year and fell to around $13 a year after that. Benjamin Bristol, the smith's son, extended the metalworking knowledge he gained from his father by working for the Platts, and by 1854 he was responsible for the rolling operations in the zinc shop.[42]

As the metalworking business grew, Platt frequently hired carpenter Thomas Upson and his helpers. In early 1850, Alfred Platt owed Upson almost $200 for labor and materials used in fitting up the buttonmaking, zinc-rolling, and japanning shops. In 1851, Upson and his crew put in twenty-one days' work on Platt's "Bank and Mill." Platt also hired Upson's helper for seven weeks, paying Upson the weekly rate of $2.25 for his time. Over the next five years Upson and his employees made doors and repaired windows for Platt's houses and shops, worked on Platt's bridge over the Naugatuck, repaired the headgates of the waterpower system, and made the wooden crates for shipping buttons. In 1852, Upson began performing some of the woodworking functions of the zinc business: making the flasks that held molds for pouring zinc billets and the patterns used in the mold-making process. Platt often compensated Upson with sawn lumber used in his work and with feed orders from the gristmill for Upson's livestock (as much as four hundred pounds at a time). But with lumber priced at less than a penny a foot and meal at $1.56 per hundred pounds, Upson's services far outpaced such payment, and Platt had to make up the difference in cash. Cash payments to Upson were usually no less than $20, several times a year; in some years he received more than $100 in cash. Upson reaped greater benefit than most of the neighbors from the economic growth based on metalworking in Platts Mills.[43]

Alfred Platt dealt individually with each neighbor and with each task. In the years for which his daily records survive (1850 and after), Platt made no less than nine transactions a week and as many as forty or more a week when he settled accounts with gristmill customers. Dickering was woven into the fabric of his life. Though Platt resented the manipulations of commercial men, he never lost his taste for one-on-one bargaining.[44]

The Platts were better off than their neighbors because the gristmill and sawmill served as the principal suppliers of flour and lumber for about a square mile of area, where between two hundred and three hundred people lived. The mills provided indispensable materials that neighbors had to pay for in scarce cash if they could offer no goods or services that Platt needed. For dozens of nearby families the obligations ran between $7 and $20 a year in the early 1850s. In 1850, Platt's property was valued at $16,000, more than triple the next-highest valuations in the vicinity.[45]

Income from the sawmill and gristmill depended on specialized labor. While Platt oversaw the mills and frequently worked in them, and his sons operated the mills too, the family alone could not keep them going after buttonmaking picked up in the early 1840s. Alfred then trained selected individuals to run the mills. Abel Turney had charge of the sawmill from the mid-1840s through the late 1850s. Platt paid him piece rates in the early 1850s, such as $1 per thousand feet of lumber, and wages only rarely took the form of cash paid directly from Platt to Turney. When Turney bought groceries and other household goods on credit from Nirom Platt or Eli Curtis, the storekeepers charged Alfred, who then usually paid with flour from his gristmill. Alfred also allowed Turney to bargain directly with saw-mill customers and to collect, and keep, the cash paid for lumber, then deducting those amounts from the money he owed to Turney.[46]

Abijah Crofut, who boarded in Alfred's household throughout the 1840s, was a valued gristmill hand. He probably had major responsibility for the mill in the latter years of the decade, when Alfred turned his atten-tion to developing the metalworking business. Crofut's wages reached $1.62 a day, and he also traveled to West Stockbridge to help out with Charles Platt's gristmill. But he spent less time at milling as the 1850s progressed; in 1855, Crofut only worked about six weeks in Platt's gristmill. As Crofut's par-ticipation declined, Platt took an unusual course for his day by training Daniel Bergan, a recent immigrant from Ireland, in the operation of the mill.[47]

New Neighbors: The Irish

Bergan was among the hundreds of Irish people who began arriving in Waterbury in the late 1840s. They were a small part of the massive emigra-tion from that famine-stricken country after blight decimated the potato crops of 1845, 1846, and 1847. Many Irish helped to build the Naugatuck Railroad, then stayed in Waterbury to work in the growing metals indus-tries and as farm laborers. Of nearly four hundred people in the eighty households in and around Platts Mills in 1850, about 20 percent (seventy-seven people) claimed Irish birth. While representing a less dramatic change than that which occurred near the center of Waterbury—where Irish people were a substantial majority in some neighborhoods—these immigrants brought a new labor force to Platts Mills.[48]

Most of the Irish living near Alfred Platt in 1850 worked as farm laborers and lived in tenant houses. Six families lived south of Platts Mills, near Union City; all of the employed people worked as laborers, probably in the nearby foundry as well as on local farms. North of Platts Mills were four Irish households, twenty-four people in all. Edmond Fitzpatrick and his family rented a house from Thomas Upson. The households headed by Patrick Reed, John Phalen, and Patrick Welch rented quarters from Yankee farmers. Reed's household included only his wife and baby, but the others had a variety of adult relatives and boarders. Phalen and his wife lived with their three young children and four Phalen siblings between the ages of sixteen and thirty. Patrick Welch, his wife, and his daughter shared their house with four unrelated Irishmen between the ages of thirty and forty. These people, without any land or businesses of their own, were more available for temporary work than the Yankee farmers. Since all worked as laborers, they apparently had no special capacity to offer and therefore scant bargaining power. Low-paid, available, and willing to take on the most arduous physical tasks, Irish immigrants supplanted the extensive network of neighbors in fulfilling many of the Platts' labor requirements in the 1850s.[49]

At a time when many Yankees wanted nothing to do with Irish people, Alfred and Irene Platt boarded the twenty-year-old Daniel Bergan in their home. He worked as a laborer, probably on the farm, and Alfred came to respect his abilities enough to train Bergan to tend the gristmill. In 1851 Platt hired Bergan to run the mill full-time in the fall and winter and evenings for the rest of the year, for an annual salary of $156; combined with the $1 a day Bergan earned for agricultural labor in spring and summer, this salary made for a substantial income. In his agreement with Bergan, Platt dealt with his Irish employee as an individual and compensated him according to the value of his work, much as he negotiated with his Yankee neighbors for the special aptitudes they offered.[50]

In the early 1850s, teaching an Irish immigrant a special skill was even less common than boarding an Irish employee in the home, and all in Platt's family may not have agreed with him regarding the treatment of Bergan and the other Irish. William seems to have viewed them as a mass of people indistinct from one another, tolerable only because they were an available labor force. In 1856 he wrote, "A multitude of Irishmen each with a name dear to himself but which are mainly unknown to me, are employed in excavating for the ditch." And when William made fun of a cousin who was willing to take on any task, he called him a "Bogtrotter." It is hard to imagine Alfred Platt disdaining any task or anyone who worked hard.[51]

The compensation that Alfred Platt charged for his own labor demonstrates further how he perceived an intrinsic value in work, regardless of who performed it. In fulfilling the metalworking agreement with his sons, Alfred undertook many tasks for no additional pay beyond profits from the partnership and rent on the shop. But for other tasks, such as taking a wagon to Union City to pick up a load of spelter or stacking wood for the shop's stove, he charged the firm $1 a day. To Alfred, the value of a day's work depended on the task, not the man who did it. (As will be seen, Platt did place different values on work according to the gender of the worker.) A job had the same worth whether it was done by a newly arrived Irish day laborer or a sixth-generation Yankee proprietor.[52]

The Metalworking Shop

When the metalworking business began in 1847, Platt had Turney to run the sawmill, Crofut (and later Bergan) in the gristmill, and neighbors and neighbors' sons helping out with specialized farming chores and common labor. But the growth of the zinc business upset any balance he had achieved in the distribution of his family's efforts and those of his neighbor-employees. It increased the demand for the highly skilled tasks involved in casting zinc, making and setting up metalworking machinery, and operating the critical processes such as rolling. A. Platt and Company also created an entirely new type of labor in Platts Mills: the repetitive tasks of tending production machines and packaging their products, tasks that required neither a high degree of skill nor much muscle power. Alfred Platt tended to place a very low value on these jobs.

The Platts set up and maintained the machinery, and in the 1850s they devised new equipment for buttons and other products. They ordered the critical parts from the region's machine builders, and occasionally a skilled hand from The Foundry Company worked in the shop for a week or two to help install a new piece of equipment. For the continuous responsibilities of tending the casting shop, rolling mill, and japanning shop, the Platts trained a small group of relatives and neighbors. Alfred boarded his nephew Truman Judd in his home and trained him to work in the casting shop as a "melter." Franklin Thomas, the son of local farmer Mansfield Thomas, ran the japanning operation from 1847 through 1849. Truman Judd's brother Franklin, who ran the stamping machinery, then took over the japan shop.[53]

William Platt probably handled the rolling mill by himself until 1854, when the seventeen-year-old Benjamin Bristol began rolling zinc. The Platts made this assignment very carefully because rolling, the core operation of their firm, demanded a high degree of judgment to handle material with different and unknown impurities. The considerable time variations in Bristol's account reveal the unpredictability of rolling in relation to other jobs. The Platts paid him according to the time he put in and expected him to produce one or two "batches" in a standard week of six ten-hour days; the number of batches differed according to the quality of the incoming spelter and the specifications for Bristol's output. In two successive two-batch weeks in August 1854, Bristol took fifty-five hours and sixty-five hours to finish the work; the following March, two successive one-batch weeks ran fifty-two and sixty-five hours. Since constant oversight would have defeated the purpose of hiring and training a skilled roller hand, the Platts must have trusted that young Bristol had good reasons for time variations as high as 25 percent from week to week.[54]

A. Platt and Company needed people to pack buttons into cardboard boxes and to make the boxes. (Standard packaging was a small gross, or 144 buttons, to a box, and twelve boxes, or a great gross, to a case.) Alfred saw little skill in these tasks, and the low wages he set made them hard to fill: $.06 for making a hundred boxes; for packing, less than $80 per year. Local families with their own farms or businesses did not have much labor to spare, and the pay did not make it worth taking time from farming or other activities. Alfred prevailed on his wife Irene to make some 47,500 boxes in the late 1840s, enough for several years' production. The first packers were Lorraine and Cynthia Lawrence, who worked for about six months in 1847 while boarding with Clark Platt and his family.[55]

Over the next five years Platt hired local Yankee farm girls to pack the buttons: George Roberts's daughters Catherine and Susy and Mansfield Thomas's daughters Sarah and Mary. The work was uneven before the J. C. Welton contract. In 1849, Sarah Thomas packed only eight great gross in a month between the two busy seasons and almost four times as many when the Platts prepared for the January rush. Hiring local people as packers was an advantage for the Platts because the workers were close by when needed and the Platts did not have to make boarding arrangements when they had to get some buttons packed.[56]

Irish people eventually worked in the button factory, but Alfred hired them for other jobs initially. Edmond Fitzpatrick began in April 1849 as Alfred Platt's full-time farmhand and wagon driver. Platt paid him $125 a year and paid rent to Thomas Upson for the house the Fitzpatricks lived in. In 1850, Fitzpatrick's eighteen-year-old daughter Ellen worked as a live-in maid for Alfred and Irene Platt, and sixteen-year-old Patrick as a farmhand. In 1852 Platt started hiring Fitzpatrick children to perform the packing and other less-skilled jobs in the metalworking shop, the first step in establishing the Irish labor force to support the expansion of the business in the following years.[57]

Years of Transition, 1853–1858

Alfred Platt turned sixty-four in 1853. A vigorous man who had worked six days a week for his entire adulthood, he nonetheless began to experience some of the minor health problems of advancing age. He apparently suffered from an upper respiratory ailment as well as some stiffness in his joints, and he copied home remedies on the flyleaf of his daily account book. One recipe contained molasses, ginger, and other spices, with the principal ingredient "1 Pint of Rum." Although Clark and probably some of the other Platts advocated temperance, Alfred prescribed for himself a daily dose of this spiced rum. Alfred's advancing years and declining health brought a certain immediacy to his concerns over the property and businesses, and the mid-1850s were among the busiest years of his life.[58]

A. Platt and Company produced fewer zinc buttons after the loss of the Welton contract. The dividend for 1853 was $192.63, the lowest since the start of the partnership in 1847. Short of sending out one of the partners to market the buttons, the Platts had no choice but to sell through commission merchants. They used two houses, L. B. Horton and Company of Boston and E. S. Wheeler and Company of New York. In 1854, Wheeler moved some 2,500 great gross, about half of the peak annual sales of Welton. Horton never ordered more than one hundred great gross of mixed types and finish every few months.[59]

The merchants pressured the Platts in familiar ways. Delivery schedules were a frequent irritant, as when Horton wrote, "We want them immediately if at all." Nor did Horton hesitate to raise the issue of alternative suppliers in his effort to push prices lower: "We are receiving the Straps from another party at 95 cts. How does that agree with your present price? Can you sell us at a less price—say 85 cts. nett cash?" They compromised at $.90, payable in eight months.[60]

The Platts' continued naïveté regarding marketing impaired their relations with merchants. They granted Wheeler the exclusive right to sell their buttons in New York and "Southern markets" but did not protect Horton from Wheeler's incursions into Boston. The Platts also gave Wheeler, their highest-volume seller in the mid-1850s, a lower price and more favorable terms. Not only did they risk offending Horton, but they lost the chance to establish a higher-priced territory for their buttons when Wheeler offered his discounted Platt buttons to the Boston merchants. "Why is it that we cannot get your buttons as cheap as E. S. Wheeler and Co.?" wrote Horton in 1855. "They offer us your buttons at 90 cts." Since Horton paid the Platts $.90 for a great gross, the Bostonians knew that Wheeler had a better deal from the Platts if Wheeler could offer the same price that the factory did.[61]

Alfred Platt's distaste for the trials of selling did not turn him away from the business, but he did turn over to his sons the negotiations with merchants. In the first years of the business, the sales correspondence featured Alfred's spindly script. In 1852 the company's letters began to bear the bolder characters of Clark's handwriting, and after 1853 Clark had primary responsibility for relations with sellers.[62]

While they continued to make buttons, Alfred, Clark, and William stepped up their efforts to develop new uses for zinc. The first result was weather stripping for windows and doors. Starting with rolled zinc in the proper thickness and width, it was a relatively easy product to make with minimal adaptations to existing equipment, requiring only cutting to length, punching some holes for attaching the strips, and bending them to fit window and door frames.[63]

The next product, seamless zinc pipe, demanded complicated new equipment with high power requirements. The product of William Platt's innovative mind, the pipe machine featured four dies working against a mandrel in the longitudinal hole of a round zinc billet. In a rocking motion, the dies elongated the billet, reduced its wall thickness, and advanced it into position for the next stroke. The Platts applied the process to zinc because they were familiar with it and to avoid competing with the brass firms, whose brazed tubing was used for gas and kerosene lamps and for decoration. To capitalize on zinc's noncorrosive property, the Platts envisioned a market in plumbing, where they would compete against lead pipe.[64]

Through 1854 and 1855 the Platts worked to build the seamless pipe machine, buying castings, gears, and pulleys from The Foundry Company, Naugatuck Machine Company, and the machine works of Scovill Manufacturing. The pipe machine's carefully integrated timing of precise motions represented a new level of mechanical sophistication for Platts Mills. The mandrel and the threaded hole it ran in took three and a half days for Naugatuck Machine Company to cut and fit. Also in 1854, the Platts worked on making a new button press, a huge machine whose bed alone weighed over 2,100 pounds and cost nearly $100 for The Foundry Company to cast and machine. From November 1855 through February 1856 the Platts revamped their zinc-rolling process; Naugatuck Machine provided the key components, the "chilled rolls" that were the center of the operation. While the mill was down, the Platts rented machine time from Scovill to keep rolling zinc.[65]

The pipe machine and the new button and rolling equipment elevated the power requirements of the metalworking business. Alfred also continued to operate his grist- and sawmills, and he upgraded or added to the sawmill equipment in early 1856. The waterpower system of the mid-1830s no longer sufficed. Between late 1855 and late 1856 Alfred had "the water shut out of the ditch" while he worked to increase the power supply. The irregular plan of the dam probably dates from this construction job; it zigzagged across the stream in order to maximize the length of the spillway, letting more water flow over the dam during floods and minimizing the pressure on its upstream face. In 1856, Platt also installed the stone apron of the downstream face, to prevent undercutting. Alfred eliminated the older west headrace (the one closer to the river) and completely rebuilt the east race and headgates for higher capacity. Work on the race also included building a long, arched masonry culvert to conduct the race under the road, and a means to prevent ice damming. The greater height of the new headrace walls protected against flood and accommodated increased flow volume from the consolidation into a single race. The three feet Platt gained brought the head of his waterpower system to seventeen feet. He also dug a new wheelpit and tailrace in order to install a small turbine "for the purpose of driving our button machinery," as Clark reported.[66]

The turbine came from another country mechanic, John Tyler of West Lebanon, New Hampshire. Though small, at fourteen inches diameter and under five horsepower, it offered several advantages. The Naugatuck provided very uneven flow over the course of a year, with abrupt rises in volume. In high-volume conditions the river would rise into the tailrace, creating backwater that would slow or even stop a breast wheel. To counter this, breast wheels were usually placed one to three feet above the normal tailwater level, sacrificing some of the fall to assure more days of operation each year. Nor did waterwheels take full advantage of periodic higher water levels since their effective head was determined by the fixed distance the water fell between entering and leaving the wheel. Alfred Platt sought reassurance from Tyler on precisely these matters related to water level. Tyler advised him to "have the wheel [i.e., turbine] fully underwater that you may get all the head." The turbine, which operated submerged without hampering its efficiency, could run during the occasional higher water levels when elevated tailwater would impede a waterwheel. Thus the periodically higher flow would be put to use.[67]

The Tyler wheel had other advantages. Made of iron, it required much less maintenance than a wooden wheel. It came in a watertight iron "draft box," with an "apron" at the top that was simply bolted to the wooden curb of the wheelpit. Installing it was easy, and there was no need for expensive masonry lining in the pit. The turbine ran at 316 revolutions per minute, at least thirty times faster than the old waterwheels, minimizing the need for gearing to get the shafting up to the proper speed for button machinery, which ran faster than grindstones.[68]

Like the new machinery it drove, the turbine represented increasing technological sophistication and a more important role for metalworking in the lives of the Platts. With its own dedicated prime mover, buttonmaking no longer had to share power with Alfred's other processing enterprises. The turbine's ability to run under a greater variety of stream conditions began to move buttonmaking more fully away from the seasonal rhythm of farming and gristmilling and toward those other seasons determined by the garment trade. By installing a power source independent from the other

This c. 1890 photograph shows the gristmill that Alfred Platt enlarged in the mid-1850s. The bearded man at the extreme right is Alfred's son, Legrand Platt. (Mattatuck Museum)

processes, the Platts improved their ability to respond quickly to orders generated by commission merchants, with less concern for coordinating buttonmaking with the gristmill and sawmill. At $55, Tyler's turbine was not cheap, but equal to about one-quarter of Alfred Platt's annual profit on the button shop. Alfred's willingness to absorb the expense further indicates the importance of metalworking to the family's economic circumstances.[69]

The construction work and new machinery drove metalworking expenditures beyond the ability of Alfred's collateral activities to support them. Besides the cash he earned from the gristmill and sawmill, Platt had often used produce, lumber, or flour to buy materials and services for the metal business and to pay the employees. In 1847 and 1848, for instance, Platt received materials and services worth $124.13 from The Foundry Company. In return he supplied wood for use in the foundry, and flour and produce the foundry used to pay its workers; Platt's cash balance came to only $14.39. Platt defrayed his own labor cost by supplying buckwheat flour to a general store to settle up for shoes and cloth his employees bought on credit. In the mid-1850s, however, capital expenditures such as the $100 press bed and the $55 turbine, and increasing wages to support the expanded work force, pushed Platt's finances into a different realm.[70]

The Waterbury Savings Bank, established in 1851, offered an alternative to the personal loans and mortgages that the Platts had depended on since their arrival in Waterbury. Nirom established the family's relationship with the bank, soon after it opened, by borrowing $1,000 in the form of a one-year note. In September 1851, requiring a constant line of credit to stock his store, Nirom began taking out three-month $1,000 notes in a series of routine transactions. He took out two more of the standard loans in December 1851 and a total of fifteen in 1852. From 1853 through 1855, Nirom paid interest every two to three weeks, on average, then rolled over the balance to begin another three-month term. In late 1855, Waterbury Savings Bank doubled Nirom's credit line to $2,000. Alfred co-signed all of these transactions, almost a hundred in all, but did not immediately follow Nirom's example in financing his own enterprises. Alfred's only bank loan in the early 1850s was for $500 in June 1852, when the button shop was adding new equipment to satisfy J. C. Welton's orders. Nonetheless, Nirom's experience allayed any doubts Alfred might have had about the bank, and he needed money to fund the improvements of 1855 and 1856.[71]

In June 1856, Alfred Platt approached Waterbury Savings Bank with a plan to replace his three existing mortgages with a single loan from the bank. On June 8 the bank lent Alfred $8,000 against his property, and the next day he paid off the Benedict and Burnham mortgage of 1841. On June 12, Alfred gathered his brothers together to resolve the obligations on Platts Mills. He repaid Leonard's loan of 1840 and retired that mortgage, then paid Almon for his share of the land from their father's will. Alfred owed the bank $8,000 and held an otherwise clear title to all of the land, water rights, buildings, and equipment on the east side of the river.[72]

The bank loan solidified the business but made Alfred's personal situation far less secure, since mortgages held by family members had been part of the debt replaced by the loan. Alfred stood to gain from expansion in metalworking, but if the hoped-for profits did not materialize, he faced the loss of his property. His $8,000 loan obligated him to pay some $400 each year in interest alone, which would take most or all of the cash earned from the gristmill and sawmill. He then found another way to extract value from technological expertise by selling the rights to use his patented buckwheat fans. In late March of 1857 he traveled to West Stockbridge to negotiate with Platt and Barnes, his son Charles's company. Alfred received $3,000 for the patent, reserving for himself the right to use it in Connecticut. Combined with his refinancing, this sale enabled Alfred to pay for the new power system and machinery and to set aside a small cash reserve. He had secured the financing for the next stage of industrial growth.[73]

Alfred did not relate to his sons the details of his financial dealings. Clark learned about the sale of the buckwheat fan patent and discerned its benefit to Platts Mills, but not from what Alfred told him: "I have no positive information respecting the matter but from what I have seen and heard have got the impression that they know nearly at least how they are going to do it." Nor could Clark have known about his father's payment to Leonard to retire that mortgage. Clark was mystified when Leonard, who neither had nor sought any work, headed south for the winter. "Think he must be rather short for funds; know not how he will contrive to keep his big Belly full," wrote Clark in December 1856.[74]

Alfred's secrecy spared his worried sons from further concern over the uncertain financial outlook. Clark and William did not appreciate the lack of income combined with the rigorous labor of this transition period. William had hoped that "when the water was shut off in our ditch I should have an abundance of leisure time." Instead, he was "very busy indeed doing . . . hand work." William found manual labor in metalworking "a heavy job."[75]

The local Irish did not hesitate to accept the work when the Platts began to offer it. Edmond Fitzpatrick's son Richard began packing buttons in 1852 at the age of eleven; a year later the Platts had him "Cutting Buttons" on the stamping machine. Mary Fitzpatrick, age fourteen, worked forty days during 1853 making weather strip and a year later started packing buttons along with her younger sister Bridget. The Fitzpatricks were the first Irish family to move to Platts Mills. In April 1853 they rented from Alfred the house that stood next door to his own, paying $1 a month plus another $.50 for a half-acre kitchen garden.[76]

Besides his annual laborer's salary ($216 in 1854), Edmond Fitzpatrick made extra money when Alfred Platt assigned him teamster work for A. Platt and Company. Edmond was known to have a fondness for liquor, and some of his "days sick and absent" were attributed to his less than sober state. On one trip to Massachusetts, Alfred docked Edmond for five days that appear to have been spent on a drunken binge. Indeed, alcohol seems to have killed Fitzpatrick, as the disapproving William Platt reported in the summer of 1856: "His body was found (after having been absent four days) lying straightly upon its back in [a neighbor's] barn. He had a bottle in one hand about one fourth full of liquor as firmly secured upon his breast as complete rottenness superseded to the death grasp could well make it."[77]

Alfred Platt, who favored spiced rum, did not seem to mind Fitzpatrick's bouts with the bottle so long as Platt did not have to pay for the time. Fitzpatrick, the oldest Irishman in the area, may have been a leader among his countrymen. After he moved next door to Platt, many more Irish people appeared on the payroll, perhaps after introductions furnished by Fitzpatrick. Fitzpatrick also seems to have acted as a wholesaler between Alfred Platt and the local Irish, reselling them flour from Platt's gristmill.[78]

With the new product lines and machinery in the mid-1850s, the Platts started hiring Irish people for metalworking jobs. In 1854, Franklin Judd supervised four Irish boys working at stamping. The carpenter Thomas Upson renovated one of Alfred's dwellings into a boardinghouse for hired hands in 1855, and over the next four years Irish women began performing press work, earning the lowest wages paid by the Platts. Jane Falen started running a press in July 1858 at the annual rate of $62.50, less than half of the $132 per year that Alfred paid male Irish factory workers. (A male Yankee machinist earned $1.75 a day.) By the end of the 1850s the shop had a differentiated work force of low-paid Irish labor for the less-skilled tasks and high-paid Yankee skilled workers and supervisors. It was still small, however, with under a dozen workers most of the time, including the Platts.[79]

In adjusting to this new work force Alfred Platt changed some of the procedures he had followed for thirty years. He began separating the labor accounts of wage-earning employees from the daybooks in which he recorded all of his other transactions, keeping a "time book" to record hours worked. Platt's Irish employees surprised him by taking a day off to celebrate Christmas. Since he assumed that his salary agreements covered work on December 25, Platt deducted a day's pay for the new holiday. After he started hiring machine operators with no prior manufacturing experience, Platt realized the need to begin inspecting the work more closely. When he deemed Jane Falen's press work to be "shattered and partially damaged," Platt deducted half of her wages. He must have regretted not catching the problem more quickly because the half pay covered twenty-four weeks of deficient work.[80]

As the work in Platts Mills evolved and the people who performed it changed, the community comprised by the family's holdings and the surrounding farms began to assume a different character. In 1860, Irish people were 30 percent of the residents in and around Platts Mills, up from 20 percent in 1850. More Yankee family farms came to resemble that of Mansfield Thomas, with fewer acres under cultivation as the younger generation took manufacturing jobs. In the Platt enclave, Daniel Bergan and his family moved into the house formerly occupied by the Fitzpatricks. Perhaps influenced by Jane Falen's dismal results as a machine operator, Alfred put her to work as his household's live-in maid. Alfred and Irene had four boarders in their home, an English immigrant factory hand, two Irish farmhands, and a teamster who was probably Irish. In the twenty years from 1840 to 1860, less than a generation, an exclusively Yankee community became a multiethnic one. Once a place of landowning families, by 1860 the number of tenants in the area rivaled the number of property holders. The neighbor-employees of the early 1840s all held some bargaining power, but by 1860 the residents included immigrants who, except Bergan, had no skill or property with which to trade.[81]

The quickening pace of industrialization at Platts Mills—higher investment and risk, new equipment, new construction, new workers and new
neighbors—exacted an emotional toll. In 1856, when A. Platt and Company
had paid no dividend for a year and its power system was shut down, Clark's
worry occasionally overtook his hope for the button business. "At the best
you know it is a very small affair for 3 . . . proprietors," he wrote to Legrand.
"And requires that I should labor pretty constantly and secure the wages
therefor with the proffits [sic] of the business in order to get a deasent [sic]
living." While Alfred risked everything to build up the business, Clark had
a young family and wanted more income. Alfred was devoted to proprietorship, but Clark did not value the role of proprietor by itself, especially
when the business was "very small." Though Clark may not have realized
it in 1856, his experience mirrored Alfred's. When Alfred was in his early
thirties and awoke each morning to a houseful of young children, he had
been a partner of Benedict rather than an independent manufacturer assuming all of the risk for his undertakings. In 1856, Alfred's view reflected
the experience of a long, difficult career. His appreciation of independence
in business had deepened with maturity and required some success for reinforcement. Decades later, when Clark was the patriarch and new circumstances threatened the family's control over its enterprises, Clark had fully
absorbed the lessons of his father and presided over another unprecedented
expansion of productive capacity at Platts Mills. Clark had already learned
to value hard work, however, and despite his gloom resolved "not to suffer
myself to cry for the milk that has been spilt but shall set myself to pulling
the teats of the animal with as much or more vigor than before."[82]

By the end of 1856, A. Platt and Company had the financial stability, the
machinery, and the independent power system adequate to fill high-volume
button orders in a timely fashion, but lacked a source for such orders.
Wheeler continued to sell less than half the volume that J. C. Welton had
generated. The most promising part of the business in 1856 and 1857 was
the "Thin Zinc," or rolled strip, used as blanks for cloth buttons. R. Hitchcock and Company, a principal customer for the strip, bought two thousand to three thousand pounds a year, always ordering five hundred pounds
at a time.[83]

Zinc pipe did little to alleviate the kinds of sales difficulties the firm had
experienced earlier with buttons. Though pipe was aimed at builders and
plumbers and not tied to a fast-changing consumer market, it nonetheless
demanded the attention to customers and their needs that could not be
provided from Platts Mills. Alfred Platt traveled to New York in October
1855 and March 1856 to select an agent. He again relied on his relationship
with Timothy Porter by choosing the firm of A. W. Welton and Porters,

the commission house that Arad Welton had started in Boston in 1853 and expanded in 1854 by taking two of Porter's sons as partners to set up a New York office.[84]

Thomas and Nathan Porter carefully explored the market for zinc pipe, but their report in May 1856 was not heartening. Querying builders, the Porters learned "that the usual way was for them to contract with a Plumber to furnish pipe and do a job." They found that in New York City only a licensed plumber could tap the water mains, that licenses were few because they required a $1,000 bond, and that licensed plumbers spurned zinc pipe because it was so much cheaper than lead: "Plumbers we think generally regard the thing with jealousy knowing that if it is generally introduced the best part of their trade will be gone." When a plumber agreed to scrutinize the pipe, he feared that the pipe wall was too thin for soldered joints to hold up: "A blow or anything of the kind would be apt to make it leak." He thought that the pipe would not take a bend and suggested making cast elbows "twice as heavy" as the pipe. Installation also required a greater variety of "couplings and tees" than the Platts had furnished, and the agents reported a difference between the threads in the Platts' fittings and those cut in the field: "A thread cut by their plate will not enter your coupling."[85]

The Platts' lack of market awareness made the pipe venture futile. Production-based insight had triggered the experiment: they could make pipe more cheaply than other manufacturers, and they could lower the cost further by making it from zinc. Such thinking had worked for zinc buttons, but the Platts did not understand the difference between selling buttons and pipe. Garment makers could use low-cost buttons on work clothes and other unpretentious apparel, but plumbers passed the high cost of pipe through to their customers and would not risk their bonds to install a questionable product. Sewn-on buttons had no requirements for technical compatibility, whereas pipe was useless without an array of related products, and it had to conform to established standards of performance and fit.

"The prospects of our being able to dispose of much Zinc Tubing are not very flatering [*sic*]," wrote Clark in 1857. The Platts attempted to adapt their process to make stronger pipe of copper and brass. When the difficulty of competing with the tubing made by the larger metals firms stilled that attempt, the Platts began experimenting with zinc pipe lined with tin. Not easily abandoning the investment of more than $2,500 in machinery, they continued trying to sell pipe in New York. A plumbing supplier in Brooklyn disposed of several thousand feet of it between 1859 and 1861, but sales never recouped the investment.[86]

Despite the ultimate disappointment, the pipe venture had an enormous impact on the Platts' metalworking enterprise by opening their relationship with A. W. Welton and Porters. In early 1858, Clark Platt asked the Porters to sell zinc buttons, and Thomas Porter agreed to try. His response lacked promotional zeal: "We do not suppose that we could sell a good many of your goods at first. We should have to work into it." Porter's candor would continue to characterize the dealings between maker and seller for many years to come, as the sons of the two deacons built the zinc firm into a resilient and profitable enterprise.[87]

CHAPTER THREE

"Taking Down the Whole U.S."

D U R I N G the Civil War the Platts' metalworking business broke from its past as a single component within the many-faceted family economic system. The new technology, labor force, and financing put in place during the mid-1850s supported a massive production surge based on government purchases during the Civil War, which propelled the business beyond the scope that Alfred preferred. He tolerated but did not participate in the expansion to downtown Waterbury that Clark and William undertook during the latter years of the war.

The Porter brothers contributed the commercial insight and managed the distribution system necessary to profit from the niche production the Platts had established with their specialty in zinc. The Porters' long view of the markets, awareness of the Platts' full capability, and constant probing for exclusive offerings produced a spectacularly profitable niche in zinc buttons for army tents. The proceeds from this burst of output secured the business for the next generation, and the experience provided the model that Clark and William would follow after their father's passing.

Though able and perceptive wholesalers, the crucial difference between the Porters and other merchants was that the Platts trusted deeply these sons of Timothy Porter. Alfred followed their advice, if grudgingly at times, and allowed his sons to follow it too. William Platt's wife, Caroline Orton, was raised in Timothy Porter's household. William viewed Thomas and Nathan Porter and their brother Samuel, who joined them in 1860, as his brothers-in-law.[1]

The Porters repaid the Platts' trust by establishing a fundamentally different kind of relationship than the Platts had experienced with other merchants. The Porters viewed the Platts as partners and never set the Platts against other manufacturers to keep their own costs down. On this basis of mutual benefit the Porters brought to the button business the marketing and management functions that larger firms such as Benedict's had put in place a generation earlier. They performed all of the tasks that Alfred Platt spurned and that his sons never had an opportunity to learn. The Porters also improved those functions that the Platts had handled themselves, such as purchasing materials and scheduling production.

In their most important job—selling buttons—the Porters devised and implemented a broad strategy for building up the business. From their New York base they gathered comprehensive information on the button market to offer the Platts an assessment of which customers and which products had the best prospects for sales. As the product line expanded and the Porters shopped the new buttons around, they wrote back to Waterbury frequently to readjust tactics. They sized up which customers were worth pursuing, discussed the offerings of competing buttonmakers, assessed the quality of the Platts' goods in relation to competitors', and suggested new materials, machinery, and techniques that would improve the Platts' position. In the first two years of selling for the Platts, the Porters identified the two critical competitors in the field of low-cost pants buttons and targeted their own efforts and those of the Platts against them. By cajoling, encouraging, pleading, and scolding, the aggressive and ambitious Porters pulled the Platts into their grand strategy: explore the widest possibilities, focus on the main suppliers to the largest customers, and then devote all resources and ingenuity to "take them down," in the commercial parlance of the day.

Family Business

Alfred Platt never wavered in his insistence on retaining the family-based partnership as the structure of his enterprises, and his frank assessments of his sons' respective abilities sometimes caused jealously and discord. These occasional difficulties illuminate an important aspect of Alfred Platt as both a person and an industrialist. Though he was tolerant of other views, fair in his dealings, and disdainful of those who profited but did not produce, he was a competitive businessman and not a high-minded idealist.

As William worked to improve the ill-fated pipe manufacture he devoted less time to his partnership with Alfred and Clark, and in 1858 the partners dissolved A. Platt and Company. Alfred and Clark then ran the button and rolling business as A. and C. M. Platt. The division was not strict, as Clark still handled much of the pipe correspondence and William still spent at least one-quarter of his time working on behalf of A. and C. M. Platt. Thus,

William S. Platt. (Mattatuck Museum)   Clark M. Platt. (Mattatuck Museum)

no significant change occurred when William ceased making pipe in 1861, and the three reinstituted their partnership as A. Platt and Sons.[2]

Legrand Platt posed a more intractable problem. The failure of L. L. Platt and Company in 1855 left him unemployed and indebted. He reluctantly moved to Leominster, Massachusetts, to run a small bone-button shop for one of L. L. Platt's creditors, a Mr. Lomas. He disparaged his small business as the "crumbs of L. L. Platt." Even when the business picked up, Legrand could not report his success without also decrying the slights he suffered: "[I] sell enough so as to have what money we want to use in our business. . . . Ther[e]fore no trouble to raise money, a trouble that I have always had ever since I wanted money to do business with." Legrand expressed his desire for wealth more baldly than his brothers did, sometimes with a resentful tone. After accompanying Mr. Lomas on a trip to the Midwest, Legrand remarked that he could afford a good farm in Illinois, but not without adding that "I should have enough money to stay here in the East."[3]

Even if Alfred did not want Legrand as a partner, he did not repudiate his son. When Legrand's work in Leominster slowed to a halt in the fall of 1860, Alfred accepted him back into the family enclave, though Alfred charged him for the use of the wagon and team to fetch his furniture from the depot. Legrand and his wife, Sarah, with their two children, rented a house from Alfred for the going rate of $4 a month. Alfred put Legrand to work in the gristmill for $1.75 a day and in the fields for $1.50, more than regular hired hands received. For those times when Alfred did not supervise the gristmill, Legrand and Daniel Bergan split the responsibility. Finally at home in Platts Mills after more than a decade away, Legrand had steady work and economic security. But he must have bridled at his dependent status, especially as the button business expanded and Legrand, despite his experience in buttonmaking, did not participate. That resentment would surface later, during the resolution of his father's will.[4]

The Porters and the Platts

As the Porters had warned when agreeing to sell the Platt buttons, success did not come immediately. In the first half of 1858 the Porters moved just 130 great gross of the old standbys, japanned suspender buttons, and netted only $121. During the first year of the relationship, however, the merchants offered observations on the market and suggested new products that began to alter the way the Platts operated. By October 1858 the Porters had persuaded the Platts to offer buttons with tinplated and brass ("gilt") fronts for the fall clothing trade. The next month they asked about the possibility of customizing buttons with the name of the clothing manufacturer in "raised letters" on the front. The statement of sales by A. W. Welton and Porters for the second half of 1858 included nine different types of buttons, including some of brass, compared with only two types at midyear. But net sales came to only $146 on 155 great gross, bringing the Platt's total proceeds for the year to just $267.[5]

Urging patience and trying to justify the cost of diversifying, at the end of the year Samuel Porter wrote: "We are sorry that our sales have not been larger but the fact is that the Naugatuck Button sells so low that they are used more than formerly & this makes it more difficult to sell other buttons about the same cost." The Naugatuck pants button consisted of one piece of formed and japanned brass with holes punched through it for attachment to the garment. The Platt buttons, with wire eyes for attachment, cost more to fabricate but came close in price because zinc cost less than the other metals. To poach some of the Naugatuck customers the Platts tooled up to make four-hole and two-hole pants buttons out of zinc, with fronts finished in japan or tinplate. In early 1859 the Porters sold over two hundred great gross of them, nearly as many as they sold of the old types. The product line included twelve different buttons, but adjustment came quickly as the Platts dropped the two-hole varieties for the second half of the year. In September 1859 the national scope of the Porters' efforts came home to

Waterbury with the first order for buttons with a name stamped on the front, for a clothing manufacturer in New Orleans. The new products and the more thorough marketing showed up in the Platts' proceeds of $1,670 from the Porters for 1859, compared with the total of $267 for the prior year. The partners took no dividend because costs also had risen, especially in connection with new materials—brass, block tin for plating, and new plating equipment. Clark received $145 in salary for the year; Alfred, $78 for rent on the shop.[6]

These results might have reminded the Platts of their earlier experience of rising sales accompanied by level income, and during the few years it took for the Porters' strategy to pay off, the Platts protected themselves by maintaining diverse ties to their markets. Clark tried to open a wholesale outlet with a Philadelphia merchant in 1859, but the poor results only underscored the value of the Porters as the Philadelphian tried to drive the wholesale price down. Noting that a competing button sold for around the same price, the Philadelphian asked Clark, "[P]lease let me know if you can reduce them somewhat." The effort was nonetheless valuable for giving the Platts more information on their competition: "'Hatches Patent' [buttons] can be bought for very little more and which buyers generally prefer." Though this was the first the Platts had heard of the Hatch patent, the Porters soon encountered it too, and it joined the Naugatuck button as the chief opponents in their marketing strategy.[7]

The Platts continued to stock E. S. Wheeler and Company with their old-style buttons, and for 1859 Wheeler yielded them about the same revenue as did the Porters. When Wheeler saw the success of the Platts' gilt button, he sought a portion of the output. In October 1859, William Platt asked the Porters if they would mind. The response demonstrated the distinctive relationship the Porters were trying to build. Nathan Porter opened his letter by noting that they did not want to profit at the expense of the Platts: "Thos. Porter has written us saying that you wish to have Wheeler sell the Gilt Buttons for you & wished me to write you in regard to the matter. We prefer to have the sale of them and would prefer the exclusive sale but if you think it will be for your interest to have Wheeler sell them we ought not to be selfish enough to object to it." Porter asked for no special treatment but did insist that both merchants be treated equally. He closed by describing Wheeler's predatory practices and noted that the main competition the Platts then faced was the result of Wheeler's pursuit of his own short-term gain: "The only trouble we expect in case they sell the buttons is that they will on the sly sell under price to some party who buys of us both just for effect. In case this should take place we shall not care to sell the buttons at all. Wheeler has done more to run the price down on the Japann[d] Button made at Naugatuck than all others put together." On this advice the Platts rejected the Wheeler request. As their production rose over the following five years, their involvement with Wheeler declined and then halted altogether.[8]

The Porters could prevail because they had already begun to offer services beyond those of the normal commission merchant. In September 1859, for instance, the Platts queried them about the reliability of a Philadelphia buttonmaker who had requested credit on the purchase of zinc strip. Drawing on the unparalleled information available in New York—from the records of the Mercantile Agency to the gossip of other merchants—the Porters reported in detail on the character and capital of the Philadelphians and offered their own recommendations on credit limits and terms. They connected the Platts with the nation's commercial pulse without requiring the Platts to abandon their rural location.[9]

During 1860 the Porters started to give a general reading of the market rather than simply suggesting specific product innovations, stimulating the Platts to develop their own ideas about new products. When the Platts sent a sample button with a "star pattern" on the front, the Porters assessed its chances: "We like the button very much and think they will sell some . . . as we have had nothing of the type." Not stopping with a simple view of the button's prospects, the Porters went to on to remind the Platts that their general market was in low-cost buttons and advised them not to produce for an exclusive clientele but for a volume market: "We should think it would be best for you to put the price at a fair profit above cost as the button will have a larger sale at a low price, than at a high price. We should think the button would sell so as to pay you a fair profit in considerable quantities. We think that it would be best all things considered to put up these buttons in the cheapest way." Their explanation of wholesale pricing might appear obvious and simplistic, but the Porters had to explain impersonal big-city ways to Alfred Platt, whose deal making took place face-to-face. "You might give us two prices & if it did not go at the higher we could make it less," they explained. "There is no trouble in making the price lower, but the price cannot be raised."[10]

The Porters alone received the Platts' permission to adjust prices at the point of sale, another manifestation of the trust that underlay the relationship. This policy equipped the Porters with an agility in response to market conditions that was helpful in seeking the broadest possible markets for the buttons. It also complicated the accounting in the semiannual sales statements. From the start the Porters listed sales by type of button, multiplied volume by price for each type, and then added up the dollar amounts for the types to arrive at gross sales. When they started varying prices in 1860, the Porters reported individual prices as weighted averages, apparently confusing the Platts and requiring a somewhat patronizing explanation in the year-end statement.[11]

During 1860 the Porters adopted new merchandising tactics corresponding to the proliferation of button types, which included fifteen styles at the end of the year. They assigned the different patterns into numbered groups that included suspender and fly buttons of similar design. Like their pricing advice, the Porters' instructions on product numbering and packaging might seem so basic as to be unnecessary. But the Platts' utter lack of marketing savvy truly frustrated the Porters, as the chiding nature of their letters makes clear:

It is the worst possible way to put the labels on the [packages of] new buttons like the old as it looks like the old style & what is worse they cannot be told from each other unless the buttons are seen, consequently they are liable to be sent for the old ones in packing goods [i.e., assembling orders in the Porter warehouse]. Where several kinds of buttons are made by one maker the best way is to distinguish them by numbers. . . . We have numbered the Fig[rd] star pat. Fronts same as the Suspender, viz. #150. Always No. the Sus. and Fronts of the same Pat. [with the] same No.[12]

The Porters also addressed the usual concerns of the commission merchant, such as alarm over the speed of deliveries and notice of shortages in the stock of a particular item. The results were still modest, amounting to $880 net sales for all of 1860, followed by a dividend of about $120 for each partner. But Porters' efforts to establish up-to-date commercial practices had begun to prepare the Platts for the sharply accelerating pace of change that would come during the Civil War.[13]

Army Buttons

To fund the war effort, the federal government adopted fiscal and monetary policies that supercharged the northern economy. The government sold bonds and levied taxes on income and manufactured goods, then put most of that money back into the economy by buying arms, uniforms, tents, and the other gear to equip armies. By permitting banks to issue notes backed by federal bonds, the government made credit more available for manufacturers seeking to expand. Printing more paper money also made the northern economy more liquid; by February 1863, three-quarters of the greenbacks in circulation were of Civil War origin.[14]

The wartime economy affected every aspect of the Platts' metalworking business. Raw material grew more scarce and expensive. Machinery became easier to purchase after machine builders began completing equipment in anticipation of orders. Production increases exceeded the labor available in Platts Mills and forced expansion to downtown Waterbury. The markets for buttons rose in volume, and the number of sales went down: the Porters sold more buttons to fewer customers, and army uniforms and tents accounted for the largest sales.

When the government started to equip the Union army, the Porters reacted quickly by tracking the award of contracts for making uniforms. Before clothing houses would buy the buttons, the army had to approve them, and Nathan Porter sent for William Platt to give technical explanations to officials in the Quartermaster General's Office. On July 23, two days after the first Battle of Bull Run, when the news of Confederate victory dominated public and private discourse, the Porters wrote a calm assessment of their chances of selling directly to the government: "Mr. Wm. S. Platt has been investigating the Button bid advertised by Government and finds as we have before that Hatches Patent White [i.e., tinplated] Button is the kind used. It is very doubtful whether any other kind will answer but a button as good at less Price might do."[15]

The Hatch patent covered a two-piece metal button with holes for attachment. Its great advantage was the shape inside the holes; the holes were punched into the front and back pieces with countersunk (or chamfered) edges to offer a smooth surface against the thread that sewed the buttons to the garment. This design, patented in 1845, overcame the chief problem with four-hole metal buttons—the sharp edges of the holes severed the thread. The government preferred metal buttons for Civil War uniforms, and buttons with holes were cheaper than buttons with eyes. The Hatch button, made by Robinson and Company of Attleboro, Massachusetts, won early favor among four-hole metal buttons because it stayed on the garments longer.[16]

The Porters suggested that the Platts encroach on the patent: "You had better get up samples of a double button similar to Hatches." The finish was critical: "They must be White—made of [Tin-]Plated metal & we think it would be best to have both Back & Face Plated." The Porters realized that the lower cost of zinc might allow the Platts some price advantage but cautioned that unplated zinc be confined to the backs because its dull white color was less attractive than tinplate.[17]

When the Platts could not produce a Hatch button quickly enough, the Porters halfheartedly submitted the old-style four-hole button for the government bid in early August. As expected, the Hatch button won out. But the Porters renewed their request for "samples of the Plated Button both Sus. and Fronts like Hatches Patent. . . . if the Gov. will not use your buttons we think contractors will."[18] Two weeks later they reported "an order from a House (who has a Gov. contract) for some goods and they will want some 200 Gt. Gro. of Front buttons soon and our chance for getting in your front Buttons in place of Hatches we think is fair."[19]

Duplicating the Hatch button gave the Platts more trouble than the Porters had hoped. "We think the trade for these buttons will all be over before you send any," they wrote on August 15, adding not to take trouble with packing as "Hatch puts his up in 1 Gt. gro. in a bundle loose and yours for army contractors would do as well." At the end of the month they advised again: "These buttons may not sell as well *after the War is over*." Too busy trying to perfect the tooling to stamp out Hatch-like parts and the assembly process to join them, the Platts did not take the time to write about their progress. The lack of news troubled Samuel Porter as he tried to balance his promises to customers with his reputation for reliability, and he offered the Platts a chance to back out: "If you are not going to send any buttons please let us know."[20]

After the Platts reassured them, the merchants began taking orders from uniform makers. By September 20 the backlog was more than five hundred great gross, and the Platts had not yet started shipping the Hatch buttons. In his letter of October 15, Samuel Porter dropped his stern instructions in favor of a more benign and helpful attitude toward the Platts. He understood that the wartime commercial frenzy of the New York garment district was difficult to grasp from the rural vantage point of Platts Mills and that the personal feelings between maker and seller were all-important in this relationship. Porter mildly reproached them for prior assurances: "You talked so encouragingly about getting the goods out *fast*." Then he set a production schedule to work off the backlog, advising the Platts that half of one order could be shipped to keep the customer working, and planning a sequence for the remaining orders. He ended with a gentle recommendation that the shop work overtime: "Some of the buttonmakers do a little over work if they are hurried."[21]

The first week of November the Platts began shipping uniform buttons. Clark Platt accompanied the order to New York and assured the Porters that the shop would work overtime. Buoyed by Clark's statements, the Porters accepted more orders and on November 8 reported sales of an additional 150 great gross. Clark's visit also alleviated their concern about antagonizing the Platts, and forceful insistence slipped back into the correspondence: "Work overtime and get them out as *fast as possible*."[22]

Over the next seven weeks the Porters, and Arad Welton in Boston, sold more than 750 great gross to producers of army clothing by touting the Platt buttons as a moderate-quality, lower-priced alternative to the Hatch button. "People cannot get as many of the cheap ones as they want and are obliged to buy some better," they reported. "Yours come out at [a] better rate than Hatches Patent." The profit potential they saw within their grasp drove the merchants to fits of shrill urgency. "[Welton] wants them *immediately* as they are for *Army contracts*," they wrote on November 11, followed by similar pleadings: "It is necessary to get the Buttons. *Hurry them along,*" on the 12th, and "Send along the buttons fast as possible," on the twentieth. After two weeks of fervid hammering they shifted to a more collegial approach, trying to entice the Platts to greater speed with the promise of a big payday. "We . . . could have taken an order for *5 times as many* if we would agree to furnish them in a day or two," came word on November 21, followed two days later by the polite appraisal that "We think it a good plan to do all possible when goods sell at a fair profit." The Porters used these abrupt shifts in tone as a tactic to get more work out of their country cousins.[23]

Speed of communication grew more critical. Welton started telegraphing his orders to the Porters for forwarding to the shop, rather than mailing them to New York as before. Samuel Porter instructed the Platts to "send to the P.O. each day as we may be writing." Porter could abide the three-day interval for a letter between New York and Waterbury, but not if the letter languished at the post office for several days before the Platts saw it.[24]

In the last weeks of 1861, the army clothing market moved the Porters to take on much greater responsibility on behalf of the Platts. They provided an unlimited line of credit: "If you want any money we can let you have all you want." After the Platts reported difficulty in getting the tinplated iron they used for the uniform buttons, the Porters threw themselves into the effort by buying any scrap that came up for sale in New York. Through their contacts with other merchants selling Connecticut-made metal goods, the Porters located a shop in Meriden with scrap tinplate the Platts could use. The Porters obtained nearly nine thousand pounds by the end of the year, financing the purchases and deducting the cost from the Platts' button receipts.[25]

Acquiring the raw material enabled the Porters to improve scheduling by coordinating among marketing, manufacturing, and material supply. Concerned by the scarcity of tinplate and the low quality of much that was available, they persuaded some makers of army trousers to use japanned buttons. Thus diversifying the market, the Porters enabled the Platts to keep a steady flow of work moving through the shop. In late November the Porters instructed the Platts to fill orders with poor-quality tinplate, hiding it by japanning: "If you get out of Bright Tin use rusty tin and make Blk. [japanned] buttons." Later in the week, after failing to find any tin at all, the Porters suggested switching production over to japanned zinc, "if stock gives out."[26]

The Porters understood but could not solve technological bottlenecks as easily they could solve problems in financing or material supply. The months of delay before the Platts sent the first uniform buttons resulted from the exacting process of making metal-forming punches and dies, then setting up, testing, and adjusting them. It was precisely this ability to produce the buttons that made the Platts such valuable allies, and central to their capacity was the stamping press that Alfred and his sons had designed and built five years earlier. Ordering the castings from vendors, making the other components, and assembling the machine had consumed months. In early November 1861, when the Platts suggested building another stamping press to help fill war orders, the Porters recommended against it, preferring instead that the Platts spend their time producing buttons on the existing equipment rather than making another machine. "You had better run your machine 24 hours a day," they wrote. To judge from the increased outlays for candles that month, the Platts must have done so. Clark and William, and perhaps their father, must have taken shifts at the press to spell Franklin Judd, the regular press hand.[27]

In 1861 manufacturers could not simply go out and buy another stamping press. Machine builders in the Naugatuck Valley serving fabricated metal-goods producers, in Hartford serving arms makers, and in New Haven serving carriage and hardware producers surpassed most of the nation in their metalworking sophistication. But none of them made stock equipment for off-the-shelf sale. Most worked as Farrel Foundry had for the Platts, making critical parts, and sometimes whole machines, on a custom basis. The unprecedented demand of the Civil War created the steady market for capital goods that solidly established the Connecticut machine builders.

By 1863 the Platts could get rapid delivery of whole machines from local firms such as Farrel and Blake and Johnson, but during the initial rush of military orders they had to depend on their own capability. In their search for another press in November 1861 the Platts wrote to Milo Peck and Company of New Haven. The local specialization of Connecticut metalworking made it difficult for Peck to help. The Waterbury buttonmakers stamped small, precise parts from soft metals, while Peck concentrated in heavier and slower equipment to forge carriage parts from iron. "The manufacturing in this vicinity is of that kind which requires a different class of tools," responded Peck. Peck had patterns to make castings for a small press, but starting from castings he offered no saving in time because the Platts could order their own castings and build a press that fit their own special needs. They did just that, but it took three months to finish the new press for Hatch buttons. The decision to make another stamping press pleased the Porters, although they displayed no patience in their eagerness to double sales and production: "Fit up another machine *at once*. We can sell all one machine can make."[28]

The year-end accounting showed remarkable results. In the second half of 1861 the Platts made 63 percent more buttons than they had produced for all of 1860. Second-half net sales of over $1,706 also outpaced the highest annual revenue of any preceding year. Three-quarters of the sales consisted of uniform buttons, which the Porters coyly called "Extra Countersunk" on their statement instead of referring directly to the Hatch patent.[29]

The Platts accomplished the increase without great changes in their business, in part because the Porters took on so many diverse responsibilities that the Platts otherwise would have had to fulfill. The metalworking labor force stayed the same through this period of rising output. Bristol ran the rolling mill, Judd operated the stamp, and six to ten women at a time worked on assembly presses and packed the buttons. The principal change was that everyone worked longer hours. The female employees—Daniel Bergan's wife, Ann; Catherine and Susy Roberts; Sarah and Mary Thomas; and new hands Maggie Duff and Ann Riley worked almost every month—earned $10 a month or less in early 1861 and from $12 to $15 at the end of the year. Some of their jobs drew piecework; some, day wages. The precise distribution is not known, but either way the increased wages show they performed more labor. Monthly payments to Bristol, based on hours worked, rose from $20 to $25 early in the year, to over $30, and as high as $42 at the end.[30]

The Platts too spent more time at metalworking, making new equipment and putting in turns at the rolling mill and stamp, as well as handling the more voluminous correspondence. While the nature of their tasks and their basic approach to the business remained consistent, metalworking assumed a larger role in their lives, and this represented the most significant change for them. Alfred continued some farming and milling, but Clark and William had to devote all of their energies to metalworking to keep up with the Porters' success in selling their goods. For them, the rise in production meant that they did not have time to pursue the multiple activities that their father had throughout his life. And they had to trust that the income would eventually repay their efforts; in 1861 the business distributed no dividend, although the sons each received more than $300 of intermittently paid salary. That was twice a laborer's pay, but in 1861 Ben Bristol made more than his employers did.[31]

The pace and volume of business exploded to higher levels in 1862, when the Porters' button orders reached the unprecedented level of over six thousand great gross. The average order size of 170 great gross surpassed all prior performance, pulled upward by massive military sales. The Porters moved the Extra Countersunk buttons in hundreds of great gross at a time, including 620 in two orders during the first week of September alone—more than half a year's output before the war. The first big payoff also came in 1862, when net revenues from the Porters reached $6,487. The partners each took a $600 dividend, and the sons received salaries that pushed their income over $1,000 for the year. The Platts tied their business more fully to the Porters, making only some eight hundred great gross for other agents and discouraging the others by requiring guaranteed payment.[32]

During 1862 the Porters' strategic planning and management advice grew more frequent, diverse, and comprehensive. They took a longer view of the market and corresponding production needs. They bought scrap tin throughout the year as it became available. By mid-March, with the second press operating and government orders falling off, Samuel Porter foresaw a problem in keeping the shop running at the newly established level. He turned his attention back to civilian clothing with the suggestion to stamp out an old product on the new machine: "Could you not make a cheaper Gilt Sus. Button by making them on the machine you make the extra Countersunk Buttons on . . . and using a tin back?"[33]

In early April he reported "good demand" for the gilt suspender buttons, but a month later the Platts' higher production capacity had outpaced the market. May went by without a single order, the only dry month of the year. On May 16 the Porters explained that pricing was the problem. Significantly, rather than asking for a reduction in price, they advised adjusting production methods to meet the market: "We think it would be worthwhile to get up a cheaper Gilt Sus. & F[ron]t Button if you can." Pursuit of mutual interest also included criticizing the Platts' use of cheap and unattractive brass for the fronts. "Your Gilt Buttons are not quite so good color as some people make," came word in early June. "We send you a [competitor's] sample wh[ich] are rather better color." Not waiting for the Platts to perfect the gilt button, the Porters switched their emphasis to the japanned goods and sold over two hundred great gross by the end of June.[34]

Through constant communication with clothing makers and government purchasing agents, the Porters knew that military orders would pick up in early autumn, and in midsummer they started positioning for that market. In early August they negotiated with Clark Platt to set lower prices for the tinplated uniform buttons by reiterating the argument of profit through volume. This pricing strategy targeted the costlier Hatch buttons made by Robinson. Then the Porters attacked on the basis of quality their lower-priced competition, the Naugatuck button, which did not have the countersunk thread holes. In mid-August they reported their discussions with the Quartermaster General's Office: "We are doing all we can to get the Naugatuck Button rejected and we think there is a fair chance of doing it. If some of the cheap buttons are rejected on clothing now being made, we can sell all of the Buttons you can get out & more to[o]. The prospect is very good we think."[35]

While these marketing tactics took their course, the Porters started the Platts working, for the first time, in anticipation of orders. The Porters suggested how far to proceed through the manufacturing process before the specifications of individual orders would make a difference. "If you would get a lot . . . made up and not packed we think it would be a good plan," they wrote on August 14. "Then you could put them up in packages or bulk as wanted. Or you might black them." Within the week the Porters sold over two hundred great gross of military buttons, which they took as a sign of the impending rush, as they advised on the 21st: "You should be in full operation *now,* a week now may be worth more than a mo. some time hence." The next three days proved them correct, and word came to "*Let it come*" and to "Run your machines nights a little while."[36]

As the September orders rolled in, the Platts experienced the first setback of their wartime expansion. Henry Roberts quit running the second stamping press to help with the harvest on his family's farm. The Porters blamed the Platts by suggesting that more pay would have kept Roberts working: "You should use better Generalship than to let your best hands go at this time." Since no new names appeared on the payroll, the Platts themselves probably operated a stamp through the fall.[37]

Running full out for the rest of the year, switching quickly among products, and shipping partial orders without being asked, the Platts met the delivery schedule the Porters desired, and exhortations to speed up came less frequently than before. In a sure sign of more rapid production the Porters began sending orders to the shop via telegram, which had hardly been necessary in the days when manufacturing had lagged so far behind.[38]

The Platts used some of the zinc strip they made for their own button backs, but their increasing use of brass and tinplate for buttons meant that more of their twenty thousand pounds of annual strip output went to covered-button makers. The Porters resented any time the Platts spent away from the button trade, but the Platts doggedly insisted on retaining the diversity of production that the rolling business provided. Out of their general concern for the Platts, and perhaps their reluctance to antagonize the source of substantial commissions, the Porters helped to advance the zinc business. Their few zinc orders were less important than the communication the Porters offered from their more central position in the nation's commercial network. Thanks to the Porters' spreading the word about zinc, the Platts began fielding unsolicited inquiries: "I have been informed that you are in the habit of working zinc" began a letter from a Jersey City manufacturer. William and Alfred Platt negotiated zinc sales, a service the Porters provided for buttons, but the Porters gained enough familiarity with the metal to develop new markets for it in the coming years.[39]

In mid-November 1862, during the height of military-button production but when new orders had already abated, Samuel Porter again considered the long term. He asked for a new civilian button, made of a single piece with four holes and a different geometric pattern on its face. Foreseeing higher volume in all markets, he recommended that the Platts start making another machine. Praising the hoped-for conjunction of his own selling ability and the Platts' metalworking capacity, Porter set out the goal of market dominance: "We hope you will succeed in making a handsome button of the style of the figured one sent up and then we will give you credit for taking down the whole U.S. in making pant button[s]."[40]

Porter saw the button trade as an integrated whole. He consistently sought to link success in the uniform market to opportunities in civilian clothing. Making the Hatch button and building an additional machine had opened up new civilian markets in 1862, and attacking the Naugatuck button for army use had improved the Platt/Porter competitive position in nonmilitary trade. In 1863, Porter would work the relationship between markets in the opposite direction by taking the first steps toward establishing a vast new military application for the most recently developed one-piece button. Early in the war, army buttons were his immediate vehicle for growth, but Porter's ultimate aim was to establish a major and permanent position in the industry.

Lacking dramatic uniform orders in 1863, the Platts' production grew by only 13 percent over 1862. Net proceeds rose more sharply, by 18 percent, because the Porters charged more for civilian than for military buttons. The Platts each took a $1,000 dividend from 1863 revenues; each son also received some $550 in salary, and Alfred realized over $200 from renting the shop to the partnership.[41]

The business did not simply grow but continued to evolve under the Porters' direction. In two years the product line had undergone virtually complete turnover, as the Hatch-type buttons accounted for 96 percent of the work in 1863. The number of different button styles rose to twenty-four. All but four represented variations in finish or material used for the Hatch buttons, which had enormous potential in the civilian market, as the Porters wrote in the summer: "We . . . have succeeded after working at Brooks Brothers for more than a year to get the promise of an order. . . . We are now selling [to] all of the clothing houses in N.Y. who have heretofore used Hatches." Such results depended in part on further improvement in merchandising tactics. Early in the year the Porters asked for ten buttons of every type so they could make up the Platts' first sample cards. The merchants also redesigned the button label, with "the object being to give it a French look." This was the type of commercial advice that Aaron Benedict had begun receiving from Garret Smith more than forty years earlier.[42]

In pushing nonmilitary sales the Porters managed the many-faceted process of developing new products, assessing them, and bringing them to market. In 1863 the Platts made prototype lots of twelve different types, which the Porters shopped around in the consumer clothing market. The

Platts' brass-front buttons continued to fall short of the Porters' expectations, although as the year progressed, the criticism grew more helpfully specific. In February they wrote, "If your Gilts were a little better color they would look better," but by November the comments singled out the most troublesome competitor. "I got samples of Gilt Sus. Buttons of Anson Bronson when in Waterbury—something to sell cheap. . . . I inclose [sic] samples. . . . I think he takes you down on the color by using low brass," reported Samuel Porter, who, feeling compelled to reassure the Platts about his contact with Bronson, added, "We did not buy any but mearly [sic] got samples."[43]

As orders increased for buttons with names stamped on the front, the Platts contracted out the necessary diemaking. Frugality led them to a diemaker who charged only $.50 for the job, but his work enraged the Porters:

The button will not do and even if the [customer] would take them we think it would not be good policy to send him these buttons. . . . The letters are not nearly large enough. Any man who makes dies should have known to make a better job of lettering. We do not recollect what the abbreviation for Philadelphia was on the button [we] sent, but it should have been *Phila.* and not *Phild* as the button [you] sent. . . . You better make a better job of the lettering.

It took almost three months to get a lettered button that the Porters approved.[44]

To complement their constant probing for consumer button opportunities, the merchants took a more encompassing view of the manufacturing operation and offered more detailed advice on production techniques. After visiting with metal brokers to find a substitute for the chronically scarce tinplated sheet iron, in March the Porters suggested English "taggers tin," very thin tinplated sheet iron so named for its use as tags for marking textiles. The Porters' solution to the high cost of imported taggers tin was to diversify the product line further by reserving the expensive material for the already high-priced figured buttons and making the plain fronts out of zinc, "if you can make it look as well." When the Platts found the taggers tin difficult to work, Samuel Porter proposed a solution based on the methods of another shop whose goods he sold: "I do not see why you cannot do your cutting out and forming shells [i.e., fronts] out of taggers sheets . . . on a power press that [sic] same that the Cheshire Co. do." Porter himself questioned the experiment because "Taggers tin costs too much to use for Buttons," but in midsummer he worked out another way to use it—as a covering on a solid button of zinc, much the way that cloth buttons were made. It would be worth the trouble, Porter claimed, since he could charge more for the heftier solid buttons: "We thought we might get more for them in this way than for a double button and thought they would not cost you any more." The Platts, accustomed to working thicker metal, found that their dies did not stand up well against the taggers tin. Porter referred the problem to his brother Nathan, who gathered data for the Platts on die geometry and stamping lubricants from his clients who made covered buttons.[45]

To introduce this new material, the Porters addressed the full range of interrelated problems and made adjustments in every area: material supply and price, market potential, price potential, product design, machinery, and tooling. In early 1864 the development paid off in the Porters' ability to peddle a unique button. "It is quite probable," wrote Samuel Porter, "that some one else will get to making the buttons of taggers by another season and we hope you will get what advantage you can while there is no competition in this line."[46]

The low cost of zinc in relation to other metals offered unique opportunities to the imaginative Porters in their probing for advantageous niches. Besides recommending inexpensive zinc blanks in the button covered with taggers tin, they began routinely to specify zinc for the metal in japanned buttons. They continued to sell rolled strip and became acquainted with zinc's availability and pricing by occasionally placing orders with New York metal dealers for the Platts.[47]

In April 1863, Samuel Porter combined his knowledge of zinc, his awareness of the military supply situation, and the low production cost of the single-piece figured-front button the Platts had recently developed to discern an entirely new market for metal buttons. "We are trying to get the Government to accept your fig'd Suspender Button for tents & if they take them 1000 Gt. Gro. will be wanted," he wrote. The Platts made that button from brass, but Porter wanted to see how they looked in zinc because, in this application, zinc's distinctive noncorrosive quality offered a special advantage: "Send us a sample of them say one or two buttons *not* Japanned, so we can show they will not rust." After calling at the Quartermaster General's Office he raised his estimate to two thousand great gross and noted that, if successful, they would have the field of metal tent buttons to themselves because the current specification called for bone buttons.[48] The government did not order tents over the next six months, and the project receded in favor of more immediate concerns until November, when Porter wrote: "A house in this city has an order for Tents which will require over 1000 Gt. Gro. of Buttons. They have agreed to wait until we can get a small Gro. of buttons from you. *Solid figured* such as you sent a sample of the color of zinc [i.e., not japanned]. . . . If the Government will accept your buttons it will give you a great deal of work."[49] Another eight months would pass before the Platts produced zinc tent buttons in large quantity, almost a year and a half from the time that Porter first thought to make them.

The idea's long gestation period overlapped with the introduction of other new buttons, such as the taggers tin buttons and the dozen different civilian button types that came and went during 1863. Together, these efforts constituted a broad product development program that went along at the same time that the shop turned out thousands of great gross of the established types. Simultaneously with their most forward-looking efforts, the Porters' ability to forecast more immediate demand and plan the manufacturing schedule smoothed out the flow of work in the shop. Certain of sales, they began ordering fifty and one hundred great gross at a time for their own stock; for the first time since Alfred set up a stamping press, in 1863 the Platts received new orders every month of the year. As their seasons of production blended into one another, the Platts expanded their plant not in response to a particular order or a specific manufacturing problem but rather to sustain the overall pattern of growth they had achieved. Neither the Platts nor the Porters foresaw that the tent-button market would take off—they simply figured that something would.

In 1863, A. Platt and Sons became an enterprise with its own momentum. The Platts clearly understood this, and welcomed it, although the zealous merchants always wanted to expand farther and faster than did the conservative manufacturers. The Porters took care to comfort the Platts when confidence faltered. "We are constantly getting new customers," wrote Samuel Porter in September 1863. "You need not be afraid of branching out too fast."[50]

The Platts' more deliberate approach showed in the way they added equipment. Though the year had opened with Samuel Porter's urging construction of a new press, the Platts delayed it in favor of building up their own machine-making capacity: rather than ordering the key parts for a new press, they ordered a lathe on which to make some of the parts themselves. When it arrived in March, they ordered the press castings; and late in May, William had the new press nearly completed. The Porters preferred to have the Platts order a complete press, but the Platts did not want to grow more dependent on outsiders for the technology that was at the heart of their business. For simpler equipment, like the kick presses to assemble two-part buttons, the Platts were happy to buy complete machines from Naugatuck Machine Company.[51]

Employment in the shop rose slowly, partly because of Waterbury's wartime labor shortage. The brass mills hired workers away from other local industries, and employment in the city's button shops declined. In this highly competitive labor market the Platts had an additional disadvantage because of their location one mile north and three miles south of the population centers. Platt employees lived close by, either with their families or in tenant houses. To hire more workers the Platts had to house them, but

Alfred was unwilling to build more dwellings. He continued to view the land rather than the business as his central asset, using his wartime metalworking dividends to reduce the principal owed on the $8,000 mortgage from 1856. Farmer and miller as well as buttonmaker, he reserved his land as field and pasture and effectively limited the work force to neighbors and people who could board with them.[52]

Those who came to work had some relationship other than employment already established with the Platts or their neighbors, or by living with them they soon would. The work force was not the anonymous class that Aaron Benedict's workers were to him. The problem of recruitment, combined with the personal relationships that developed in the close quarters of Platts Mills, made the Platts very reluctant to lay people off. They built the work force very slowly and tended to keep people working once hired.[53]

In late 1862, when the existing work force could no longer handle the production increase, the Platts added female employees by hiring more members of those families already present, including their own. A cousin from Middlebury, Adelah Platt, came to pack buttons. Ben Bristol's wife spent half-time at packing, and another Thomas sister, Cassie, began work. In 1863 hiring expanded to include those with no relatives in the shop. Clark's house boarded five women who spent their days assembling Hatch buttons on kick presses, packing them into boxes, or affixing those labels with the "French look." Two new press operators, John Osborn and Hubert Chamberlain, were sons-in-law of Nirom Platt; the company also hired their wives, Nirom's daughters, for a few days each month. At the end of 1863, ten women and five men worked full-time in the shop. Except for Bristol, their wages remained at approximately the same level they had reached during the earlier rush. The Porters' increasing call for button parts of zinc meant more work for the rolling mill, and Bristol received around $50 most months; his earnings no longer exceeded his employers', but $600 a year made him a wealthy man for the time.[54]

To minimize the addition of new employees while keeping up with demand, the Platts started to let subcontracts for some operations. The largest subcontractor in 1863, Griggs Brothers on South Main Street, formed and japanned button parts for the Platts. The Platts assigned subcontracts not on an emergency basis but as a regular part of production, using Griggs Brothers every month of the year. This relationship hints at the complexity in the web of interfirm linkages in a specialized industrial region such as Waterbury. The Platts served as both source and vendor in subcontracting relationships, shifting between these roles as their sales and production capacity demanded.[55]

Steady industrial production at unprecedented levels inexorably altered the texture of life at Platts Mills. The enclave grew less self-sufficient as more diverse commercial ties moved Platts Mills more fully into the larger economy. The Platts recognized that the frequent half-day round trips to the Union City railroad depot represented a chance to save substantial time. They accordingly upgraded their bridge to the west bank of the Naugatuck River so that it could carry a wagon with a ton or more of zinc slabs and then arranged with the railroad for a flag stop. The Platts did not make the lumber for the bridge at their own sawmill but bought it for $300 from Waterbury Lumber and Coal Company. They needed all available power and labor for metalworking; the rhythmic pounding of button presses became the dominant sound in the vale, and the whine of the saw receded into memory. Platts Mills was a busy place, with direct rail access, less diversity of production, and greater reliance on materials and services purchased from outside. It was no longer a farm with a collection of rural industries and a little commercial metalworking; it was a small manufacturing community.[56]

In September 1863 the Platts required another type of service they could not provide for themselves—legal counsel. Their success with Hatch buttons had attracted the attention of the patent holder, whose lawyer wrote: "I am instructed to make known to you that buttons manufactured & sold by you . . . are believed to be infringements of the Hatch Patent owned by Mr. Robinson of Attleborough. You are called upon to settle with Mr. Robinson for all such buttons made and sold by you & to discontinue further sales of them. Otherwise the claim will be presented at law." There is no record of Robinson's bringing suit nor of the Platts' paying damages. It seems likely that the Porters or Arad Welton, their Boston partner, somehow settled with Robinson. This threat to the largest portion of the new product line did not pass, however, without affecting the business. The Porters' product recommendations grew more circumspect, as in this November letter: "I inclose [sic] samples [of a competitor's buttons] not to give you any new ideas about *countersinking* for I mistrust it is an infringement on Hatches patent but I think he takes you down." The Porters also stepped up their efforts to design and sell different kinds of buttons, and tent buttons assumed greater importance in their planning.[57]

The year 1863 brought to a close the founding era of A. Platt and Sons as a business rooted in the diverse interests of Alfred Platt, and in 1864 William, Clark, and the Porters took the first steps toward shaping the firm's next era. In their most significant change, the Platt sons began the transfer of button manufacturing to the center of Waterbury. They nonetheless maintained strong continuity with the homestead, its role in their industrial fortunes, and their father's approach to business.

The Porters' planning for material supply achieved the utmost in sophistication. Uncomfortable with the Platts' seat-of-the-pants estimates of output per pound of raw material, the merchants began to calculate how many button blanks could be cut from a length of brass or zinc strip, or from a sheet of taggers, and related the numbers to unit cost. In March 1864 they related that every extra dollar for a box of taggers meant a $.015 increase in production cost per great gross of buttons. To complement the cost accounting the Porters reported weekly on general economic conditions, especially the price of gold, the most sensitive indicator of commodities prices. Then they factored in their own sense of what the garment shops would pay for buttons months into the future and offered recommendations on when to buy raw material and how much to buy.[58]

The Porters took charge of purchasing most shop materials—tinplate, chemicals, labels, steel for tools—generally from New York sources. They sought out suppliers, bargained over the costs, and assessed the quality of the materials; all the Platts had to do was take delivery and pay for the goods. Despite the Porters' frequent offers to serve in the same capacity for buying spelter, the Platts did not delegate this important function. They accepted the Porters' recommendations and advice but corresponded directly with Phelps, Dodge and with Hendricks Brothers. Besides checking on the Porters' price predictions, the Platts' received independent estimates of availability and, most important, applied their own unparalleled expertise on the quality of the spelter.[59]

In almost twenty years' experience with the metal, the Platts had worked spelter from all of the European and American sources, knew which brands worked best for stamping, and had developed their own "peculiar treatment to make it [both] soft and tough." Dependent on accurate representations of the contents of the slabs they bought and on a reliable supply, they placed standing orders with their regular vendors, who in turn usually gave advance notice of price increases and shipped what they could to the Platts before raising the price. The Platts sometimes assigned clerical functions to the Porters in connection with spelter purchases but never the purchasing decisions.[60]

In guarding the ties to their most important raw material just as carefully as they retained control over their production technology, the Platts adhered to Alfred's original sense of the firm's strength as an integrated metalworking operation with command of its own distinctive processes. They would cede direction to the Porters in everything but the metal itself and the means to work it. The Platts' approach to material supply also followed Alfred's preference for steady, long-term relationships. He valued reliability more than short-term price advantage, and if he demanded such behavior from his agents, he just as readily offered it to his suppliers.

During 1864, with the relationship between makers and sellers well defined and the Platts adequately schooled in the wholesale trade, the Porters no longer had to give advice about the workings of the button market. They frequently sent samples of competing buttons and assumed that the Platts knew what to do with them: make something better for the same price or something cheaper that would serve. Samuel Porter adopted a familiar, jocular tone in his letters. Instead of demands and complaints when deliveries fell behind, he resorted to friendly sarcasm, as when he asked for either a case of buttons or "a new story to tell." He even let down his confident salesman's facade after a particularly trying week: "If you have any consolation to give it helps a fellow[']s pluck when he is in low spirits."[61]

Porter's moods did not interfere with his selling, however, and in late January he reported sales averaging one hundred great gross a day, thanks to government uniform orders and the start of the winter clothing season, as well as the Porters' new policy of sending a representative on regular trips to Philadelphia and Cincinnati. In the first half of the year production again reached a new high for a six-month period, 5,128 great gross, and no single pattern or finish dominated. The biggest seller, brass-front Hatch-type fly buttons, accounted for only 18 percent of shipments, and five other types each represented between 8 percent and 13 percent. The Platts made test batches of six new designs. The Porters constantly watched for the chance to push prices up, which, combined with unprecedented volume, meant higher revenues for the manufacturers—$9,424 for January to June. In May 1864, just four months after the $1,000 dividend for 1863 had been distributed, the Platts awarded themselves another dividend of $750 each.[62]

The Platts' labor shortage limited any further growth beyond the rate of orders generated in January. The Porters refused to accept a ceiling on production and urged instead, "Do all you can to increase your help." When fully apprised of the difficulty, in early March they wrote, "We regret that you have so much trouble . . . in getting help," and rested their hopes on a technological solution to the problem of increasing production.[63]

In 1863, William Platt had raised the idea of rolling the designs for button fronts into the strip before blanking, rather than pressing them on the individual pieces. By eliminating one press operation, this process would reduce the need for experienced press hands, the most difficult job to fill. With zinc buttons, for which the shop made its own strip, rolling did not add any jobs, as Ben Bristol simply made his final pass with rolls that had the required pattern cut in them. For brass buttons made from purchased strip, Bristol's work at pattern rolling was substituted for scarce stamping labor. William had the new rolling mill running in late February 1864, but not perfected. Ben Bristol stopped his regular rolling duties to help work out the bugs. Samuel Porter could hardly believe the news. "Tell Ben that we don't care whether he makes them on the *old* or the *new* machine," wrote

Porter, "only [that] we want them *at once.*" The first buttons with rolled designs, sent at the end of March, did not impress Porter: "Do not think the rolling is any improvement." Faster or cheaper production meant little if the buttons would not sell, and Porter still favored assigning Bristol to production: "Would not advise you to spend much time experimenting at present as we can sell them much faster than we can get them."[64]

At the end of April, convinced that the new process would not substantially raise production, the Porters suggested moving the shop to a location that would ease recruitment. They favored New York, and Samuel Porter found a loft to rent, with power from a central steam engine. On labor, he reported, "It would be safe to calculate on getting all the help you want at $4.00 pr. week and at this price they say you could choose the best of them." The Platts cited problems with the room, discomfort about moving to the big city, and the high cost of space. After Porter conceded that "There are reasons why Waterbury would be preferable and you can best judge about it," Clark and William leased from Green Kendrick a small factory complex near downtown Waterbury. Alfred Platt would not stand in the way of this expansion and would share in any increased profits, but he would not put any of his own money or time into the move away from Platts Mills. Just as his own development of the waterpower at Platts Mills had exceeded his father's ambition for the property, the expansion to downtown represented the plans of the next generation.[65]

The leased buildings stood in a line of factories along Great Brook, about two hundred yards east of Center Square. The brook bounded the east and south sides of the rented parcel and provided waterpower. Brown and Brothers, Lane Manufacturing Company, Mattatuck Manufacturing Company, and a host of smaller firms owned or rented facilities in the neighborhood. Before the Platts came, Kendrick had rented the buildings to Porcelain Manufacturing Company, a glass-button maker. He charged the Platts $150 per year for the five-year lease, a low rent that allowed them to spend liberally to improve the property and equip the shop. Citing imminent orders for tent buttons, the Porters wrote in June to suggest that the Platts "facilitate things in getting to work up to Waterbury."[66]

Clark and William Platt spent their May dividend to fit up the new shop. It came with a waterwheel, but they had to install all of the shafting and pulleys for power transmission. They bought stoves for heat and hired carpenters to patch the walls and put in windows and partitions. They built a new japanning oven and ordered castings for new blanking presses. They installed twelve new "lever presses" for button assembly and other light presswork. By summer, when all of the new machinery was installed, the production capacity of A. Platt and Sons had more than doubled.[67]

Tent Buttons

The Platts barely had the new shop ready when the tent button market took off. The government had agreed to use zinc, but the tentmaker the Porters had been cultivating wanted a lower price than was quoted for the samples he had. The Porters' material-cost accounting pointed to a solution: they calculated that by rolling the strip 20 percent thinner the Platts could meet the requested price by using a lower weight of zinc. The thinner samples met with approval, and on August 17 an order came for 2,300 great gross, all due by October 1. By early September the Platts were shipping fifty great gross a day. As the deadline loomed, the Porters reminded the Platts several times not to bother about quality: "We are not very particular about the finish or make of these as they are for army use."[68]

A few smaller tent orders came in October, totaling some 1,500 great gross. Samuel Porter correctly predicted that the government's procurement schedule would accelerate after the national election in early November. Calling for two hundred and three hundred great gross at a time, tentmakers ordered over nine hundred great gross by the first of December, and the pace kept up through the month. On the 29th the Porters telegraphed the largest order yet received, 7,002 great gross, and in their follow-up letter they reported turning down orders for a hundred great gross at a time.[69]

In the second half of 1864 the Platts shipped 8,582 great gross to the Porters and received $11,947 in net receipts. The product line had turned over again, as almost half of the buttons made between July and December were either for tents (31 percent) or had the rolled-pattern fronts (15 percent), two types that the Platts had not even made a year earlier. While the tent buttons represented an entirely new application and the rolled-fronts helped to alleviate the labor shortage, both new products also helped minimize exposure to legal action from the Hatch patent holder. The Hatch copies comprised 96 percent of output in 1863 but only around half by the end of 1864.[70]

In January 1865 more orders for tent buttons came in every week, and at the end of the month Samuel Porter proudly announced that "we have now all the orders for tent buttons that have been given out." Reminding the Platts that further orders would depend on rapid delivery, he suggested refitting one of the civilian-button machines to make tent buttons and invoked a self-interested patriotism to spur further efforts: "Run day and night and make money and help the Govt. while you can."[71]

The Porters could win every order for metal tent buttons because they had spent almost two years touting the positive qualities of zinc to the army and the tentmakers. Then, after establishing the market, the Platts' unique

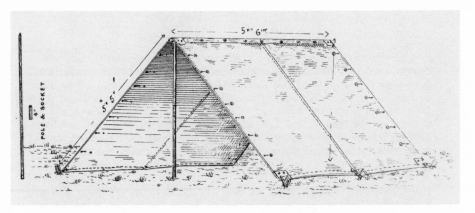

The U.S. Army shelter tent was two rectangles of cotton duck buttoned together. Each half had nine buttons along the top and seven at each end, twenty-three in all. A soldier received one "shelter half " and teamed with a partner to make a complete tent. Civil War troops made poles from branches; the standard-issue poles were a later refinement. This drawing is the first official depiction of the shelter tent, from the Quartermaster General's *Specifications for Clothing, Camp and Garrison Equipage* (1889). (Dean Nelson photograph)

capacity of zinc rolling enabled the Porters to keep the competition at bay. And competition came quickly, because the massive tent button orders did not go unnoticed, nor were tentmakers content with having a single source of supply that could dictate prices.

In early January two Philadelphia firms, a buttonmaker and a tentmaker, tried to break the monopoly. The buttonmaker, a Mr. Ivins, wrote to the Platts on January 5 requesting information on zinc strip for buttons. The Platts responded on the 9th with their scheduling and delivery data but held off quoting a price until they could learn what the slabs of spelter would cost. Ivins might have succeeded but for his mistake of also writing to the Porters to inquire about zinc. After mailing their letter to Ivins, the Platts received word from the Porters about the zinc inquiry from "a house in Phil." The Porters were alarmed: "We think it may be wanted for Tent buttons as a house [i.e., a tentmaker] wrote us 2 or 3 weeks ago that a party had offered to make them!" When the Platts communicated their intent to supply the zinc, Samuel Porter responded at length, first providing full information on the situation: "The party who wrote to us about Zinc is the same who wrote to you, although they did not say what they wanted to do with the zinc. We think it would be most decidedly bad policy to let them have Zinc at a price at which they could make anything at making the Buttons. A [tentmaking] House in Philadelphia have threatened to buy of someone else unless we give them an advantage [in price]. This we declined to do." Then he reminded the Platts of the long effort behind the zinc tent buttons and the advantage of working without competition:

We have spent a great deal of time & some money to get these tent Buttons introduced & we do not think it for your interest to help anybody else into this business & we *know it is not for ours*. This Zinc Button has been accepted and will be used by the Gov. as long as they want buttons for this purpose & you can make all that are wanted & we can sell them, each of us making something by the business. If competition is started we shall lose part of the trade at least, & you will not have *all* of the buttons to make. As soon as competition is started prices will come down & the business will be just where it is on the cheap Naugatuc[k] buttons.

While he conceded the benefit to the Platts of integrated operation, Porter also for the first time declared his own interest to be more closely tied to buttons than to rolling metal: "*You* may make all you want to make on the rolled Zinc but we do not see how that would help us. It appears to us that it would be better for you to make the profit on *both* the Zinc & Buttons than on the Zinc only. Our opinion is that it is better for you and *us* to decline furnishing this or any other party Zinc for this purpose for reasons already stated."[72]

Porter's letter and Ivins's order for one thousand pounds of zinc arrived in Waterbury within a day of each other. The Platts decided not to fill the order but had to invent an excuse. They claimed mechanical difficulties: "When we wrote to you in answer to your first letter we thought we could fill any order for Rolled zinc that you might give, but our Water Wheel shaft has given out." The turbine, however, must have been rumbling along in the wheelpit while Clark wrote the letter. The week before he wrote it, the Platts had shipped two cases (fifty great gross each) of tent buttons every day; the day he wrote it and for a week following, shipments climbed to five cases a day. They could not have made the rolled zinc for those buttons without the turbine running every day.[73]

The ruse paid off in early February, when the Porters reported that the Philadelphia tentmaker had an army order for 100,000 tents and "we stand the best chance" to supply the buttons. They also learned of an order for 140,000 tents placed with a New York maker and calculated that to make the 6,300 great gross of buttons for all of those tents by the May deadline, the Platts would have to produce an additional 160 great gross a day. When the telegram came on February 11 confirming the orders, the Platts immediately began shipping 300 great gross a day, and 450 by the end of the month. In mid-April, after the Confederate surrender, the Porters fretted that the unshipped portion of the orders might be countermanded, but the army reconfirmed the tent orders and even made further small purchases in May and June. From January through June 1865, the Platts made 16,230 great gross of tent buttons. The Porters also kept the shop busy by selling 2,000 great gross of uniform buttons and 6,000 for civilian clothing. The Platts' net proceeds for the first half of the year exceeded $34,300, more than $22,000 of it from tent buttons.[74]

The wartime demand enriched the Platts. The partners took a $2,000 dividend in May 1865 and another $3,000 in August. Though less than a tenth of the $59,000 that Aaron Benedict reported as his annual income during the war years, profits from army buttons allowed Alfred Platt to pay off the obligations on his cherished property. And his sons established a downtown factory as large as the one in Platts Mills, financing it from button proceeds rather than borrowing. The Porters rapidly adjusted to the end of the war. Before the ink was dry on the Confederate surrender, they called for switching tent button production to the old equipment and devoting the newer machinery to "regular work." Not that there was any particular deadline; they just wanted to enhance their reputation for quick delivery. Thus did the Platts and their valuable allies, the Porter brothers, begin the search for new peacetime markets.[75]

CHAPTER FOUR

"For Purposes of Experiment"

B E T W E E N the end of the Civil War and Alfred Platt's death in 1872, his sons and the Porters established the metalworking business as a steadily profitable venture. The rise in national population and the growing acceptance of men's ready-made clothing expanded the market for buttons, and the Platts were well placed to take advantage of the trend. Waterbury offered a host of specialized vendors and customers and convenient access to the rolled brass and other alloys used in buttons. The local labor base included increasing numbers of unskilled workers, as well as mechanics whose innovations helped to multiply productivity.

The most striking distinction between the Platts and their fellow manufacturers was their satisfaction in the effort itself. Like Alfred, who worked until he was no longer able, his sons did not take their fortune as an invitation to leisure. Aaron Benedict's son Charles, upon his father's death, tore down his half-built mansion to erect a more opulent one, and indulged in grand tours of Europe,[1] but Clark and William Platt spent their days in their rolling mill, button shop, and factory offices.

By continuing in the business, rather than retiring as his own father had, Alfred Platt caused enormous problems to occur after his death. The family-based partnership structure caused legal confusion and harsh contention in the settlement of his estate. His sons argued not over succession in the business—the roles of Clark and William were unquestioned—but over distributing its value. Once the bitter struggle ended, Clark and William established a new structure to smooth subsequent transitions. Alfred Platt built for the future and instilled that ambition in his sons. It fell to Clark and William, however, to institutionalize the accomplishment in the reality of a new age.

Postwar Expansion

Samuel Porter's close guess as to the date of Confederate surrender and his advice on how to take advantage of it helped A. Platt and Sons adjust to peacetime. Constantly tracking the civilian clothing trade in the early spring of 1865, Porter reported that business was "very very dull." The garment makers also foresaw the end of hostilities and the dwindling of the government orders that had pushed up button demand and prices. "People are waiting for goods to 'touch bottom' before buying," he wrote. Porter preferred to wait until prices advanced before taking civilian orders.[2]

Porter saw depressed markets as an opportunity to buy commodities cheaply. He alerted the Platts that as Union victories brought the end of the war ever closer, the price of spelter would continue to decline: "If Sherman keeps on taking rebel Cities, it will continue to go down we think," he wrote in late February. With tent-button orders to fill, at the end of the war the Platts and Porters could afford to wait a few weeks or a few months for button demand to rise, while using some wartime profits to buy material for the coming season. The Porters telegraphed dips in spelter prices and made substantial purchases on instruction from the shop via return telegraph. The Platts stockpiled spelter far in advance of orders for buttons or zinc strip as the price fell to half of its wartime high. Between March and June they bought nearly twenty thousand pounds, more than a half-year's supply.[3]

In early May the Porters began taking orders for pants buttons of every type and material. At the end of the month the business resumed a familiar character, with the Porters providing advice on quality and materials, evaluating competitors' offerings, and urging "a little night work for a week or so until we get the goods."[4]

But much had changed in the button trade and for the firm of A. Platt and Sons. Volume in nonmilitary markets was higher than before the war, and competitors fewer. Buttonmakers who had won large military contracts used those revenues to subsidize civilian production by charging very low prices, while shops without a pool of cash from wartime profits struggled to maintain a foothold. The Porters could gleefully report by late summer that smaller producers had to price goods virtually at cost to get any business at all. The Porters hurried the demise of some competing shops, taking over their customers by offering longer payment schedules or promising higher volume in shorter time. In July 1865 the Porters booked several hundred great gross per week for the Platts, a volume they sustained through the fall and early winter. Pleas for overtime focused on filling orders for thousands of great gross in a matter of weeks, rather than the hundreds over several months that had characterized the business only a few years earlier. The large postwar market was also extremely diverse. The Platts made smaller amounts of many different types—purchases of less than fifty great gross were common—including numerous orders with die-stamped fronts bearing the name of the garment maker. Smaller orders meant more frequent setups, causing downtime that cut into production and revenues. Net sales for second half of 1865 were about $22,000, some $12,000 less than the first half, which had been boosted by the tent-button bonanza.[5]

The Platts knew all of their postwar competitors, a sign of both consolidation in the industry and the Platts' long and diverse experience. Their knowledge came in several ways beyond the Porters' continuing market intelligence. The Platts' new shop in downtown Waterbury, managed by Clark, ended the family's isolation in Platts Mills. The zinc business—selling rolled strip to other button fabricators—provided another conduit of industry data that was not available to other button shops. During 1865 any new pants-button competitor that alarmed the Porters was already known to the Platts as a customer for zinc strip of several years' standing. The competition did not move the Platts to cut off the supply, as they had in the face of potential competition in tent buttons. Perhaps losing the sale of a few thousand buttons did not bother them when they were working off back orders. Also, the Porters sold enough to keep the shop busy, and the Platts made money on the zinc sales in any case. The policy of integrated operations—primary processing and fabricating—gave the Platts both knowledge of their field and some insurance against seasonal downturns that was otherwise available only to the integrated brass firms a hundred times larger.[6]

The downtown Waterbury shop, originally opened to ease the wartime labor shortage, continued in operation for postwar civilian production. The casting and rolling processes for zinc remained at Platts Mills; the stamping presses that made blanks probably stayed there too, along with the old japanning oven and some of the smaller press operations. The Waterbury shop housed much of the new capacity in the less-skilled processes: japanning, burnishing and packing, and light presswork for punching holes in the one-piece sewn-on buttons, for assembling ("covering") the two-piece buttons, for edge trimming, and for stamping patterns and names on the button fronts. The process division between the two shops resulted from power needs and the minimizing of capital expenditures rather than a strict operating policy. At Platts Mills, the Naugatuck River offered some three times the potential power (theoretically 145 horsepower, about a third of which was used in this period) as that of the downtown site on Great Brook. Since zinc rolling drew the most power among the firm's processes, and Ben Bristol, the key roller hand, lived right nearby, there was no good reason to move the rolling mill and associated casting shop. But neither was there a clear identity of the older shop as a primary processing site and the new shop as a fabricating and finishing site. Late in 1865 a functional distinction between the two shops began to emerge, as most new button-making equipment went into the downtown factory: small presses for assembly, another japanning oven, and an innovative new stamping press.[7]

Edward Brown's machine shop took three months to build the expensive new press; at $400 it cost more than twice the annual rent on the shop that housed it. Its critical feature was a rotating "dial plate," a round table with eight radially arranged positions for holding stamped blanks in place for a press operation such as edge finishing, hole punching, or pattern stamping. The dial plate allowed speedier performance of a semiskilled job. Instead of placing a button between the punch and die, actuating the press, and then placing another button, the operator placed the work in the inactive plate positions while the press was running; then the plate rotated to bring a new position under the punch. This type of innovation in work feeding and positioning accounted for the substantial industry-wide productivity increases in small metal-goods fabrication in late-nineteenth-century Waterbury. The central process of a press—shaping sheet metal with punch-and-dies—changed only slightly as improvements in steel, lubrication, and geometry for tooling made for incrementally faster operation. However, roll feeds for strip, coil feeds for wire, dial plates, automatic ejection mechanisms, and later, bulk hopper feeds for buttons, eliminated most of the need for operatives to handle the work.[8]

Complicated new machinery and the frequent setups required by the more diverse product line increased the need for the skilled work of machinists and toolmakers. The Platts sent out most of their tool- and die-making to local job shops. Lettered or patterned button dies cost between $1 and $5, which the Platts usually passed on at or near cost to the customer. But the postwar business also demanded full-time, in-house machinist help to set the tooling, modify existing equipment, and build new machines; A. Platt and Sons struggled to fill this need. Lack of a machinist delayed button deliveries throughout the summer and fall of 1865 and remained a problem for many years to come.[9]

Even while the business adapted successfully to the postwar situation, the Platts and the Porters recognized the better profit potential in high-volume manufacture of a more limited product line, such as tent buttons. Besides the income falloff in postwar 1865, operational problems such as the scarcity of skilled machinists drove this lesson home. After a trip to Philadelphia in June 1865, Samuel Porter reported an interesting prospect in a new business promoted by William H. Reed, a button merchant. Reed based his plan on the novel idea of a metal button with a single large hole, attached to the garment with a rivet driven through the cloth, into the back of the button, by a kick press. The leg of the rivet would crumple up in the button hole, and Reed claimed the binding of metal on metal in the hole would make a far stronger attachment than any thread. Even more innovative was Reed's marketing plan: he would make the single-purpose kick presses and lease them at modest rates to garment houses, then sell the buttons and rivets to use on the machines. Reed thought, and Porter agreed, that if garment makers already had the attaching machines, repeat button sales would come much more easily than under the normal practice of starting with new designs every season.[10]

With his customary thoroughness, Porter identified the advantages to the Platts of working with Reed. The Platts made pants buttons both for fashionable men's clothing and for work clothing; by emphasizing a stronger means of attachment rather than selling primarily on the basis of style, the Reed button would appeal to makers of work clothing and minimize the Platts' exposure to the volatility of the fashion trade. Because neither the button nor machine design were yet perfected, the Platts' technical competence and willingness to tinker could help Reed bring off the plan. Porter noted that such help could be handsomely compensated if the Platts bought a share of Reed's company. He considered buying in himself, but only "if we think we can get the Acct. [of] buttons to sell thereby." Porter also outlined the details of corporate structure, equity financing, stock valuation and the difference between authorized and paid-in shares, all of which was anathema to Alfred but profitably applied by his sons in later years. Porter noted in closing that Reed wanted to use a rustproof white metal rivet, and he urged the Platts to patent one of zinc that would work with Reed's buttons.[11]

Clark Platt immediately wrote to Reed, who came to visit the shop in July 1865. Drawing on their experience with the Hatch button, the Platts advised Reed on the forming of the countersunk hole in the back of his button, which so pleased Reed that he ordered samples "for purposes of experiment": fifteen great gross each of suspender buttons in four different finishes—gilt, tinplated, japanned, and zinc, which Reed had not encountered previously and called "white silvery looking metal." Over the rest of the summer the Platts worked to improve the manufacture of Reed's fly button. The fly button posed an intricate challenge because its overall diameter was smaller than the suspender button, and the raised and countersunk "hub" that took the rivet could not be substantially reduced in diameter or it would be too weak. By adjusting the angle of the countersink and redesigning the rivet, they got it to work on a trial basis.[12]

William and Clark sought to secure the benefit of their innovations by patenting the improved button. Reed's prior patent did not deter them, although the fine points of the Platts' work eluded their patent attorney,

Lemuel Serrell of New York. Serrell advised that Reed's patent covered rivet attachment and that the manufacturing process of cupping the shell and then folding down the edge also appeared in earlier claims. Convinced that patenting any part of the process as an invention was futile, Serrell finally determined that he could patent the button as a proprietary design: "The claim must be to the *article* as a novelty in itself." He submitted the application in October 1865, and the patent came through the following July.[13]

Reed kept ordering small lots of buttons to use for experimentation and sales samples through the first half of 1866. He moved his office to the center of the nation's garment trade in lower Manhattan and negotiated with vendors to make his machines and the button rivets. He ended up buying the machines in Philadelphia and the rivets from Connecticut hardware firms in Wallingford and Ansonia. Before establishing regular production of his button presses, Reed moved his few prototype machines around to different garment houses so that they could try the new buttons. The fly buttons continued to bedevil the project because the combination of a small front and a large hub made them difficult to button and unbutton. Reed garnered suggestions from everyone—makers of garments, machines, and rivets— to pass along to the Platts. After a great deal of trial and error they improved it by reducing the hub diameter and compensating for the reduction in strength by also lengthening it, thereby using the same amount of metal as in the shorter, thicker hubs. The change reduced the margin for error in punching the hole in the hub (a process called piercing). If not precisely concentric and properly sized, the hole would cut into the hub wall and turn the button into an expensive piece of scrap. Reed and the Platts continued for several years to refine the hub design.[14]

In late June 1866, Reed began leasing his machines to garment factories on a long-term basis. He warned the Platts that each placement meant an immediate order for at least one hundred great gross of buttons and worried about their ability to keep up: "I should like to know how you are to supply me and get me out of difficulties when these little [sample] orders are so very slow coming along. . . . I fear sometimes you do not properly appreciate that this one holed Button is *sure* to revolutionize your Button trade & drive out the sewed Button so that it will never be heard of." Reed underestimated the Platts. They had heeded the lessons of their Civil War experience, when huge leaps of production were delayed by lack of enough machinery, long lead times to perfect tooling, and labor shortages. Moreover, they had wartime profits to invest, they had seen the benefit of expansion, and they had the advice of the Porters to guide them.[15]

Even though the Platts sold the riveted buttons directly to Reed, the Porters helped with the Reed project. The Porters provided independent confirmation of Reed's claims as to the growing acceptance of the buttons and encouraged appropriate expansion. They also welcomed the Platts' diversification, which afforded some protection from price cutting. Writing in February 1866, Samuel Porter noted that the Platt buttons he sold were "above the market," but he did not recommend reductions as long as the development work and sample production for Reed kept "running strong."[16]

For their part, the Platts took full advantage of Waterbury's burgeoning machine-building sector, buying more machinery of greater sophistication. They doubled the capacity of their basic buttonmaking process in March 1866 by purchasing four stamping presses from the firm of Blake and Johnson, a neighbor of their downtown factory. The new machines came equipped with Charles Johnson's patented automatic strip-feeding device, which reduced the time, judgment, and physical endurance necessary to feed sheet metal into a button stamp by hand. Formerly assigned to the most experienced and trusted employees, such as Alfred's cousin Franklin Judd, stamping became, at most, a semiskilled job. The Blake and Johnson presses also featured a patented stop-motion attachment, which halted the machine in the event of a jam or if stock ran out, eliminating the need for constant attention and allowing press operators to run more than one machine at a time. Even though the new machinery might have aggravated the problem of scarce machinist help for setup, adjustment, and repairs—which would have accompanied any expansion—the overall skill level in the factory did not increase in proportion to output. If anything, it declined. The new machines also brought change in the material used to make button fronts, or shells: because the new feeds were set for regular-width coils of strip, they eliminated the use of scrap sheet metal. This change did not create any difficulty in material supply because the Platts rolled their own zinc strip, and getting brass strip was hardly a problem in Waterbury.[17]

Thus, the Platts were prepared when Reed signaled in September 1866 that massive orders were imminent. He asked for a production estimate in order to schedule deliveries: "Would like to have some idea from you as regards the quantities you are prepared to produce, whether one, two, or three hundred [great gross] per day." Reed was correct about the eventual volume of demand but grossly overoptimistic on the timing. By the time orders reached a steady rate of more than one hundred great gross per day, Reed was no longer in a position to benefit from it. But the future looked rosy in September 1866, when Reed filed the incorporation papers for his firm, the United States Patent Button, Rivet, Needle and Machine Manufacturing Company (U.S. Patent Button).[18]

The comfortable regularity of business with the Porters helped the Platts build up the U.S. Patent Button production without sacrificing their other work. The Porters continued to aid the Platts in stockpiling metal by recommending large purchases when commodity prices fell. They routinely monitored customer needs and inventory, factored in the Platts' reports on the Reed orders, anticipated overall production needs, and helped adjust the schedule of work in the shop accordingly. As the orders still outpaced expansion in manufacturing capacity, the Platts regularly subcontracted some operations to prevent orders from piling up, notably the fabrication of shells for the buttons the Porters sold. Major subcontractors besides Griggs Brothers (and its successor Smith and Griggs Company) included Thomas Manufacturing, a subsidiary of Seth Thomas Clock Company in Thomaston, and Lane Manufacturing Company, a buttonmaker next door to the Platts' downtown shop. Lane also performed gilding and japanning. A relatively even pace of production resulted from all of these tactics even while the different market segments fluctuated. For the busy months when garment makers readied their fall and spring lines, the Porters' efforts yielded average monthly revenue around $2,000; during slow months, net from the Porters dipped below $1,000. Production for U.S. Patent Button rose and fell much more precipitously (a danger sign that did not escape the notice of Clark Platt and Samuel Porter). Nonetheless, with reliable information looking at least several weeks forward, the Platts could orchestrate the work in their own two shops with assignments to subcontractors, keeping all of their customers supplied without working overtime. In the busy month of December 1866, for instance, they shipped the first big orders for U.S. Patent Button and restocked the Porters' inventory for the coming spring season. Though subcontracts for fabrication and finishing ran high for the month, the month's shipments of $3,586 worth were unprecedented for peacetime ($2,732 worth to U.S. Patent Button and $854 to the Porters).[19]

The Platts continued to spend freely on new equipment as the business expanded in 1867 and 1868. They bought two secondhand stamping presses and a small double-action press from another button shop. Kirk and Welton, the firm founded by former Platts Mills resident Thomas Kirk, provided kick presses for button assembly. Kirk also charged the Platts for a total of several weeks' labor in 1868, probably for setup, adjustment, and repairs beyond the skill or time available from in-house help. The Platts built up their own tool and machine making too, buying toolroom equipment fitted for single-piece rather than high-production operation. Every new machine also required about $30 in capital cost for the pulleys, shafting, and related hardware to drive it.[20]

In early 1869, with the end of the five-year lease on the downtown shop approaching, Clark and William Platt began looking to buy property for a larger factory. In 1866 and 1867 they had assembled a small parcel on the east side of Elm Street, one block southeast of the leased shop. But land was scarce in this neighborhood, one of Waterbury's two rapidly growing industrial districts. Their new property, totaling less than one-quarter acre, was bounded on the north by the Brown and Brothers brass mill and on the south by the Hayden hardware factory; neither would limit their own expansion by selling any land to the Platts. Alfred still wanted to build up the Platts Mills plant and would shortly do so, but his sons valued the convenience of downtown, with material suppliers, machine builders, and subcontractors within a two-minute walk.[21]

Their solution to the difficulty of securing space for downtown expansion began with the financial difficulties of Merritt Lane, proprietor of Lane Manufacturing. If Clark and William were reluctant to take advantage of a fellow buttonmaker's troubles, Lane would have been the last to benefit. In 1866, when Lane started making shells for the Platts' buttons, he ran off a few for himself, made up some samples, and tried to sell them through the leading pants-button wholesale merchants in New York—Porter Brothers, who quashed the scheme. Lane's property, an acre of land with a two-story frame shop, a one-story brick shop, and a waterwheel, was immediately south of the Platts' leased quarters on Great Brook. Lane, who had also expanded sharply during the war, had bought the property in 1864. But his firm lost business during the postwar consolidation of the trade (which probably lay behind his try at taking down the Platts), and in early 1869 he did not have enough cash or credit to continue operating.[22]

Lane approached a source for money that might seem unusual anywhere but Waterbury: the city's Library Fund endowment. The trustees of the Library Fund, a group of brass manufacturers headed by Frederick Kingsbury, no doubt viewed their own industry as an excellent way to invest the public funds under their guardianship. Unfortunately for Lane, the trustees also knew his situation and would not approve his loan without a co-signer of ample means, even though the factory Lane offered as security was probably worth the $10,000 he requested; Lane had paid $15,000 for it in 1864.[23]

Lane asked the Platts for help, and in March 1869 he accepted their offer. They took title to the property in return for an unknown amount of cash, then used the factory to secure two $5,000 notes of obligation to Lane, one payable in 1872 and one a year later. Lane sold the notes to the Library Fund to obtain the cash he used to continue operations. The Platts leased the second floor of the frame building to Lane for $675 a year, along with five horsepower for $525 annually. They also agreed to continue the lease of the tenant in the brick shop, Kirk and Welton, which paid $375 annual rent. The Platts obtained a factory far larger and with more power than they needed, land for future downtown expansion, and rental income of $1,575 that was approximately three times the annual interest the Platts owed the Library Fund. And in their own buildings they housed one of their leading

Brick factory built at Platts Mills in 1869. From left to right: Walter Harrison (boy on horse), Mary Bergan, Alice Thomas, Antoinette Tolles, Lillie Davis, Emma Barcley, Eva Pape, Anna Judd, Annie Bergan, John Harrison, Fred Harrison (boy on wheelbarrow), Ida Pape, Maggie Bergan, Vill Williams, Benjamin Bristol (on fence), Sam Miller, unknown young man on fence, William Platt, Irving Platt (on fence), Edgar Bristol. (Mattatuck Museum)

subcontractors and one of their leading equipment suppliers. (Lane recovered fully and in 1873 built his own new factory on North Elm Street.)[24]

Alfred Platt's interest in real estate remained closer to home. Two months after the Civil War ended, he used his share of the tent-button profits to pay off the balance of the 1856 mortgage of $8,000 on his Platts Mills holdings. In 1869, the year of his eighty-first birthday, Platt took the forward-looking step of building a brick factory at Platts Mills to house the buttonmaking operations that remained there. The one-story factory cost some $4,600, $3,500 of it to mason Ben Chatfield. The balance was for Alfred to provide and prepare the stone to build the foundation, retaining wall along the river bank, wheelpit, and new races. He oversaw and paid for quarrying, dressing, and moving the stone from his quarry. He also paid Chatfield's bill and then charged A. Platt and Sons for his "Expenses on Brick Shop."[25]

Impetus for acquiring the downtown factory and further developing Platts Mills might have come from the prospects for the Reed button, but by 1869 the plans did not include Reed himself. Reed's firm ran into problems after the heady days of late 1866 and early 1867, when the Platts' monthly net from his buttons averaged nearly $2,000. The fly buttons had never been perfected, and Reed kept suggesting adjustments that would make them easier to use, usually some variation on lengthening the hub or further reducing its diameter. The imperfections of the fly button cut deeply into sales, which, after the first half of 1867, fell to a monthly average of under $1,000 net to the Platts. At the same time, Reed stretched out his payment term.[26]

The Platts eventually took over Reed's idea, although they did not abandon him hastily. Starting in August 1868, they discounted every month's invoice by 20 percent. When Reed failed to pay them anything at all during March 1869, they stopped sending buttons. At the end of April, Reed scraped together a payment of about one-quarter of the $7,456 he owed, but the Platts had run out of patience and started to develop the business on their own. The Platt riveted-button patent of 1866, as well as their soon-to-be-patented rivet and attaching-machine improvements, gave them a legal and technological basis to pursue the project. The loss of U.S. Patent Button revenues did not hurt the Platts because the Porters accelerated their sales efforts for the sewn-on buttons, yielding more than $4,000 a month net revenues for the first half of 1869 and some $3,000 a month for the second half. The Platts made two final shipments to U.S. Patent Button, some 200 great gross in July 1869 and another 250 in December. During 1870 the relationship with Reed's firm consisted entirely of collection notices and legal wrangling. In his last transaction with the Platts, in February 1871, Reed reimbursed them $138 for attorney's fees.[27]

A. Platt and Sons could absorb their new building costs in 1869 and 1870, but taking over the entire riveted-button business strained their capital. Solving the problem of the fly button and completing development of the rivet and the attaching machine—Clark's rivet and William's machine both received patents in 1871—occupied the Platt brothers and perhaps a machinist but did not demand major new expenditure. Establishing the capacity to make the rivets and machines and to enlarge the button output required substantial outlays, however, and the Lane notes limited the company's ability to borrow. Furthermore, when the Platts started this effort in early 1869, the Reed situation was still unsettled and they did not know when they would see the first income from the project. The Porters stepped in again, agreeing to absorb half of the "expense on Pat. Butt." development and to sell the buttons for less than their standard 10 percent commission.[28]

The two firms spent more than $5,600 on the project during 1869 and 1870, with no income from it. The development work took place in the downtown shop, where the Platts made full use of Thomas Kirk's machine shop and expert services. A. Platt and Sons paid him $504 for "Labor, Presses &c &c for Patent Button" in 1869 and another $396 in 1870, some 16 percent of the total development cost. The most important part of Kirk's work was helping the Platts devise and build a specialized press "for making

TABLE I[31]
A. Platt and Sons Net Button Revenues from Sales by Porter Brothers
(Dollars)

Year	Sewn Buttons	Patent Buttons
1869		
Jan.–June	26,903	—
July–Dec.	18,272	—
1870		
Jan.–June	23,660	—
July–Dec.	20,592	—
1871		
Jan.–June	23,991	8,085
July–Dec.	23,611	9,676
1872		
Jan.–June	37,032	12,990
July–Dec.	28,154	22,480
1873		
Jan.–June	33,809	22,024
July–Dec.	24,518	24,733

Patent Buttons." (The distribution of the remaining cost among wages for new workers, contracting, equipment, and tooling is unknown.) Toward the end of 1870, many of the increased purchases from Benedict and Burnham, Brown and Brothers, and Waterbury Brass were probably brass strip for making the buttons and rivets. Kirk's work was mostly done—his fees for the year included only $46 after June—and A. Platt and Sons had probably started producing the buttons and rivets at the new, higher level.[29]

The long development process yielded dramatic results when the Porters started offering the buttons in 1871 (see Table 1). During the first six months of sales they more than recouped the entire experimentation and capital expense. In 1872 the Platts and Porters invested another $9,600 in new equipment for the patent buttons (some $1,500 of it paid to Kirk), almost tripling manufacturing capacity; and again the results soon reflected the investment: for the second half of 1873 sales tripled those of early 1871. At the end of 1873, after three years on the market, net revenue from the riveted buttons equaled that of the sewn buttons, the market for which had taken more than a decade to cultivate.[30]

The rolled-zinc business proceeded on a more regular pace of production and income than did the button side, with its ups and downs from the Reed venture. The backs of sewn-on buttons remained the principal market, and the Platts' own button works consumed at least half of the rolling mill's output. Led by this internal use, the zinc trade enjoyed steady levels of repeat business. At least partly due to the lack of many competitors in supplying rolled zinc, once a firm became an established customer, it tended to remain so for many years. Goddard Brothers of New York began in 1860 to buy three hundred to five hundred pounds of zinc strip a year for their "clothiers' trimmings" and maintained that same consumption into the mid-1870s. Even when the Platts lost customers, they usually got them back. G. H. Smith, a buttonmaker in nearby Woodbury, bought between three hundred and one thousand pounds until 1864, when his New York agent found a source that was $.03 a pound cheaper. But by late 1865, Smith had resumed ordering from the Platts and kept it up until his firm closed in 1875. After the war there were at least ten major continuing customers, including Newell Brothers of Longmeadow, Massachusetts; Giershofer, Leowi and Company of Philadelphia; Bridgeport Button Company; and U.S. Button Company of Waterbury. They each bought several thousand pounds a year at prices that fluctuated between $.20 and $.35 a pound.[32]

The primary zinc operation grew more metallurgically complex as new American and European sources of metal were opened up. Until the mid-1860s, metals brokers generally supplied one type of European spelter ("Silesian") and one American ("New Jersey"). "Lehigh," from Pennsylvania, became available during the war; "Springfield," from Missouri, and "Sicilian," from the Mediterranean, after the war. The Platts did not know in any exact fashion the type and extent of impurities in the slabs, nor did they have the ability to analyze the metal. However, from their own observations and the reports of their customers, they could determine how the different types performed under various operations. They selected the metal for a particular job according to its label. When making what they called "Tough metal" (presumably high in tensile strength), they used only the American Zinc Company's "Lehigh" brand.[33]

The proliferation of metal-fabricating shops in postwar Waterbury gave William Platt the chance to apply his expertise with zinc to uses other than buttons. Carrington Company made hardware for saddles and harnesses, products subject to outdoor exposure that could benefit from zinc's non-corrosive property. Carrington began buying thirty to fifty pounds a month and occasionally ordered more than two hundred pounds. American Ring Company, which provided a wide variety of hardware items to makers of clothing, jewelry, machinery, and weapons, found many uses for zinc, normally using at least two hundred pounds a month and sometimes as much as one thousand.[34]

American Ring was also the Platts' largest early customer for a third line of business beyond buttons and rolled zinc: brass stampings either resold by American Ring or used as component parts in American Ring products. Known generically as "shells" or "eyelets," these products featured neither a distinctive material, like the zinc-rolling business, nor distinctive designs, like the button business. The Platts' only edge over dozens of other local eyelet shops was their ability to handle tricky shapes and close specifications,

TABLE 2[36]
A. Platt and Sons Income and Dividends, 1866–1872

Year	Net Income	Dividend	Dividend Date
1866	Not known	6,000	July 1866
1867	Not known	0	—
1868	6,115	6,000	December 1868
1869	14,169	4,500	January 1870
1870	8,932	0	—
1871	15,560	7,500	July 1871
1872	20,000 +	9,000	August 1872
		6,000	September 1872

an ability they had developed in the work on the riveted fly button. Most eyelet customers were local firms that probably had some knowledge of the Platts' particular capability, such as American Suspender Company and Matthews and Stanley, both of Waterbury. Opportunity to exploit this advantage did not come frequently, however, and the Platts continued to spend more on subcontracting than they made as parts suppliers.[35]

A. Platt and Sons produced substantial profits between 1866 and 1872, as it evolved into a larger, more diversified firm. Vastly increased capital expenditure and the deferral of profit-taking while pursuing the development work on the riveted button made for several long intervals between dividends (see Table 2). Alfred, William, and Clark Platt each received a dividend of $2,000 in July 1866. The costs of expansion and diversification delayed the next payout until December 1868, after the money had started rolling in from Reed's early success. Though revenues continued to rise, investment did too; buying and equipping the new downtown factory in 1869 reduced the year-end dividend for each Platt to $1,500. Paying for the brick shop at Platts Mills, as well as rising expenditures for equipment, labor, and subcontracting, eliminated any dividend for 1870. The partners took $2,500 each in July 1871. In August and September 1872, they each received two dividends totaling $5,000, or some ten times more than the annual income of the highest-paid wage earners. In addition to these proceeds, Clark and William each received an annual salary of $1,500, and Alfred took some $600 for use of his property and waterpower, $400 for the brick shop alone.

In the twenty-five years since their first venture together, the Platts' work force had grown from the owners themselves to dozens of full-time employees. Their equipment had come to embody the most sophisticated process innovations in consumer metal-goods production. Their total revenues rose from a few hundred dollars a year to tens of thousands. And Alfred, William, and Clark Platt amassed a small fortune.

The Legacy of Alfred Platt

Alfred Platt died in his bed on December 29, 1872. For the last year of his life a lingering respiratory ailment forced him to quit his accustomed daily exertions on the farm, in the gristmill, and in the Platts Mills metal shop. From outward appearances it would have been difficult to know that this small old man wearing a homemade beaverskin cap was one of the wealthiest people in Waterbury. Though he had spent a long lifetime at hard work, only during his last eight years did he make his fortune.[37]

Platt liked to work and enjoyed farm life. After he got rich, he still spent many days in his fields, although in his seventies he had more help with the heavy labor. He would have needed more farmhands anyway because he bought more land with his metalworking profits, including some twenty acres on the west bank, across the Naugatuck from Platts Mills. Platt's grandsons-in-law, the husbands of Nirom's daughters, worked the west-side land. The money Alfred did not put into land around his homestead he put into the bank or into his various enterprises. He never took part in financial machinations that did not depend centrally upon his own expertise in farming, Platts Mills real estate, or manufacturing. The biggest difference money made in his life was that he no longer had to mortgage his property.[38]

William and Clark invested more widely, and for a time less conservatively, than did their father. Encouraged by the Porters, who made many of the purchases for them in New York, Clark and William bought financial assets with their dividends between 1865 and 1867. The investments ranged from secure government bonds to speculative western mining stocks, such as Star City Mill and Mining Company, shares of which declined from $1,000 to $30 after William and Clark bought them. Perhaps sobered by that experience, they subsequently bought stock only in companies they knew something about, such as Cheshire Watch Company and the brass firm of Plume and Atwood. They also started following their father's example by devoting most of their investments to real estate. Clark and William each established holdings throughout Waterbury that would eventually rival their industrial pursuits in value and income. In 1866 William lent millwright Charles Miller the money to build a house on Grand Street. This transaction introduced William to the business of private mortgage lending, which he and his children would pursue to great benefit in later years.[39]

In early 1867, Clark bought a house downtown so that he could move close to the leased button shop. He sold his house and garden in Platts Mills to William, who moved there with his family. For $20 a month William rented his former dwelling to the company for use as a boardinghouse.

At the end of 1867, William vastly expanded the family's holdings at Platts Mills by buying Henry Matthews's farm, thirty-six acres immediately north of Alfred's land, for $2,200 in cash.[40]

The younger Platts continued to accumulate property that became available in the neighborhood of their downtown shop, both as an investment and toward further expansion. They were especially interested in land on the large block their factory occupied—north of East Main and west of Elm. The factory they bought from Lane had been built to take advantage of Great Brook and had no street frontage, merely the right to use a fifteen-foot-wide private passway running south to East Main Street. In the mid-1880s the passway would become Brown Street, a public right-of-way; but until then the Platts preserved their ability to use the passway by taking every opportunity to obtain land along it, whether or not the land directly abutted their factory.[41]

While Clark and William built the metalworking business and their personal real estate holdings, their brother Legrand continued to work at the family gristmill. Alfred had softened his opinion of Legrand enough to make him a partner in 1863. Unlike the metal shop when Clark and William had joined it, the gristmill was well established, and Legrand had to pay for his ownership interest out of his share of the milling proceeds. It took four years, but in 1867 Legrand owned half of a business that netted some $2,000 a year. Alfred still owned the mill, had responsibility for maintaining it, and charged the business for its use. Since the gristmill often received immediate cash payment, but the metal shop had to wait several months for payment of its invoices, Alfred frequently had Legrand lend from milling proceeds to carry A. Platt and Sons through periods of cash shortage. A. Platt and Sons never paid interest on these loans, which ran between $100 and $900, with terms ranging from a week to six months. Apparently, Legrand also served as the button shop's unpaid shipping clerk, as A. Platt and Sons often reimbursed him for railroad freight charges but did not pay him a salary.[42]

In rewriting his will in May 1871, Alfred Platt tried to assure an even distribution of his estate while also bequeathing separately to Clark and William those assets that they had helped to build. He stipulated six equal shares, one to each of his five surviving sons and one to the heirs of Nirom, who had died in 1863. It would have been difficult to make six equal shares of an estate consisting mostly of land, water rights, buildings, and machinery under any circumstances short of liquidation. But Alfred complicated the estate further by specifying Clark's and William's parts of it. They would get Alfred's share of A. Platt and Sons' assets; if the appraised value of Alfred's third of the firm exceeded that of the two sons' third of his total estate, they were to pay the difference to the estate. Alfred anticipated some contention over the Platts Mills waterpower and devoted the longest section of the will to an arbitration procedure for settling disputes over apportioning it between the metal shops and the gristmill. What he did not foresee was jealousy over the most profitable enterprise, which pitted Charles, Legrand, and Seabury against Clark and William.[43]

Charles, Legrand, and Seabury hired Seabury's law firm, which filed a petition listing sixteen claims against the estate: the division into six equal shares overrode the specific legacies to Clark and William, implicit conditions governed Clark and William's conduct of the business, the business could be taken from them for nonperformance, and so forth. It all amounted to Charles, Legrand, and Seabury wanting to share in Alfred's portion of the profits from A. Platt and Sons, while Clark and William wanted to split the profits down the middle for themselves. Clark and William retained the Waterbury law firm that had helped Alfred write the will. They defended the specific legacy and bluntly dismissed the other claims: "As to the residue of the allegations of said petition the respondents say that they are not true." The Waterbury probate judge upheld Clark and William, as did the New Haven County Superior Court in 1874, after Charles, Legrand, and Seabury appealed. In appealing further to the State Supreme Court, Charles, Legrand, and Seabury added a claim on the profits of the business during the time since Alfred's death. Also, because Clark and William had refused to let their brothers examine the accounts, their brothers had to ask the court to grant that access. The Supreme Court finally settled the mess in April 1875. The justices confirmed the specific legacy to Clark and William and awarded to their brothers a third of the profits for the two and a half years of delay in settlement, as well as a look at the books. Reappraisals and audits consumed another year, and the final distribution came in April 1876.[44]

The final appraisal of A. Platt and Sons put the firm's worth at $100,817. Alfred's estate, including a third of the metal business, came to $112,960. Thus Clark's and William's combined share of the total estate was a little over $37,000, and the other heirs' share of the business was a little under $34,000: Clark and William would not have to reimburse the estate. The audit of A. Platt and Sons revealed undistributed dividends of about $39,000 because after Alfred died, Clark and William had not taken any dividends from the company's rising net income. Some complicated negotiation then ensued. In the distribution, Clark and William received clear title to the downtown factory and the Platts Mills button shop, casting shop, and rolling mill; they also had rights to an eighth of the water privilege and about an eighth of the nonindustrial property at Platts Mills. They traded their interest in the nonindustrial holdings for a greater share of the waterpower, a little more land near the metalworking shops, and a reduction in the $13,000 dividend owed their brothers.[45]

In their squabbling over Alfred Platt's share of the metalworking profits his sons shattered his vision of family-centered enterprise based on everyone working together. Alfred had set the pattern for the undoing of his hopes by establishing different businesses in which he was the only common participant; he alone shared in the metalworking business, in the Platts Mills gristmill, and in Charles's gristmill in Massachusetts. For Alfred, the success of A. Platt and Sons was a happy circumstance that provided more resources for all of his other activities—more land to farm and more money to pay off his mortgages and equip all of his enterprises. But his sons diverged in their view of A. Platt and Sons. To Clark and William its profits were a reward for their own efforts, and to their brothers the profits were their due as heirs, from which they should continue to benefit.

The estate battle did not leave any of them destitute. Charles still had his profitable store and milling business, and Seabury had his law practice. As part of the distribution Legrand got the gristmill business, which he named the Platts Mills Company and built into a prosperous wholesale operation, including a warehouse close to downtown. He closed the sawmill to devote his share of the waterpower fully to grinding grain, but he continued to serve as a wholesale lumber merchant on a resale basis and added coal and ice to his offerings.[46]

Alfred Platt cared as much about how he conducted his affairs as he did about their outcome, with the result that his legacy was rich in seeming contradictions. Platt relished bargaining and pursued it down to the half-penny, yet he disdained those who bargained only, who traded on the value others created without creating anything themselves. He manipulated the credit he could obtain in the emerging market economy but not for gain alone and always toward keeping or improving the farm and mills that he enjoyed working himself. Nor did he hesitate to risk his holdings in support of what he viewed as a higher purpose, his Baptist church and parish; Platt's piety did not begin and end on Sunday. As a Baptist in his youth Platt belonged to a group that suffered from official discrimination, perhaps helping to explain his unusually fair treatment of the principal victims of prejudice in mid-nineteenth-century Connecticut, the Irish Catholics. Ambitious, shrewd, technically adept, and a hard bargainer, yet also pious, tolerant, egalitarian, and disdainful of financial chicanery, Platt was motivated by more than profit alone, and the business he founded reflected the man.

Two other traits stand out in the life of Alfred Platt—independence and satisfaction in work. Platt could have devoted his shop and his effort solely to Aaron Benedict's ventures and realized far greater gain with much less risk. But he left Benedict after fifteen years to apply those ideas of Benedict's that suited him best and to live the life he loved—that of a farmer, a miller, and a buttonmaker too. Platt valued his days as much as his bank account, and he spent them at the work he enjoyed.

In the estate battle Clark and William contributed to the dissolution of Alfred's family-based economic vision, but their conduct of the metal-working business continued to embody many of the ideas that had guided their father and set him apart from the Waterbury moguls of that earlier generation. Their brothers might have disagreed, but "family" actually meant the same thing to Clark and William as it did to Alfred—themselves and their children, not their siblings—and they valued family-based organization just as highly. They did share ownership, on very generous terms, with unrelated people who made significant contributions to the business, but they did not let control pass out of the family. Clark and William never disdained the factory floor, never delegated entirely the technical and direct supervisory work to retreat into less involved and more prestigious management positions. Their roles reflected the respect for work that Alfred had inculcated in them, and allowed them to keep close control over the core processes and materials on which the business relied. They also inherited some of Alfred's suspicion of "commercial men": with the special exception of the Porter brothers, the sons never dealt with commission merchants. Like their father, Clark and William also felt responsible to the wider community that helped make their wealth possible; they did not pursue wealth as a sole end in itself. Although none could ever match the depth of commitment to the parish that Alfred had demonstrated, William became the Baptist church's largest benefactor of his generation.[47]

Clark and William Platt also followed their father's example regarding industrial property. Alfred had always viewed his waterpower and mills as the heart of his working life and his prospects for prosperity and had pursued any tactic necessary to hold onto them. His sons never risked their industrial real estate in speculation; once they owned factory property, they kept it. Even when they could have raised money for outside investments by borrowing against the factories, they borrowed on personal accounts rather than leverage the manufacturing holdings. They placed a high priority on sustaining the business and never risked its steadiness and reliability as a vendor, a customer, and an employer for short-term gain.

The Family Corporations

William Platt was fifty years old when his father died in 1872, Clark was forty-eight, and their children had reached or were approaching maturity. William and Caroline's daughter Helen was twenty-four; Caroline A., known as Carrie, was nineteen; and their son Irving was thirteen. Clark and Amelia had a daughter, Bertha, age twenty-one, and a son, Lewis, eighteen. As Alfred was the last Platt to engage extensively in agriculture, his sons were the last generation raised to the rigors of farm life. Clark's and William's children, in their early years at Platts Mills, no doubt knew the smell of manure and new-mown hay, but they did not work in the fields from dawn to dusk at harvest time or churn butter or smoke pork. Clark had left the farm when he moved with his family to the city in 1867. William and his family stayed near the old homestead; late in her life his daughter Helen recalled with some regret both the lack of urbanity and the remoteness from her friends connected with her girlhood in Platts Mills. The family's concern for education spanned the generations. Sons and daughters alike completed the full courses offered at the Waterbury public schools. Irving went on to Eastman's Business College in Poughkeepsie, New York. Lewis studied at Yale, graduating in 1879.[48]

Like their fathers before them, Irving and Lewis Platt began working in the family business as young adults and assumed continually increasing responsibility in the following years. But even before they took over, the business had grown too large for their fathers to manage completely by themselves. Soon after Alfred's death Clark and William widened the circle of responsibility at the downtown shop, although not too far beyond the immediate family. Their first "foreman," in 1873, was F. E. Porter, a relative of the button merchants. A few months before Alfred died, the company hired a young man to handle the shipping chores at the downtown shop, Jay H. Hart. Hart, reared on a farm in Berkshire County, Massachusetts, had moved to Waterbury in 1869 as the local agent for a railroad freight-forwarding firm, then worked for two years as head of shipping operations for one of the large brass mills before coming to A. Platt and Sons. Though he did not start out as a family member, he soon became one by marrying Clark's daughter Bertha in May 1873. Hart's job changed to "foreman" that same year. Hart shared many characteristics with Wallace H. Camp, the husband of William Platt's daughter Helen. Camp moved to Waterbury in 1870 from his family's farm in Harwinton, Connecticut, and worked in shipping for Scovill Manufacturing. He continued to work at Scovill after marrying Helen in 1878, but he participated in the important decisions governing the Platts' business. These four men—Irving Platt, Lewis Platt, Jay Hart, and Wallace Camp—formed the cadre of owner-managers for the following generation.[49]

To prepare for transition to the next generation without the disputes that attended their father's passing, Clark and William established a corporate structure that provided an unquestioned basis of ownership while preserving the personal control and rewards of the earlier partnership. On 22 January 1876, three months before the final distribution of Alfred's estate, Clark and William filed incorporation papers for the two firms that would

Platts Mills, 1876, viewed from the west. The large building to the right, on the riverbank, is the Platt gristmill. Surrounding it are frame additions built for casting and rolling zinc, the one-story brick shop built in 1869, and the homes and barns of the family enclave. (Platt Brothers and Co.)

succeed A. Platt and Sons: The Platt Brothers and Company and Patent Button Company. Initially, no strict division existed between the functions performed by the two new companies; the major distinctions concerned property and share ownership. Patent Button occupied the downtown shop; Platt Brothers, the Platts Mills facilities. The distribution of Patent Button's 480 shares reflected the all-important role of the Porters in building up the riveted-button business for which it was named. Nathan, Thomas, and Samuel Porter together owned half of the business, with 80 shares each; Clark and William also held half of the total, with 120 shares each. In contrast, most of the original 1,200 shares of Platt Brothers stayed in the family: 520 to William, 520 to Clark, 100 to Samuel Porter, and 60 to Jay H. Hart. Unlike the corporations of Aaron Benedict and his peers, those established by the Platts had no provision for raising capital and dispersing ownership by the sale of shares. Indeed, the incorporation documents included only the minimal provisions necessary under state statutes to set up a corporation, such as frequency and location of meetings (once a year in Waterbury) and number of directors (three to five). The new form of organization was clearly intended as a legal device to substantially maintain the approach to business that had brought so much success. Platt Brothers and Patent Button had the status of corporations, but still they were family businesses.[50]

CHAPTER FIVE

Small Business in the Gilded Age

C L A R K and William Platt initially envisioned Platt Brothers and Company and Patent Button Company as two parts of the same business. They planned to keep most manufacturing under Platt Brothers, while Patent Button would market the riveted buttons and manufacture only the attaching machines. During the first four years after incorporation, however, the Platts' success in developing new uses for zinc and new markets for their expertise in metal fabricating transformed Platt Brothers into something very different from its original role as the manufacturing arm of Patent Button. Patent Button, in turn, had to assume increasing responsibility for its own manufacturing; by 1880, Patent Button employed more production workers than Platt Brothers did and directly owned much of the buttonmaking machinery. Clark and William then focused their own energies more on the core businesses remaining in Platt Brothers, which were centered around expertise in particular technology rather than a certain line of goods. This fundamental divergence between the two firms continually widened after 1876, but Clark and William never completed the complex process of untangling Platt Brothers and Patent Button. The next generation would have to finish that job.

The Relationship between Platt Brothers and Patent Button

Patent Button had the responsibility for selling the riveted buttons, and the selection of Samuel Porter as its first president signified the importance of Porter Brothers' expert marketing efforts in the finished-button trade. After Porter's untimely death in 1876, his brother Thomas was chosen to succeed him; twenty years later Thomas's son, Thomas W. Porter, would follow. At the start Patent Button depended almost exclusively upon Porter Brothers to sell its output to clothing manufacturers. For the Porters, Patent

Button was the culmination of a long-standing ambition: an entire factory devoted to filling its orders. Though several steady customers did not buy through Porter Brothers (mostly local firms such as Waterbury Brass Company), these sales were minuscule compared to the business generated by the Porters: in 1876 the $74,000 in orders from Porter Brothers was over 90 percent of Patent Button's sales. Porter Brothers more than doubled their sales over the next three years, to more than $162,000 worth of buttons in 1879.[1]

The new corporate structure and changes in the men's clothing sector both contributed to a decline in the Porters' selling role after 1880. After incorporation the Porters no longer received a 10 percent commission on the sales but half of the dividends from Patent Button's manufacturing profits (when dividends started in 1878). The new arrangement let them relax any objection to Patent Button's selling directly to manufacturers. The incorporation of Patent Button occurred during a period of consolidation in the ready-made menswear industry. When the Platts started making buttons in the 1840s, highly capitalized clothing manufacturers had emerged in the major cities, but these garment makers still faced strong competition from small-scale tailors and from production by retailers such as Brooks Brothers (a Platt customer). In the 1870s and 1880s the garment firms that could afford the new production technology, especially sewing machines and mechanical cloth-cutting knives, pulled away from their smaller competitors. The menswear industry as a whole grew more complex, with many different combinations of production by wage earners and contractors; but the assembly of garments—the step in which buttons were used—took place in fewer and larger shops than had earlier been the case. For Patent Button this evolution in its market meant that a vigorous sales effort targeting a host of potential customers, such as the Porters had undertaken in the late 1850s and the 1860s, was no longer necessary. Contacts with the few dozen largest garment makers would suffice.[2]

Thomas Porter, the Patent Button president, still had authority to negotiate sales and continued for a time to lead the efforts to find new customers. But the Porter Brothers commission house in New York no longer took all of the shipments, warehoused all of the buttons, nor distributed them to the garment shops. Patent Button dealt directly with clothing manufacturers, particularly with established customers, and the proportion of buttons handled by Porter Brothers and Company declined. When substantial direct marketing began in 1880, sales through the Porters fell to some $90,000. They booked $102,000 in 1881 and $96,000 in 1882, but only one more time, in 1887, would the Porters' sales again reach that level. Through the rest of the 1880s their orders ranged between $55,000 and $77,000 a year. During the 1890s, even while Patent Button's total output continued to rise, the Porters' orders slid further, to less than $50,000 in every year but one.[3]

When the corporations began, the fabricating machinery at the downtown factory included thirty-four presses for blanking, pattern-stamping, and flanging button parts as well as assembling finished buttons; four edging presses; two presses equipped with dial plates; and four "eyelet machines." These eyelet presses, another innovation from Waterbury's brilliant machine builders, made finished pieces from a roll of metal strip without any need for handling of the work piece. After cutting the blank, the eyelet machine completed the piece with a variety of operations, such as drawing (or cupping), flanging, coining (or pattern stamping), and piercing. The machine had multiple stations, one for each operation, and a system of "fingers" that closed to grip the piece, advanced it to successive stations, and opened to release it. At Platts Mills the brick shop held four "hole button machines" that made the one-piece sewn-on buttons used on army tents; three "capping," or assembling, presses; two general-purpose presses; one piercing machine; one machine to make a new one-piece sewn-on button; eighteen assembly presses (including six new ones awaiting installation); five blanking presses; and three "clutch punches" to perform heavy forming operations such as blanking.[4]

During 1876, Platt Brothers nominally performed virtually all of the button production. This was necessary if only for bookkeeping purposes because in distributing the partnerships' assets Platt Brothers had received both factories and all of the machinery. But the accounting system reflected a functional separation. Platt Brothers charged Patent Button directly, by the piece or by weight, for metalworking tasks that were not distinctive to buttons but that were applied to many other fabricated metal products too: blanking shells, roll-forming patterns into strip, japanning and plating. For processes unique to buttons—notably the assembly of two-piece buttons and stamping customers' names on the shells—Platt Brothers simply charged Patent Button a fee for the use of machinery, with no labor costs included in the direct charges; Patent Button had its own employees to run the machines. Slightly less than half of the machinery was the responsibility of Patent Button, even though Platt Brothers held title to all of it.[5]

The practice of dividing button production costs into different types of charges ended (briefly) in December 1876, when Platt Brothers sold most of the buttonmaking machinery to Patent Button. Included were seventeen assembly presses, fourteen presses (including the two dial presses) for stamping and blanking, five recently acquired hopper-feed devices, dozens of punch-and-die sets, and associated fixtures, furniture, and tools. Platt Brothers continued to sell blanks and finishing services to Patent Button, but in early 1877, Patent Button fully owned and managed the rest of the buttonmaking processes. The emerging difference between the two firms was further indicated by Patent Button's receiving the dial presses and the hopper feeds: Patent Button was to concentrate on high-volume production.[6]

Over the next thirty years, as sales volume multiplied for the riveted buttons, the Platts bought hundreds of high-production machines to make them. By 1880, when a button press could cost $800, the Platts had established a regular pattern of purchasing button machinery two or three times a year, steadily adding capacity but carefully spacing the expenditures. They shopped among all of the machine builders in the local area. In addition to their well-established vendors such as Farrel Foundry and Machine, Kirk and Welton, and Blake and Johnson, they began buying from Cross and Speirs and E. J. Manville Machine Company, both local firms that offered patented fabricating equipment.[7]

The high-volume button machinery went into the downtown factory on Brown Street, which was jointly occupied by both firms. Platt Brothers kept all of the furnace and casting work and all of the rolling and slitting—the operations involved in making strip from slabs of spelter—at Platts Mills. Production of eyelets and other specialized fabricated goods and the finishing operations of japanning and plating occurred at both locations. As will be seen, Platt Brothers succeeded in marketing a wide array of fabricated products, including new types of buttons and other goods manufactured by similar processes. It was therefore convenient for Platt Brothers not only to have access to the high-production button equipment but to control that access directly in order to gain the priority for machine time that could be necessary for rapid response. Thus, despite the precedent established by the 1876 sale of button machinery from Platt Brothers to Patent Button, Platt Brothers took title to all of the new equipment purchased after that.[8]

The two firms also overlapped in their labor force. In the early and mid-1880s the Platts employed three groups of people: those who worked only for Platt Brothers at Platts Mills, those who worked only for Patent Button downtown, and those who worked downtown for both. The regular work force at Platts Mills was thirty to thirty-five people, of whom a dozen or so were women. Patent Button employed 135 people, 115 women and 20 men. In both shops the female employees served as low-skilled operators who tended self-acting machinery performing high-volume repetitive operations. The men at Platts Mills were a versatile and highly skilled group (detailed below). The men at Brown Street made the button-attaching machines that were sent out to the garment shops and made the tooling and set up the presses for buttonmaking. The group that shifted between the two firms consisted of between fifty and sixty female production workers.

The two firms assigned the charges for this group's labor on a monthly basis. Though the charge to Patent Button fluctuated between extremes of under $400 to over $3,000, it ran toward the high end, indicating that most of the time these women did Patent Button work. Only Clark and William, who kept the respective records for Patent Button and Platt Brothers, could have known the precise distribution of assignments for this group of workers. The workers themselves must often have wondered which firm they were working for; machine operator Lizzie Rich resolved the confusion in her own way when she listed her employer as "Platt Button Co.," which did not exist.[9]

Both firms paid the same wages: an average of $1.50 per day for production work, termed "ordinary labor," and $2.95 for a "skilled mechanic." The ordinary labor rate was at the top of the local scale; no factory in town exceeded it, and most were $.10 to $.45 lower. The mechanics' rate was in the midrange for Waterbury, where most shops paid skilled hands around $3.00 and some as high as $3.50. Jay H. Hart and F. E. Porter continued as salaried supervisors at Brown Street and were joined in that capacity by Frederick Minnaman. Minnaman probably helped too with the important job of recruitment among his fellow Irish Americans. People of Irish descent continued to be the predominant ethnic group in the Patent Button work force in succeeding generations as well, a situation sustained in part by the frequent practice of workers passing on their jobs to relatives or neighbors.[10]

Patent Button was devoted exclusively to the men's clothing trade, while Platt Brothers sold to all of the other metal-using industries, an extremely diverse group. As Clark and William Platt developed new products, they assigned to Patent Button those that were used on garments and kept all the rest for Platt Brothers. The most significant new Patent Button product in terms of long-term sales were what became known as rivets and burrs, the small metal reinforcements for the corners of pockets on work clothing. Patent Button continued to use zinc for button backs, for some plated goods, and for special orders, but the great majority of the metal consumed was brass and tinplate. Patent Button did not exploit the specialty in zinc that would become so important for Platt Brothers. For Patent Button, expansion was driven by more thorough marketing of its eponymous product and by the needs of an established customer base; its materials and production processes resembled those of dozens of other firms in Waterbury and hundreds nationwide. Platt Brothers would follow a very different strategy.[11]

Transferring the partnership assets to the corporations proved to be difficult without crippling the new firms with massive obligations to the surviving partners. Easing this transition was another reason for assigning all

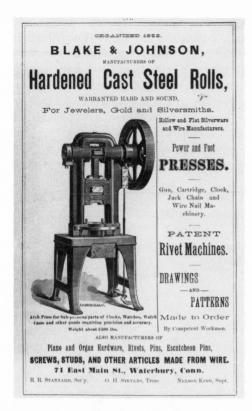

Advertisement from *Waterbury Directory,* 1886. The Waterbury machinery suppliers specialized in metal-forming equipment to work on soft metals. (Mattatuck Museum)

of the machinery and buildings to Platt Brothers; that way, only one of the firms would start out with costs for capital equipment. Patent Button received title only to finished buttons, most of them already at Porter Brothers' warehouse in New York, and invoices for finished buttons. Clark and William would get the money Patent Button owed them for the assets of the partnership when those buttons were sold and the invoices paid, but Platt Brothers presented a different problem. Since the corporate stock distribution was a paper transaction—shares in exchange for promissory notes from the shareholders—the only funds available to compensate the surviving partners were the undistributed dividends from 1873–1875 ($26,000 after settlement with Alfred's other heirs) and a bank balance of $1,833. Alfred's estate inventory placed the sons' equity in the partnership at almost $70,000. Rather than weighing down the new company with debt, William and Clark took a heavy discount in transferring assets to Platt Brothers, accepting the $27,833 cash balance as payment in full. That was serious money—the $14,000 each received was equivalent to more than $200,000 of 1990 dollars—but only about a third of what they were owed.[12]

The discount allowed Platt Brothers to begin without debt, but the payment to Clark and William depleted all of the firm's cash. Over the first thirteen months of operation, through early March 1877, Clark and William had to put their own money into the business to meet short-term obligations on twenty-five separate occasions. During March 1876 they had to refund $24,000 of the payment for the partnership assets to keep Platt Brothers afloat. At the end of April the company paid most of this money back, but hardly a month passed when the brothers did not have to lend more than a thousand dollars to the firm. Not until the end of 1877 did Clark and William get all of their money back and the company begin paying dividends.[13]

For the first time in their lives Clark and William had full responsibility for directing the business and fulfilling its obligations, with no gristmill or well-to-do father to help. Instead of retiring with their personal fortunes, they each made a substantial financial commitment to build the firm. The ready sacrifice revealed their dedication to continue the business, but it was also driven by their enthusiasm for the exciting work that lay ahead in finding new markets and developing production methods to serve them.

Selling Specialization

After Patent Button assumed high-volume button production, Platt Brothers and Company still had the specialty in zinc and a very diverse line of fabricated goods marketed directly to other factories rather than through a commission house. The range of products and processes recalled those of the old partnership from around 1850, although the corporation was more technically adept and better managed. Platt Brothers represented an opportunity for William and Clark to return to that creative work of their early careers, when they had invented the small-scale integrated metal business along with their father. It also allowed them to indulge the delight they took in working out complicated technical problems, such as producing the Hatch button and perfecting the Reed button.

Sales to Patent Button were an artificially high 70 percent of revenues in 1876. More than half of those receipts were Platt Brothers' portion of the invoices for shipments made prior to incorporation, and another fourth were at-cost resale to Patent Button of brass and tinplate and fees for use of machinery. Sales from production—rolled zinc, button shells, and japanning—were only 14 percent of Platt Brothers' revenue. As Patent Button assumed greater charge of its own manufacturing and began purchasing its metal directly, and the old partnership invoices were paid, the Patent Button share of Platt Brothers' income fell.[14]

Platt Brothers had at least seventy other customers in its first six years

TABLE 3[16]
Distribution of Materials Worked by Platt Brothers, 1877–1882
(Percent by Weight)

Material	1877	1878	1879	1880	1881	1882
Tinplate	17	23	19	18	25	23
Brass	38	27	27	30	27	27
Zinc	45	50	54	52	48	50

of operation. Only on rare occasions did any customer other than Patent Button receive more than $1,000 worth of shipments in a month. Fewer than thirty firms made more than six orders a year. The steady customers typically asked for small orders at two- to six-week intervals and usually did not order the same strip or eyelet all of the time. These frequent orders kept the shop busy but not continuously so on any single rolled or stamped product; virtually every order required skilled setup work. The small average order size indicates the highly specialized nature of the business; everything Platt Brothers made fulfilled a very tightly defined purpose. Platt Brothers did not serve any single niche market but a collection of them.[15]

The specialty in zinc assumed greater importance once Platt Brothers stood apart from the button business. In the last years of the partnership, zinc products had represented about 20 percent of the manufactured goods. After a period of adjustment in 1877, the proportions of different metals worked by Platt Brothers assumed the distribution that would continue for the rest of the nineteenth century: about half zinc, the balance split between brass and tinplate, with brass usually a little bit ahead (Table 3).

The proportions of metal worked corresponded to the relationship between primary production and fabricating: about half of the work was casting, rolling, and slitting to make zinc strip, and about half was stamping and other press operations on brass and tinplate that was purchased in strip. This division was not strict; some zinc was sold as fabricated products, and some brass or tinplate went out in strip slit to uncommon widths or otherwise different from the standard offerings of larger metal processors.

Shops making buttons and other garment trimmings were at first the largest market for zinc strip, including many long-standing customers such as Newell Brothers and Bridgeport Button. The reorganization gave the Platts the flexibility to sell zinc to more buttonmakers. Splitting the partnership provided a clear break between the Platts' primary zinc production and the direct interest of the Porters, and Patent Button did not rely substantially on access to zinc as a competitive tactic but on a novel product that was protected by patents. This new situation was most apparent in the resumption of sales to the Porters' old nemesis, the notorious price cutter E. S. Wheeler. Much more lucrative were the frequent sales to new customers such as Boston Button Company, New York Button Company, and Waterbury Button Company. Platt Brothers still protected its cousin firm when Patent Button used zinc. Patent Button bought rolled strip at a penny less than other buttonmakers and sold back its scrap for a penny more.[17]

Platt Brothers sought new markets for zinc by capitalizing on its distinctive qualities, particularly that it did not rust. The first new application was buttons for Goodyear India Rubber Glove Company in Naugatuck. Rustproof zinc hardware nicely complemented gloves with the distinguishing quality of being waterproof. When India Rubber Glove agreed to try it in March 1876, Platt Brothers made up twenty thousand of their old fly buttons, completely from zinc. The glove firm took seven months to use them up, then bought more in October and submitted three more orders in 1877. In early 1878, Platt Brothers landed another nearby customer, American Pin Company. With the business well established, Platt Brothers set up a "glove fastening" account, transferred the entire line to Patent Button, and renewed the quest to develop uses for zinc.[18]

Far larger, richer, and more durable than glove fasteners was the market for "tipping zinc," used for the reinforcements on the ends of shoelaces. Zinc strip made good shoelace tips, not only because it did not rust but because of its behavior when bent. When subjected to bending at room temperature, most metals develop minute movements in their crystalline structure, resulting in increased hardness and strength, known as "work hardening," at the bend. The tension between the work-hardened area and the unaffected area causes bent metal to spring back slightly. But zinc does not work-harden nor spring back when bent—an important feature when crimping a piece of sheet metal onto a small piece of fabric to make a shoelace. With other metals, if the tip was crimped too hard to assure that it would not spring back and lose its grip, the tip could sever the fabric; if crimped too little in order to spare the fabric, the metal could spring loose.[19]

To sell tipping zinc the Platts had to venture beyond their accustomed sources of business in the New York–based garment trade and the diverse industries of the Naugatuck Valley to the textile center of Providence, Rhode Island. The first customer for tipping zinc, Fletcher Manufacturing Company, had started out making lamp wicks and had moved into other narrow fabrics, including laces for boots and shoes. Fletcher Manufacturing (later known as International Braid) bought a sample of twenty-six pounds of zinc strip in October 1877. Platt Brothers charged a quarter-cent over that month's prevailing strip price for slitting the strip to the unusual width of six and a half inches. After testing the sample, Fletcher Manufacturing made four large orders in rapid succession, and by the end of the year Platt had shipped nearly ten thousand pounds of tipping zinc. Thereafter, Fletcher ordered tipping zinc between twenty and fifty times a year, well into the twentieth century. In 1880, Fletcher began requesting japanned strip, for which Platt Brothers charged an additional $.04 to $.06 per pound. Year in and year out the Platts could depend on revenue between $6,000 and $10,000 from Fletcher.[20]

Fletcher Manufacturing directed Platt Brothers to the second regular customer for tipping zinc, James H. Hill and Sons of Coventry, Rhode Island. Fletcher had helped James Hill, a former employee, to start his firm, which was devoted entirely to japanning the Platt strip and then slitting it to the narrower widths from which the individual tips were cut off. In 1880 Hill began to sell its reprocessed tipping zinc to other lacemakers. Its orders ran between $1,000 and $1,500 a year through the early 1890s and to more than $4,400 as the new century opened, with the same consistency, gradual rise in volume, and price variations keyed to commodity cost that characterized the Fletcher account. At least eight other narrow-fabric producers also bought Platt tipping zinc on a regular basis in the late nineteenth century.[21]

Unlike fully fabricated glove hardware, tipping zinc left the Platt Brothers factory as strip. It was not just another button variation that would logically belong at Patent Button once sales and manufacture achieved some regularity but a primary metal product matching the character that William and Clark wanted for Platt Brothers. Tipping zinc, the first successful new bulk-metal line, validated the hope that expertise in zinc held promise beyond its use in buttons. By introducing tipping zinc the company continued Alfred Platt's vision of small-scale integrated production and brought it completely up to date.

Besides inheriting a more fully developed enterprise than Alfred had, Clark and William also operated in a far more extensive, diverse, and sophisticated industrial economy. The tipping zinc was only a small and insignificant part of the production stream that resulted in a pair of shoes: it went into one small component of the lace that was itself only a component of the end product. Nationwide industrial growth and specialization was critically important for agile little Platt Brothers. In pursuing niche markets, it helped that there were many niches to fill.

Tipping zinc also fulfilled the long-term potential of certain specialized products. Clark and William Platt appreciated the difference between the tent button, which had come and gone quickly, and the riveted button that had won a steady market capable by itself of sustaining Patent Button. Niche strategy demanded rapid response when a chance arose, but the best niches evolved into a steady pace of demand over a period of decades. The challenge came not only in prolonging the advantage but in recognizing when it had faded and finding other products to replace the revenues. Successful transition after Clark and William would be delayed until their successors grasped this tempo of development.

Just as crucial to a firm whose new markets depended on tinkering was the discipline to restrain enthusiasm over novel but untimely ideas. Electricity intrigued William Platt in the late 1870s and early 1880s. Zinc's low electrochemical potential in relation to iron, carbon, and other materials made it useful in electric batteries, and kindled William's experiments with electrical applications. He devised plates, electrodes, and clips for batteries, but the market was tiny, and the only sales were to a firm that used batteries in quack medical devices. After registering the patents he moved on to other projects, much as he had abandoned the pipe venture of the late 1850s when sales did not materialize.[22]

In its other area of production—fabricating and finishing metal goods such as eyelets—Platt Brothers made substantial sales locally to such old customers as American Ring Company and Carrington Manufacturing, as well as to new ones, including most of the large diversified metals firms. Out of hundreds of jobs each year a few dozen accounted for about one-third of Platt Brothers' work in this part of the business. Waterbury Brass Company, for instance, every year bought thousands of pounds of two-inch-diameter blanks stamped from tinplate—for Platt a large account but for Waterbury Brass a trivial amount of a metal it was unaccustomed to working. The rest of the work was in small orders, such as bronze-plating about 1,800 pins that Benedict and Burnham needed for one of its many products, a job worth a little under $5.[23]

The Platts established a helpful complementarity with the region's dominant manufacturers. The integrated brass firms also employed the competitive tactic of exploring new product opportunities with the potential for large, enduring markets. The formation of Smith and Griggs after the Civil War followed the successful development of production techniques and an adequate customer base for buckles and "loops" (the bent-metal slides used on suspenders, belts, and other accessories). And by the end of the century the brass firms would establish an enormous presence in the electrical field, making lamps and fittings (and miles of copper wire). All of these products started as one-piece experiments or small lots, and Platt Brothers could serve as a prototype shop in their development. Scovill, Benedict and Burnham, and the other behemoths also accepted less than enormous orders for their fabricating departments, and the ability to sub-contract one operation or part, particularly an unfamiliar one, enhanced their ability to profit on such jobs. Thus the Platts maintained an intricate relationship with the large brass firms. They refrained from competing di-

Interior of 1869 brick shop at Platts Mills, photograph taken c. 1890. Along the right wall are small single-operation presses used for capping and coining. The machine at left, behind the grinding wheel, appears to be a horizontal wire-forming machine. (Mattatuck Museum)

rectly in high-volume lines and benefited from product differentiation on the part of the giants.[24]

Eyelets and other fabricated goods had thousands of highly specific applications in industries outside of Waterbury too. Numerous manufacturers needed an eyelet or two in everything they made but not enough to justify the cost of buying the expensive, complicated eyelet machines and learning how to use them. Platt Brothers sold to many industrial sectors: cutlery, clocks, carriages, corsets, lamps, and machinery among others. Both the number of these customers and the value of sales to them increased steadily after 1880.[25]

Platt Brothers occasionally took on specialized bulk processing in metals other than zinc. The most significant venture began in April 1876 with a subcontract from American Ring for some twenty-two great gross of the tinplate buttons, or ferrules, for the tops of umbrellas. Attracted by the possibility of another product that could benefit from a metal that would not rust, the Platts began to explore the umbrella trade. The effort took them to Baltimore, where dozens of shops turned out the majority of the nation's umbrellas. Platt Brothers found that the J. P. and D. C. Ammidon Company served as the leading wholesale metals dealer to the city's umbrella makers. Ammidon and the umbrella firms never adopted zinc for ferrules, probably because it cost at least three times more than tinplate. But Platt Brothers could offer more than access to an unfamiliar metal. Unlike the cutting-up shops in Waterbury, which had ready access to every kind of specialized machinery and metalworking expertise, the umbrella shops in Baltimore required partially processed tinplate for their buttons, not standard coils or rolls. Some bought short strips, and others bought circular blanks. In Platt Brothers, Ammidon found a bulk-metal processor that would slit and cut off strip or stamp blanks to order, a highly capable fabricating firm that would produce finished ferrules, and an extremely flexible supplier that would provide strip, blanks, or buttons in any amount, no matter how small or large. In October 1876 the first shipment to Ammidon—twenty-two thousand pounds of short tinplate strips—filled an entire railroad car. In the context of the iron industry, twenty-two thousand pounds was a small bulk-metal order. But Platt Brothers did not compete with the ironmakers that turned out tinplate by the ton. Instead, for a quarter-cent a pound it filled a reprocessing niche for an industry that was itself only a minor consumer of tinplate. Once again Platt Brothers settled into a decades-long relationship. At the end of 1878 a shipment to Ammidon took two railroad cars, although most orders were far smaller. Through the end of the century annual sales to Ammidon ranged between $2,000 and $7,000.[26]

Besides its long-established specialty in zinc, in the late nineteenth century Platt Brothers distinguished itself with its expertise in difficult or uncommon fabricating and finishing operations and in its acceptance of small orders. These attributes gave the Platts a very broad array of possible niches. Flexible, responsive, and willing to take on the smallest jobs, the firm made its size into a virtue.

The ability to respond quickly to a wide range of customers and applications depended on worker skill and worker responsibility, not just the abilities of Clark and William Platt and Benjamin Bristol. The firm purposely kept the work force at Platts Mills small and devoted mostly to highly skilled, specialized work. The Platts could do so without limiting the firm's scope by conducting the high-volume fabricating jobs at Brown Street and, if a high-volume product won a steady market, by transferring the line to Patent Button. In the 1880s the permanent work force at Platts Mills was between thirty and thirty-five people, about one-quarter the size of Patent Button's. Male workers were always a majority, and more than half of the men had skilled trades.

About half of the Platts Mills workers were either related to the Platts or were longtime neighbors or associates. Ben Bristol, by then a part owner as well as a salaried employee, had the title of superintendent and probably provided the ultimate solution for any intractable problem with the rolling operations. His son Frank was the chief machinist. The late Nirom Platt's son-in-law, Legrand Osborne, was chief roller hand, and his son, John Osborne, ran the casting shop. Around 1895, John took over the rolling mill too and later succeeded Ben Bristol as superintendent. Among the production workers were at least four of Clark and William's nieces and nephews and Daniel Bergan's son and daughter. Bergan worked for Legrand Platt in the gristmill, rented a house from Platt Brothers, and boarded two female workers with his family. This was a small and extremely close-knit group of workers. About one-quarter of them either benefited directly from any dividends or were related to someone who did. Others had decades-long relationships with the Platts. Highly motivated and personally involved, this work force enabled Platt Brothers to undertake specialized and often complicated work and deliver it quickly.[27]

The Family Fortunes

Platt Brothers consistently earned money after the transitional period following reorganization. Fluctuations in revenue and profit corresponded more to changes in expenditures than to changes in the volume of sales or production. The business was very steady, and financial management consisted largely of deciding how much to distribute to the stockholders while making sufficient capital expenditures to maintain slow growth.

Clark and William exercised virtually total control over those decisions; the initial stock distribution of 520 shares to each of them, 100 to Samuel Porter, and 60 to Jay Hart changed only slightly in the firm's early years. Porter's estate sold his 100 shares to Clark and William, who then each held 570. Hart sold 40 of his shares back to the corporation, which transferred them to Ben Bristol. Bristol paid with a note, which Platt Brothers never collected; when Bristol died, his estate returned the shares, the company retired the note, and thereafter all shares were held by Alfred Platt's descendants or their spouses.[28]

Clark and William Platt never permitted annual dividends to exceed the year's cash surplus from operations, so every year the firm's cash balance increased (see Table 4). This conservative policy reflected their experience in 1876 and 1877, when they constantly had to make loans from their personal assets to keep Platt Brothers afloat. They had done so without hesitation, but they could not have borne lightly the prospect of losing all they had accumulated. Clark and William thereafter kept money in the company so that they would not have to contribute their own. After William Platt died, in 1886, this policy was violated about half of the time, but the company nonetheless maintained a high cash balance.

TABLE 4[29]

Platt Brothers and Company Cash Performance 1876–1897

(dollars)

Year	Annual gain in cash before dividend	Dividend	Net cash gain or (loss) after dividend	Total cash balance at year end
1876	17,239	0	17,239	17,239
1877	25,884	9,000	16,884	34,123
1878	19,683	18,000	1,683	35,806
1879	39,468	16,500	22,968	58,774
1880	40,504	35,400	5,104	63,878
1881	39,654	22,800	16,854	80,732
1882	33,830	18,000	15,830	96,562
1883	41,613	40,800	813	97,375
1884	32,065	20,400	11,665	109,040
1885	46,073	42,000	4,073	113,113
1886	46,381	36,000	10,381	123,494
1887	32,268	24,000	8,268	131,762
1888	24,721	48,000	(23,279)	108,473
1889	26,400	66,000	(39,600)	68,883
1890	50,327	24,000	26,237	95,210
1891	47,920	46,800	1,120	96,330
1892	40,492	48,000	(7,508)	88,822
1893	57,753	36,000	16,753	105,575
1894	48,277	36,000	12,277	117,852
1895	64,275	54,000	10,275	128,127
1896	14,273	24,000	(9,627)	118,500
1897	59,578	63,600	(4,022)	114,478

Dividends from Patent Button also began about two years after incorporation, and the amounts were similarly bountiful after a brief adjustment to corporate status. In 1878–1880 the firm paid a total dividend of $6,000. After a year of no yield, in 1881, when the company built a new factory at Brown Street, Patent Button began to pay at levels similar to Platt Brothers (see Table 5).

The Porters had long since moved away from Waterbury to be closer to their principal business in New York. Enriched by Patent Button dividends, they bought extensive acreage in Montclair, New Jersey, a well-to-do suburb of New York. They built mansions, acquired art collections, and contributed to many community institutions and philanthropic causes. Thomas Porter, who headed Porter Brothers after Samuel's death, organized and substantially funded the Washington Memorial Association, a "company of gentlemen" who bought the site of George Washington's headquarters in Morristown, New Jersey, and erected the monument there.[31]

Ben Bristol, the blacksmith's son, became a wealthy man through his long participation in the Platt enterprises. Besides his salary (and most years a bonus) as superintendent of Platt Brothers, his share of the dividends

TABLE 5[30]
Patent Button Company Total Dividends, 1878–1888
(dollars)

Year	Dividend (dollars)
1878	6,000
1879	6,000
1880	6,000
1881	0
1882	36,000
1883	47,980
1884	58,200
1885	50,400
1886	50,400
1887	58,200
1888	57,600

usually came to over $1,000 a year after 1880. In 1884, near his sixtieth birthday, Bristol prepared for retirement by selling his farm to William Platt. Ben's youngest son, William Bristol, taught mathematics at Stevens Institute in New Jersey and tinkered in his spare time. His first invention was a system of wire clips to replace the rawhide used to lace together factory belting. As the Platts' rolling mill operator and later superintendent, Ben must have laced or instructed others to lace hundreds of belts; he well understood the greater reliability and faster installation of the clips. When his son brought the idea to him in 1889, Ben immediately bought machinery to make the wire clips and installed it in the barn of his other son, Frank, the Platts' machinist. Frank left Platt Brothers to supervise production at the newly formed Bristol Company. Like Alfred Platt, as an older man Bristol did not hesitate to invest the gains of a lifetime in what he thought was a promising industrial venture. Within three years the Bristols built a brick factory, directly across the Naugatuck from Platt Brothers, to make the clips and the small lever presses used to attach them to belts. William Bristol then devoted his scientific and mathematical training to developing recording thermometers and pressure gauges to monitor industrial processes. The Bristols did not heed the Platts' succession experience and after Ben died in 1904 his sons sued each other over the distribution of shares and the disclosure of financial records. After the case was settled (it took four years), the Bristol Company went on to even greater success making aircraft instruments developed by William Bristol.[32]

The chief beneficiaries of the Platt Brothers and Patent Button dividends—the Platts and their spouses—built new homes, supported a variety of local causes, and invested in local industries and property. In the 1870s the city's industrial gentry began building their own residential district on a hill north of downtown. Clark built a house there in 1873, on Buckingham Street, where his neighbors included Charles Benedict and the heirs of J. C. Welton, the Platts' early button agent. William bought a large lot of some four acres on nearby Woodlawn Terrace in 1879. He also bought land abutting the old family homestead whenever he could, and in the early 1880s he built a new, Queen Anne–style house at Platts Mills, where he lived for the rest of his life. His heirs and descendants would live on Woodlawn Terrace. The Baptist church remained the principal beneficiary of William's philanthropy. Clark contributed generously to the Mattatuck Historical Society, which he helped to found. Jay Hart and Lewis A. Platt (Clark's son), were active in politics; both held local offices, and Lewis served a term in the state senate. Lewis Platt also was an incorporator of the Waterbury Club, an exclusive establishment for the city's economic elite. Wallace Camp helped to start the local YMCA chapter.[33]

Clark, William, and later William's wife and children invested in dozens of private mortgages every year. The Platts loaned directly to contractors and investors building on speculation and to individuals or families building a home. Tracy Brothers, a local construction firm that built factories, hotels, and commercial blocks, regularly financed its projects through the Platts. The Platts' clientele for homeowner mortgages included every level of Waterbury society: top industrial employees such as factory superintendents Dwight Smith and Henry French, small business owners such as grocer Miles Upson and carpenter Alfred Charbonneau, skilled industrial workers such as machinist Lenthal Davis, and illiterate factory hands such as Scovill operative Patrick Malone.[34]

Clark's family invested widely in manufacturing. In 1898 his son Lewis helped start the Waterbury Battery Company (which used zinc for electrodes) and was a corporate officer during the firm's brief tenure. The Harts invested in and eventually controlled the Hawkins Company of nearby Middlebury, which made traps for the fur trade. They also owned the Waterbury Casting Company, an iron foundry established in 1903.[35]

After William's death from pneumonia, in March 1886 at the age of sixty-four, the distribution of his estate proved the value of the succession procedures that came with incorporation. His widow, Caroline, inherited 189 of his 570 Platt Brothers' shares, and the rest were split evenly among his son Irving and his daughters Carrie Platt and Helen Camp. Irving voted all 570 shares and took a seat on the board; he was also named general manager of the firm, formalizing the supervisory role he shared with Ben Bristol. Clark assumed the duties of president and treasurer. The transition went smoothly, aided by Irving's close connection with the manufacturing operations, which put him in a position to understand the value of reinvesting in the company. The first decision to come before the board after

William's death demonstrated this continuing commitment, as Platt Brothers paid over $13,000 to buy all of the equipment of Union Manufacturing Company, a bankrupt button firm near the downtown shop. Irving was nonetheless more willing than his father to take profits from manufacturing to support other ventures. When Irving, his sisters, and Wallace Camp needed money in the late 1880s to develop their East Main Street commercial property, the dividends were doubled to $48,000 in 1888 and raised again to $66,000 in 1889, even though these payouts put the firm's annual cash flow in the negative (see Table 4).[36]

Irving Platt survived his father by only ten years, perishing in 1896 at the age of thirty-six, a victim of typhus. Irving's sisters inherited his shares of Platt Brothers, maintaining parity between the families of Clark and William. But the loss of William Platt's sole male heir forced the owners to consider again how to accommodate the interests of all of participants without rancor. They did it by electing Carrie Platt a director, breaching one of the gender-based social conventions of their day, when women rarely filled positions of authority in industry. She represented William's side of the family and balanced the viewpoint of the other directors, Clark and his son Lewis. At Patent Button, Helen Camp succeeded to Irving's seat on the board.[37]

Irving's death deprived the family of its most fertile mechanical mind in his generation. He had finally solved the problem of the hub for the riveted button, starting with a patent for making the hub as a separate eyelet that was loosely secured to the button front. Collaborating with Frank White, the foreman of the downtown button shop in the 1890s, he then redesigned the riveted-button-attaching machine. The new machine incorporated a work-holding technique used on the presses that manufactured button parts: a spring-driven, cam-actuated fixture to hold the rivets. Irving completed this new system with a series of innovative rivets. Rather than a solid barrel, the rivet had two prongs; the lesser amount of metal to deform in assembling the buttons minimized the pressure on the hub during assembly. Not until after World War I, when Jay Hart's grandson, Howard Hart, assumed a position of responsibility at Platt Brothers, would a family member again provide the technological direction for the family enterprises.[38]

Monopolies Large and Small

The years between 1890 and 1910 were a perilous time for Platt Brothers and Patent Button. Both firms had to adapt to changes in their metal supply, at Patent Button because of monopolistic practices on the part of brass-makers and at Platt Brothers because of an unprecedented increase in the nation's raw zinc output. Platt Brothers also faced obsolescence and inad-

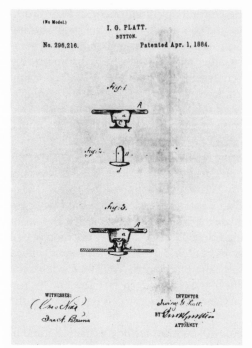

(No Model.)

I. G. PLATT.
BUTTON.

No. 296,216.   Patented Apr. 1, 1884.

fig. 1.

fig. 2.

fig. 3.

WITNESSES:

INVENTOR

ATTORNEY

With this patent Irving Platt finally solved the problem of the hub in the riveted fly button. By making the hub (*C* in the drawing) a separate eyelet, he considerably eased the button's manufacture and its assembly onto the garment. This type of button won wide use on dungarees and other work clothing and is still recognizable today on many such garments. (Mattatuck Museum)

equate capacity in its zinc-rolling mill, the same basic facility that Alfred Platt had built in the 1850s. Survival and prosperity through this period owed much to the long-standing character of each firm: integrated production, specialization in zinc, and niche marketing at Platt Brothers, and high-volume production of proprietary fabricated goods at Patent Button. Clark Platt, the last of the founding partners who had established the character of both firms, remained active in business until the end of his days. After Clark's death in 1900, his children, nieces, nephews, and in-laws applied those strategies in the face of new pressures. Their fundamental goals remained the same ones that had motivated Alfred Platt—to be independent, self-determining manufacturers and to rely on a high degree of family involvement.

Waterbury's Big Five controlled more than half of the nation's market for primary brass products (sheet, tube, wire) in the 1880s; with the four other major producers from the Naugatuck Valley and Bridgeport, the immediate region accounted for some 76 percent of the national output. These nine firms constituted the American Brass Association, which had been established in 1853 as the mechanism for agreements on pricing and production limits. Though all nine also produced finished goods, or owned fabricating companies, not until the mid-1880s did they seek to institute the same kind of pooling agreements for end products that the Brass Association had long provided for sheet, tube, and wire. These smaller pools, which the Platts did not join, included associations for buckles and loops, rivets, lamp burners, pins, and buttons. Control of the independent cutting-up shops' material supply gave the brassmakers a powerful weapon in support of their own pools for fabricated goods.[39]

The Platts had only to observe the plights of their acquaintances and customers to understand the dangers of the new situation. The Platts had a long and multifaceted relationship, for instance, with Matthews and Stanley Manufacturing Company. Henry Matthews, the firm's founder, grew up on a farm near Platts Mills; when he set up his factory at North Elm and Cherry streets in 1874, it was on land he leased from Clark Platt, upstream on Great Brook from the Brown Street shop. Matthews started out making saddlery trimmings and added stove hardware, lamps and lamp hardware, urns, and furniture trimmings when he moved downtown. Platt Brothers supplied him with brass stampings, strips of tinplate slit to special widths, and finishing services. Matthews even developed a new use for zinc (statues wrought from sheet), although brass remained by far his firm's principal material. In 1887, after a decade of steady growth, Matthews bought from Clark the land on which his factory stood. Matthews's success ended the following year, when the primary brass producers initiated a series of price increases on sheet, raising it about 10 percent annually. Matthews struggled until 1890 before going bankrupt. Scovill Manufacturing, his chief creditor, took over.[40]

Patent Button was considerably more vulnerable to the brass monopoly than was Platt Brothers. The majority of its material was brass and other copper alloys, and its products and services were less diverse than those of Platt Brothers. Its principal edge was the specialized nature of its main product, the Reed buttons that the Platts and their employees had been making since the late 1860s. Only by protecting their distinctive product line could the Platts and the Porters assure the flexibility to raise their own prices in order to pass the higher material cost through to their customers. The distinction in design that they had to retain and reinforce was functional, not decorative: the use of metal to affix the buttons to garments. And continued success depended on technical considerations: the ease of the attachment process, the strength of the connection between the rivet and the button, and the efficiency of manufacturing them. In this kind of struggle Patent Button was well equipped, not only from long experience with riveted-button technology but because Irving Platt's refinements of 1888–1890 had renewed the firm's patent protection.

After Irving died, a disagreement developed over the source for continued innovation. Thomas W. Porter, the president of Patent Button, favored financial tactics; he wanted to buy the two small firms that posed a threat in metal-attached buttons, or to license their patents. Clark Platt, who was seventy-one years old when Irving died in 1896, clung to the decades-old vision of the family tinkering its own way out of difficulty. William's heirs went along with Clark, as did Nathan Porter, Jr., the other Porter director, even though no innovative mechanics stepped forward from the family ranks. Then Clark died suddenly from a heart attack in December 1900. The stockholders, at their annual meeting a month later, appointed Lewis Platt to succeed his father as treasurer. Lewis apparently concurred with Thomas Porter's acquisition strategy and was prepared to support it at the directors' meeting that would follow immediately after the stockholders' meeting. But the other two directors, Helen Camp and Nathan Porter, Jr., left the room, preventing a quorum of three directors.[41]

Lack of board approval did not prevent Thomas Porter from negotiating with the competitors he had identified, Flagg Brothers and Company of New Jersey and Robert Amory of Maine. At a special meeting in late April in New York, the directors approved the terms he had negotiated with Flagg Brothers. Helen Camp did not attend, nor did she positively approve the sale; in a letter to Porter she agreed to accept "the judgment of the other Directors." Patent Button bought Flagg Brothers' machinery, inventory, and designs for $38,000, most of it paid out over eleven years. The proprietor, Elisha Flagg, also agreed not to engage in "the manufacture or sale of buttons to be attached by metallic fasteners" for the same eleven-year period.[42]

Amory had developed a button affixed with a staple-like wire fastener but had not patented it or begun making it. At Thomas Porter's behest in March 1901, Amory filed six patent applications covering the fasteners and the attaching tools and machines. In November the directors ratified an exclusive license for Amory's designs, agreeing to pay him $.07 for every great gross of the fasteners that Patent Button made.[43]

These transactions secured Patent Button's market position and pricing flexibility during a difficult period. By 1905 the brassmakers had driven all of the other unaffiliated button producers out of business. Much of Waterbury's buttonmaking capacity belonged to the button departments of integrated brassmakers, and there were only three local firms with the principal business of buttonmaking. Of the three, one was held by the majority owner of Bridgeport Brass, and another had interlocking ownership with two of the city's large brassmakers. Only Patent Button survived independent from the region's dominant metals firms.[44]

Despite the success of Thomas Porter's strategy, this episode deepened the fundamental divergence between him and the other owners. All seemed to agree that the future of Patent Button depended on continued techno-logical change, particularly in product development. Porter wanted to achieve it through acquisition, while the others were more reluctant to em-brace innovations from outside the family and the firm. Porter prevailed in 1901 because the acquisitions bore direct relation to the existing product line. When he later tried to expand beyond that base, he lost the support of his fellow owners.

The actions of the brass monopoly had less effect on Platt Brothers. The number of customers for strip zinc shrank, because even the heavy zinc consumers used more brass than any other metal. When the price increases for brass put these customers out of business, Platt Brothers simply started supplying the beneficiaries of the price fixing, such as the Scovill button-making department, and maintained accustomed volume. Strip-zinc sales to Scovill increased fourfold between 1890 and 1897. On the fabricating side of its business, Platt Brothers lost some customers as smaller firms suc-cumbed to the brass monopoly, and had to pay more for its brass (about 30 percent of the metal it consumed). Neither factor caused long-lasting problems for the eyelet business, because Platt Brothers' continued will-ingness to accept small orders was just as valuable to the large brassmakers as it had been to the small shops they forced out of business.[45]

More important to Platt Brothers were changes in the zinc industry that accompanied an increase in the supply of slab spelter. Until the 1890s, most slab spelter came from Europe, from one of four mining-smelting firms in New Jersey and northeastern Pennsylvania, or from two mining-smelting firms in Illinois. Most of the spelter went into making brass. Platt Brothers had few competitors in rolled zinc and only one with a comparable depth of experience: Mathiessen and Hegeler Zinc Company of LaSalle, Illinois, which had worked zinc since the 1860s and also mined and smelted it. In the 1890s the increased use of zinc sheet for roofing, and block zinc for galvanizing iron and steel, stimulated the exploitation of vast zinc deposits in the Joplin (or Tri-state) district of southwestern Missouri, northeastern Oklahoma, and southeastern Kansas. The nation had produced about 10,000 tons of slab spelter in 1870, 30,000 tons in 1880, and 60,000 tons in 1890. Joplin zinc sent the output soaring to 175,000 tons by 1900. Improved techniques for mining and treating the ore also helped push output higher, and costs went down as the smelters began to fire that process with natural gas that came out of the same holes as the zinc ore.[46]

The explosion in spelter output pushed down the cost of slab, but Platt Brothers gained little from that saving because it priced every order by fig-uring material cost plus processing cost. The lower slab prices benefited Platt customers as much as they did Platt Brothers. Nor did the firms that mined and smelted zinc succeed in their attempts to fix prices and set production limits. The chronic oversupply of zinc and the relatively low, stable pricing that resulted was a long-term benefit for Platt Brothers and every other zinc user. In the short term, however, the most significant effect of the surge in slab supply was to invite new competition in rolling zinc. One major consumer, Ball Brothers of Indiana, which used zinc for the covers of its food-preserving jars, grew frustrated with the behavior of the existing suppliers, as a memoir of the firm recalled: "Zinc sheet production was controlled by two companies [Platt Brothers and Mathiessen and Hegeler] which were unyielding and arbitrary in their pricing. . . . The Ball company was obliged to pay cash on the spot, for whatever it bought, at the arbitrary price prevailing at the time of shipping." Ball started its own zinc operation, from smelting to slitting. Platt Brothers may have been content with its existing rolled-zinc business (dominated by button strip and tipping metal) and uninterested in the new and expanding markets for it. But that business was at risk if other zinc-using industries followed the same strategy as Ball or if other metal processors moved into zinc. The company had to build on its superior expertise in working zinc and increase its bulk-processing capacity.[47]

Platt Brothers began planning that expansion in the early 1890s, at the beginning of the Joplin zinc boom. The firm could easily afford the capital investment but first had to find room to expand and an inexpensive way to increase its supply of power. The downtown property was long and narrow, with Brown Street to the east and the open headrace to the west. The Platts had purchased all of the available land north and south of the lot originally acquired from Merritt Lane, and the manufacturers that abutted on either end had built factories up to the property lines. On this tightly confined lot, the Platts too had built out to the boundaries. North of the original Lane shop they had put up a japanning building, with wings for storage and the box shop. To the south was the three-story brick factory erected in 1880, and south of that was the slightly later, one-story brick building known as the "Button Room," which housed all of the dial presses and other high-volume production machinery. In 1880 the company had also built a small boiler house and coal bunker and installed a steam engine to augment the power from Great Brook. Brown Street lacked space to expand. Moreover, the necessity of powering further Brown Street operations with steam—more expensive to operate than waterpower because of coal purchases—meant that any additional capacity in the heavily power-consuming rolling processes would be more advantageously located at Platts Mills.[48]

During Alfred's lifetime the Platts had not developed the full potential of the Naugatuck water privilege. After he died, the division of the water rights between the metalworking company and Legrand Platt's gristmill prevented any expansion. The gristmill spanned the race at precisely the location where the race rejoined the river, and the gristmill basement contained the main wheelpit for the entire complex; reconfiguring the water-power system would require reconstructing the gristmill. Worse yet, Legrand owned two-thirds of the water rights. Fortunately for Platt Brothers, in the 1880s Legrand had decreased his milling in favor of wholesaling. Thus when Clark proposed to buy the mill and water rights from his brother for $15,000, Legrand consented, and the sale went through in September 1892. At the same time, Platt Brothers bought William's house from his widow Caroline (who continued to live there), establishing undivided control of the manufacturing property and adjacent land for the first time since Alfred Platt had consolidated his holdings.[49]

In planning for expansion in Platts Mills the company still had to contend with the local labor scarcity, which had caused the original move into downtown. The solution came in 1893 with the opening of the Waterbury Traction Company's South Main Street trolley line. The Platts were aware of the plans for this line when they bought Legrand's property because they had begun negotiations to sell the trolley company some land and rights-of-way for the tracks. Running between downtown Waterbury and downtown Naugatuck, the trolley made Platts Mills accessible to people from either city, although more than a decade would pass before Platt Brothers had to hire many trolley commuters. Along with the acquisition of space and power from Legrand, resolution of the labor scarcity positioned the company for expansion.[50]

Renewing the long-term commitment to manufacturing also required Platt Brothers to anticipate issues beyond the immediate future. A forward-looking view of Platts Mills as the location of an industrial plant had to address the acquisition of more land. William's heirs owned much of the abutting acreage, and they added to it by buying more property in the area whenever it became available, effectively coordinating their private real estate investments with the company's potential requirements. In the largest of these purchases, Irving and his sister Carrie bought the portion of the old Mansfield Thomas farm that the Platts did not already own, 112 acres abutting the east boundary of the old homestead. The company, instead of spending its cash reserves to bank land, spent it to install new rolling and slitting machinery in the first floor of the gristmill.[51]

Platt Brothers received an unwanted boost to its expansion plans when a fire destroyed the gristmill and its contents on the morning of 6 February 1895. The employees tried to salvage what they could from the rubble, and the elderly Clark Platt even pitched in, but all of the contents were lost. In early April, after waiting for the ground to thaw completely and for its

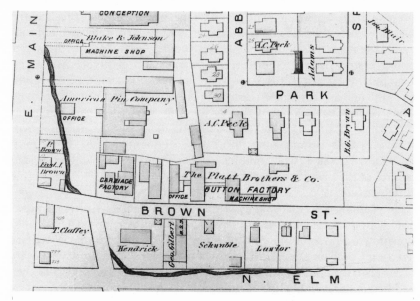

Brown Street factory property in 1879. Great Brook runs from the bottom to the left side of this view. At the extreme right, the headrace is shown as a small watercourse that disappears as it goes underground. From G. M. Hopkins, *Atlas of the City of Waterbury*, 1879. (Mattatuck Museum)

insurer to pay $8,000 for the loss, Platt Brothers began the complete reconstruction of the site.[52]

The first step, modifying the waterpower system, was completed in July. The dam had already been built to the legally permissible height, and the volume of the headrace was more than adequate; but the rest of the water-containment and channeling structures were rebuilt for higher capacity: new headgates at the dam and at the outlet of the headrace, a new culvert (under Platts Mills Road) leading from the headrace to the gristmill site, and a new forebay and wheelpit at that site. Once the power system was in place, Platt Brothers resumed zinc operations in the brick shop that Alfred had built in 1869 and started shipping rolled strip to Fletcher Manufacturing and other long-term customers. Over the next eight months Platt Brothers built a series of brick buildings connected end-to-end, west of Platts Mills Road, between the road and the river. Over the wheelpit stood a 40-by-50-foot building to hold the turbine governors, a direct current generator for the plant's new electric lighting, and the electrical switchgear. North of this powerhouse was a 160-by-55-foot building for the rundown, finish, and slitting rolls. South of the powerhouse were the casting shop and breakdown mill (80 feet by 40 feet) and then the spelter shed (72 feet by 40 feet), where

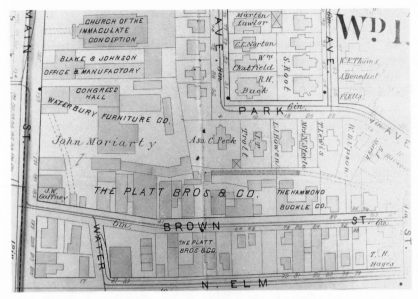

Brown Street factory property in 1896. Great Brook has been completely covered and shows only as a dotted line arcing toward East Main Street. The Platts have acquired more property and built out to the boundaries. From D. C. Miller and Co., *Atlas of the City of Waterbury,* 1896. (Mattatuck Museum)

the incoming slabs were stored. The wheelpit held four turbines, two of 24-inch runner diameter at the north side and two of 30-inch at the south side. One of the larger turbines drove the breakdown rolls; the other, the rundown, finish, and slitting rolls. One smaller turbine was connected to the direct-current generator for the arc lights; the other powered a line shaft in the north mill that ran a variety of operations. In all, Platt Brothers spent about $26,500 to build and equip the new zinc-processing facilities.[53]

In April 1896, with the zinc mill construction almost complete, the company tore down the 1869 building to make way for a new eyelet and button factory. This site was east of Platts Mills Road, across the street from the zinc mills and alongside the canal. The new factory (144 feet by 32 feet) had its own turbine in a wheelpit at the south wall. Including the purchase of new Pratt and Whitney eyelet machines, this shop cost over $24,000. To pay for all of this construction and new machinery, Platt Brothers had only to dip into its cash reserves and reduce the total dividend for 1896 to $24,000, from $54,000 the year before. In 1897 it went back up to $63,600 (see Table 4).[54]

When Platt Brothers consolidated all of the Platts Mills water rights, it also acquired the legal standing to address an enormous health problem resulting from the pollution of the Naugatuck River. Between 1884 and 1889 the City of Waterbury had built a sewage disposal system for the center of town. The new sewage channels drastically reduced the incidence of typhus, cholera, and dysentery by collecting all of the city's sewage and dumping it into the Naugatuck, which carried it down to Platts Mills. Though all of the family members who lived at Platts Mills must have been aware of the problem—the open headrace ran in front of their houses—the divided ownership of the water rights had prevented any action to correct it. In 1892, soon after buying the gristmill, Platt Brothers sued the city in state superior court to prevent the city from polluting the river. Besides claiming that the "impure, unwholesome, deleterious and offensive material" and the "vile and noxious odors emanating therefrom" made the factories and dwellings "unhealthful and unwholesome," the suit claimed that the water was so filthy that it could not be used for the manufacturing purposes of cooling and cleaning.[55]

The city's lawyers mounted a defense of questionable claims and technicalities. First they argued that Waterbury was not the proper defendant because it did not make any sewage but simply collected it, and they asked the court to rule that all of the major manufacturers whose sewage and industrial waste went into the system should be co-defendants. This tactic would have arrayed the formidable brass firms against Platt Brothers, but it failed. The city tried to invalidate the case because the Platts' Brown Street plant contributed to the sewage, so Platt Brothers was in effect suing itself; again, to no avail. Waterbury's counsel maintained unsuccessfully that the tremendous volume of sewage actually increased the flow in the Naugatuck and "made said river more valuable as a water power." Finally, the city simply admitted that it could not afford to treat the sewage, had no choice but to foul the Naugatuck, and that "the use of said river in the manner described is a reasonable and proper use of a public river."[56]

Perhaps hardened in their resolve by Irving's death from typhus, the Platts sought to force the city to treat the sewage by pushing the case to a conclusion. The Superior Court ruled in favor of Platt Brothers in 1898; after Waterbury appealed, the state supreme court upheld the decision in 1903. For remedy the city installed some filters, limited dumping during the summer, and paid damages to Platt Brothers of some $2,800 a year. Only in 1952, when the state Health Department exercised its newly expanded powers to mandate a treatment plant, did Waterbury cease dumping raw sewage into the Naugatuck and stop paying damages to Platt Brothers. Though acting in its own interest and not on behalf of the more general public good, Platt Brothers nonetheless served as Waterbury's environmental conscience at a time when manufacturers and local governments routinely polluted what the city's lawyers described as "public" rivers. The case established Connecticut's strongest legal precedent against polluters until the midtwentieth century. Though useful in antipollution lawsuits in Danbury and other cities, this precedent also limited the grounds for environmental action in the courts: only when a company (or individual) could prove specific damages would the courts restrict or punish dumping practices that affected everybody.[57]

The Emergence of Two Companies: 1901–1913

Thomas W. Porter's ambitious leadership of Patent Button eventually threatened one of the fundamental characteristics of the Platt manufacturing enterprises. Since Alfred Platt had taken his sons as partners and they started rolling zinc, the Platts had protected their independence by not competing directly against the larger non-ferrous metals firms. With riveted buttons, specialized fabricating, small-lot production, and zinc, the Platts served markets around the edges of those where the Scovills and the Benedicts worked. When Porter's continued enlargement of the Patent Button product line moved the company closer to competition it could not win and began to drain resources from Platt Brothers, the Platt family engineered a change of direction. First the family severed the existing operational ties between the two corporations and in the process gained majority ownership of Patent Button. Then the Platts reorganized the firm and eliminated Porter's role.

This struggle over the identity of the family businesses also reflected a partial vacuum of leadership in the early twentieth century. The deaths of Irving and Clark Platt had opened a gap between ownership of the firms and management of the factories. Jay Hart, Clark's son-in-law, fulfilled this dual role as the superintendent at Brown Street and an officer and director of both firms. But one family member could not command knowledge of both factories and leadership of both boards. Clark's son, Lewis, had worked in and supervised many of the manufacturing departments, was a director and officer of both firms, and succeeded to the presidency of Platt Brothers after his father's death. Even as president, however, Lewis largely concerned himself with outside interests, such as founding and managing a manufacturers' insurance cooperative. Though a lifelong resident of Waterbury, he also spent considerable time each year at homes he maintained in New York and Florida. On William's side of the family, no one served as both a policymaker and a manager in the early twentieth century. William's daughters and his son-in-law, Wallace Camp, served as corporate directors without day-to-day involvement in the manufacturing operations. Nor was the next generation, Alfred Platt's great-grandchildren, yet prepared to take over. Jay Hart's son, Lewis J. Hart, became the superintendent at Brown Street in 1905 but was only a token stockholder; most of Clark's shares of both firms had gone into a trust for which Lewis Platt had voting power. Jay Hart's other son, Howard, was still in school, as were the Camp sons, Roland and Orton. Though family members were certainly involved in the firms, none but Jay Hart could speak with the strong conviction born of long experience in both factory and boardroom, and he apparently dissented with only the greatest reluctance. Thomas Porter thus acted largely without meaningful opposition until his Waterbury colleagues perceived a crisis and found someone else from outside the family whose vision more closely matched their own.[58]

Porter continued aggressively to seek out competitors and potential competitors for acquisition by Patent Button. In one such move he widened the rift that lingered from his 1901 purchases by exploiting the overlap between the two firms, under which Platt Brothers continued to own most of Patent Button's capital equipment. A Boston company, Consolidated Fastener, had patented its own version of the riveted button, complete with attaching machines for lease to garment shops. After negotiating to buy Consolidated, Porter called a special directors meeting in March 1903 to effect the sale. Like the April 1901 meeting in which the Flagg and Amory transactions had been ratified, this one was held at the Porter Brothers offices in New York, and of the four directors only Helen Camp did not attend; the quorum consisted of Thomas Porter, Nathan Porter, Jr., and Lewis Platt. They approved the purchase of Consolidated for about $28,000, then voted to sell all of Consolidated's production equipment to Platt Brothers for $14,000. Lewis Platt, the only one present who also served on the Platt Brothers board, gave the pivotal approval to this resale. Porter thus eliminated a competitor and passed half of the cost to Platt Brothers, the firm in which he and his family did not hold any interest. This move was doubly distressing to Platt Brothers: not only did it mark a departure for a company that had always maintained strict control of its own manufacturing technology, but it was a decision determined by Lewis Platt alone, representing Clark's side of the family. By siding with Thomas Porter, Lewis Platt helped to turn the developing rift between the Porters and the Platts into one between the heirs of William and Clark or, as it would turn out, between the Camps and the Harts.[59]

As Thomas Porter continued to spend the company's money to acquire new products, the directors' meetings for these purchases always took place at the Porter Brothers offices in New York. That precaution may not have been necessary in the acquisition of such patented fasteners as the "pronged rivet button" that resembled Patent Button's existing line. But more troubling to the other directors was Porter's sales effort over several years to secure a market in buckles and loops, which were sold to the same garment makers that bought the riveted buttons. The Camps and Harts understood that this new line could change the firm's relationship with the brass monopolists. Up to that time, Patent Button's highly specialized product line did not compete directly with the clothing hardware made by the large integrated brass firms or their subsidiaries. Smith and Griggs and Waterbury Buckle, both effectively controlled by brass firms, parceled out the market for buckles and loops, along with their fellow members of the buckle association. This line could change Patent Button from a fly not worth swatting to a troublesome, but vulnerable, competitor.[60]

For Platt Brothers, the fabricating work it continued to perform for Patent Button became a burden that constrained further growth in its other fields, while parts for Patent Button accounted for a declining share of the company's profits. Platt Brothers had doubled its customer base to match the expanded capacity of the Platts Mills facility. By 1910 at least thirty more shoe companies or narrow-fabric firms bought tipping zinc than had done so in 1897, just after Platt Brothers' expansion. In 1906 and 1907, Platt Brothers bought three new sets of rolls to meet the increased demand for its tipping zinc. The eyelet business also grew steadily, selling nationwide to makers of an enormous range of products, from machinery to bullets to decorative tinsel. Around 1910, Platt Brothers received its first inquiries about the use of zinc for fuse elements, a very promising opportunity that applied yet another of the metal's unique qualities: zinc passes directly from a solid to a gas when subjected to a sudden rise in temperature through its critical range.[61]

Wallace Camp championed the argument that Platt Brothers had to disentangle its manufacturing from the Patent Button operations at Brown Street in order to develop the zinc and eyelet lines more fully. Lewis Platt, the president of Platt Brothers, eventually agreed with Camp that the relationship between the two firms had turned into a disadvantage to Platt Brothers. Convincing him took several years, but in late 1909 Lewis Platt consented to let Camp study the possibility of consolidating all of Platt Brothers' production at Platts Mills. In January 1910, Camp reported to the board that room for future expansion was the only major concern. Land itself was not the problem but rather the ability to situate new factories in the best relationship to each other. Except for the building along the canal, the factories were confined to a narrow strip between the road and the river. Moving the road would be complicated by the need to relocate the trolley tracks and alter the race and culvert. After the trolley company engineer assured Camp of his approval if Platt Brothers ever had to move the road, Camp strongly recommended locating all of Platt Brothers operations at the riverside location.[62]

Over the next nine months the board of Lewis Platt, Carrie Platt, Jay

Hart, and Camp examined the costs of factory construction, alternative trolley locations, and the disposition of the Brown Street property. They concluded that all of these matters were soluble, but none required immediate action. They briefly considered merging Platt Brothers and Patent Button but chose instead to sell Patent Button all of the machinery it used. The sale, in April 1911, included more than 250 power presses, including 108 dial presses and 49 blanking presses. Also transferred were 22 coining presses, 25 assembly presses, and 12 of the machines developed by Irving Platt to attach the hubs to the fronts of the riveted buttons. Extensive plating and finishing equipment, the steam engine, thousands of hand tools and hundreds of die sets, a shop to make the attaching machines that was equipped with some sixty machine tools, and tons of metal and work in progress also went to Patent Button.[63]

Besides taking Platt Brothers out of the riveted-button business, the sale also allowed the Platt clan to gain majority ownership of Patent Button. To pay for the contents of the Brown Street factory, Patent Button issued $36,000 worth of new stock (1,440 shares at $25), increasing the number of shares to 1,920 from the original 480, and transferred all of the new shares to the owners of Platt Brothers. Platt Brothers distributed these shares among its own stockholders in proportion to their holdings in Platt Brothers. In effect the Platt family members took money out of one pocket and put it into another. But the Porter family's 240 shares now represented only 12.5 percent of Patent Button, not the half interest they had held since 1876. Clark's heirs and William's heirs each controlled 43.75 percent of Patent Button and half of Platt Brothers.[64]

The 1911 separation brought into sharp focus the differences between the two firms. Platt Brothers enjoyed growing demand for its zinc and eyelet businesses and the potential of a new, extensive fuse market in which the firm had few competitors. Patent Button was more concerned with defending its existing market; and its new areas for growth, buckles and loops, would put the firm into competition with powerful adversaries. The Platts, Camps, and Harts preferred to develop the long-term prospects of Platt Brothers rather than preside over the decline of Patent Button or fend off that decline with acquisitions. They decided to sell Patent Button before some clever mechanic took them down or one of the integrated metal firms swallowed them up on its own terms. In July 1912 the directors offered the company to a group headed by Leonard Carley.[65]

From 1899 to 1912, Carley had run a button firm in Detroit, and he first encountered Patent Button as a customer for its riveted buttons. Thomas Porter and Lewis Platt set the sale price at $600,000 and gave Carley six months to raise the money, which he failed to do. He saw more potential in the company than its owners did, however, and persuaded them to give

Brown Street button factory, c. 1890. (Mattatuck Museum)

him an option on the firm so that he could find another buyer. But Carley could not persuade anyone to take on Patent Button.[66]

Carley's enthusiasm for the riveted button intrigued the Waterbury directors, as did his ideas about marketing the buttons. Carley would hire sales representatives to work fulltime for Patent Button, each with an exclusive territory. He was a threat to Thomas Porter because they disagreed on basic strategy: Porter wanted to sustain the level of sales by buying out competitors, but Carley would instead spend money on a more intensive sales effort. Moreover, under Carley's plan Porter Brothers would lose its remaining role in the marketing side of the business. The Platts, Camps, and Harts overcame Porter's objections by changing the makeup of the board. Since 1876 there had been four directors: two Platts and two Porters. At the annual stockholder meeting in January 1913 the heirs of Clark and William Platt amended the bylaws by expanding the board to seven members. Then they elected six directors from their own ranks, leaving only a token seat to Thomas Porter.[67]

The new board allowed Porter to continue as president and hired Carley as general manager (at $5,000 salary) to begin implementing his sales scheme. To assuage Porter the board assigned a committee to "consider some plans for the future of the affairs of the Company" and appointed him to it, along with Lewis Platt, Roland Camp, and Lewis J. Hart. The board had already decided to follow Carley's course but respected Porter's past efforts and wanted to allow him a graceful exit, which he eventually took. By December 1913, Porter had transferred all of the merchandise accounts from Porter Brothers to the new Patent Button sales department that Carley had set up. The board relieved Porter of all of authority over the company's sales and awarded him $2,500 a year for the next three years in consideration for his contributions.[68]

CHAPTER SIX

"A Pleasant Little Operation"

WALLACE Camp, Jay Hart, and the directors of Platt Brothers wanted the firm to set its own independent direction when they severed operational ties with Patent Button. They were not prepared, however, to address the difficulty in marketing that had frequently beset the Platt enterprises since the 1840s. At Patent Button, Leonard Carley compensated for the diminution of the Porters' role. But Platt Brothers faced an entirely different set of circumstances. Its collection of specialized product lines and production capabilities required more than the aggressive salesmanship that Carley would establish at Patent Button. For Platt Brothers, marketing was far more technical in nature and only began a series of tasks that penetrated far more deeply into the manufacturing operations—discerning the needs of customers and potential customers, devising products or processes to meet those needs, and implementing regular production of the resulting innovations.

Concentrated episodes of development involving all of these interlinked activities had provided the basis for the family enterprises. Identification and exploitation of diverse niche markets in the late 1870s and early 1880s had sustained Platt Brothers, notably in the establishment of the profitable specialty of zinc for lace tips. It took almost ten years after the split of the two firms for Platt Brothers to undertake a similar project. In the 1920s the company turned over its product line and thoroughly updated its production technology while retaining the key values that had informed the business since Alfred Platt had imposed his distinctive vision: long-term continuity over short-term gain, steadiness as an employer and a supplier, intensely paternalistic labor relations, and close involvement of family owners in the management of the business that in turn dictated a relatively small scale of operation.

Family-based management of Platt Brothers was difficult to achieve immediately after the split with Patent Button. By 1910 none of the family members lived in Platts Mills, and none of the younger generation was ready to take the reins. Superintendent John Osborne had run the Platts Mills factory without supervision from any of the owners since Irving Platt's death in 1896. Jay Hart's eldest son, Lewis J. Hart (known as L.J.), who was helping to run Patent Button, "would go down there by car one day a week and run the plant that way," a family member later remembered. At the time of the split such infrequent oversight had not begun to hamper profits, which for the most part were the residual rewards from prior success in establishing reliable markets for tipping zinc, rolled strip for buttons and other goods, and specialized fabricating. Also, without any special effort on the part of Platt Brothers, new applications for zinc continued to stimulate inquiries from diverse industries. One such use was the small plates, blanked out from rolled strip, that were used to store and reproduce text in mechanical addressing machines; in the first decade of this century the Addressograph Company bought $2,000 to $5,000 worth of zinc strip a year. Platt Brothers' early participation in the emerging markets for electrical products followed a similarly passive pattern. Capitalizing fully on that opportunity would require substantial improvement in the firm's metallurgical expertise and investment in new rolling technology.[1]

Even if any of the Camps or Harts had recognized the opportunity in electrical applications for zinc, no economic necessity drove them to pursue it. The owners of Platt Brothers also had substantial income from real estate and securities investments. A relative of Carrie Platt (William Platt's daughter) recalled that she had an annual income of more than $100,000 in the years leading up to World War I; despite bountiful dividends from Platt Brothers and Patent Button, less than half of her income came from manufacturing.[2]

This diversity of family income reduced earning pressure on Platt Brothers and may have prevented the owners from appreciating the looming weakness in the firm's position as new synthetic lace-tipping materials began to replace zinc. The aged directors displayed no appetite for renewal and expansion. A resolution in 1915 lamented that the company had "continued to conduct only a part of their former business," before recommending a case-by-case reconsideration of all benefits and contributions. Platt Brothers soon reaped huge profits during World War I, supplying the zinc for Patent Button's uniform and tent buttons. This market, more than sixty years old, only tied the company more closely to Patent Button, in opposition to the intentions behind the split.[3]

Orton P. Camp, Sr., who joined the firm in 1919, played the leading role in transforming Platt Brothers from a nineteenth-century company to a dynamic participant in the markets and technology of the twentieth century. His father, Wallace Camp, was the nominal president from 1919 to 1923, as was his older brother, Roland, from 1923 to 1949, when Orton succeeded him. But from the time Orton Camp joined the firm he "actually ran the place," according to his son. Camp's second cousin, Howard P. Hart, remembered by those who worked with him as a "very innovative and clever person" and a "mechanical genius," served as chief engineer and a corporate officer. He produced a continuous stream of manufacturing innovations in support of Camp's efforts.[4]

Camp's career spanned some five decades, until he retired from the presidency in 1968. When he started, the industrial sector of Waterbury stood at its all-time peak of capacity and employment, flush with the profits of wartime production. At the end of Camp's career, industrial production in the Naugatuck Valley had declined precipitously and, by all evidence, irreversibly. In the early 1920s the brass firms and their dependent or affiliated cutting-up firms struggled with the effects of overexpansion during World War I; then the Great Depression of the 1930s crippled further those that had managed to survive. World War II brought a temporary surge in metalworking production, which only masked the accumulated weaknesses from two decades of inadequate investment in plant and equipment. For companies that had lost their ties to civilian markets during the war, antiquated facilities handicapped their attempts to recapture that business. Since the late 1940s the industrial history of Waterbury has been a litany of plant closings and the relocation of vestigial operations by absentee corporate owners. This local context of disinvestment and decline serves to emphasize the accomplishment of Orton Camp, Sr., who passed on a stronger company than the one he inherited.

Camp's career began with aggressive sales and technological development in the 1920s and ended with a similar program that was accelerated by the firm's rebuilding after a disastrous flood in 1955. In between, wary of difficult business conditions during the 1930s and preoccupied with extensive involvement in civic affairs, Camp avoided growth and change. Colleagues from his later years were struck by the extreme conservatism they first encountered. Milton Grele, who joined Platt Brothers in 1954, recalled: "If it became too big, he would feel uncomfortable with it." Camp's son offered a similar characterization: "My father had the belief that the company should not get any bigger than it was. He wanted a small company making specialty items for selected good customers. The company was busy, it was profitable, but it was not expanded. It was not really looking to get into anything new or radical. . . . It was just going along very nicely at a

pleasant, gentlemanly pace. . . . It was just a nice, pleasant little operation."
This policy sprang from the generations-long tradition of family management, which limited growth to the level that the family could control; from
Camp's experience during the early years of the Depression, which made
him extremely wary of overexpansion; and from his personality, which by
all accounts was skeptical and occasionally arbitrary. Because Camp did not
trumpet his own accomplishments, those who knew him in his later years
had no knowledge of the development effort that Camp superintended in
the 1920s, when Pratt Brothers indeed got into something new. Even then
he did not change the firm in pursuit of absolute growth, but adapted it to
a changing world in order to maintain the accustomed levels of sales and
profits.[5]

Camp and Hart brought an unprecedented extent of formal engineering
education to Platt Brothers. After graduating from Yale in 1912, Camp attended Massachusetts Institute of Technology for three years to earn a bach-
elor of science degree in mechanical engineering. He then supervised crystal
production at the Waterbury Clock Company before being drafted into the
Army Signal Corps; he joined Platt Brothers upon his discharge in 1919.
Hart graduated from Yale's Sheffield Scientific School in 1914 with a degree
in mechanical engineering. He started working at Platt Brothers soon after
he graduated, then joined the navy in April 1917. After discharge in early
1919 he again entered Sheffield, for postgraduate study in mining engineering and metallurgy, and rejoined Platt Brothers in March 1920.[6]

Upon Hart's return, the two men demonstrated their commitment to
full-time management by establishing an office at Platts Mills: "[Orton
Camp] and Howard [Hart] were the first ones to be on the site. They had
a woman as their secretary, Kate Ruby, who moved from the Patent Button
plant in Waterbury to Platts Mills the same time [Orton] and Howard
started there. The three of them took over what had been William S. Platt's
house and turned that into an office." From that base, they immediately
turned their attention to the fuse business.[7]

Markets and Technology of the Twentieth Century

When Platt Brothers split from Patent Button, the complete standardization of electrical products still eluded the industry, and fuses were one
of the last areas to receive detailed attention. Only in 1903 did the Under-
writers Laboratory (which represented insurers) and a committee of electrical manufacturers agree on standard sizes and mounting clips for fuses.
Even then there was no widely accepted means of appraising fuse performance, nor definitive knowledge of the various metals and shapes for the

"links" or "elements"—the part of the fuse that would melt, or "blow," to disconnect an overloaded circuit.[8]

Zinc's ability to sublimate—to pass directly from solid to gas when heated rapidly past its melting point—assured a clean break when a zinc fuse element blew. Other metals could form a molten pool inside the fuse that would maintain the connection between the leads and fail to disconnect the circuit. Even though fuse experts grasped this capability, other factors eclipsed it in the selection of fuse metals, and zinc did not emerge as the clear preference until the years immediately following World War I, when Platt Brothers would play a critical role in its widespread acceptance.

Fuse makers selected among a handful of metals with relatively low melting points for the links in the low-capacity fuses (less than 100 amperes) that made up the great majority of the market. At 788 degrees Fahrenheit, zinc has by far the highest melting point among this group, which also included lead (621 degrees), cadmium (610), bismuth (520), and tin (449). Thus, zinc elements for low-capacity fuses had to be very thin, and the industry did not trust the dimensional accuracy of thin zinc "ribbon." In 1917 a fuse expert asserted that about one-sixteenth of an inch was the thinnest practical size, because "in attempting to secure a ribbon of less thickness difficulties in rolling are encountered." Some zinc was used for low-capacity links, although fuse industry researchers recommended various alloys of lead, tin, and bismuth despite the careful handling demanded by their lack of strength and the need for special solders. To assure a clean break, engineers focused on the cross-section of the element rather than the material (rectangular section worked better than round). The easier handling that zinc allowed would work in its favor once Platt Brothers demonstrated the ability to roll thin strip with great accuracy.[9]

Continued uncertainty over the precise composition of the raw zinc bought in slabs also deferred the adoption of zinc for fuse elements. The war in Europe brought this issue to a climax by simultaneously spurring extraordinary demand for brass firearms cartridges and closing off the supply of high-quality spelter from Belgium and Germany.[10] An excess of cadmium in the spelter used in cartridge brass made a brittle alloy that could crack when drawn to make the shells.[11] Responding to brassmakers' demands for standard specifications, the American Society for Testing Materials established four grades: High Grade, which was at least 99.9 percent zinc and had less than 0.05 percent cadmium; Intermediate, 99.5 percent zinc with the same 0.05 percent maximum for cadmium; Brass Special, 98.8 percent zinc and less than 0.75 percent cadmium; and Prime Western, with maximum amounts of lead (1.5 percent) and iron (0.08 percent), but no stated limit for cadmium and effectively no minimum zinc content. While adequate for the alloying foundries that supplied thousands of tons of cartridge brass, these standards did not provide definitions of sufficient precision for zinc fuse elements. In a fuse link that weighed a fraction of an ounce, minute impurities of unknown composition and amount could affect resistance or conductivity and therefore reliability. Wartime spelter quality even caused problems for Platt Brothers' regular business in rolled strip. In the summer of 1915 the president of Platt Brothers, Lewis A. Platt, reported to the board on the "uncertain qualities of the metal procured—and the difficulties encountered in manufacturing it to the satisfaction of customers."[12]

The huge demand for cartridge brass caused an unprecedented rise in the price of spelter. Between 1914 and 1915 the average price of Prime Western slab almost tripled, from $.05 to $.14 per pound, and it did not decline to the prewar price until 1921. The general manager of a mining and smelting firm described the boom as "the fortune of a Monte Cristo." Zinc consumers decried the "orgy in spelter" and pointed to the difficulties it caused in supply during 1915. With "customers frantically bidding up the price against each other," smelter inventories were exhausted in January and their output was presold through March. None of the smelters had orders for delivery after March, however, because the zinc users assumed the price would fall and delayed ordering. Unlike most others, Platt Brothers continued throughout 1915 to contract for spelter several months in advance, passing the price on to its customers. The Platt directors did not panic when their resulting higher price quotations for strip caused a decline in orders. Meeting in July 1915, they decided that "it is best to keep the business going." Platt Brothers continued to value long-term continuity over short-term considerations, but fuse makers did not rush to the metal under those circumstances.[13]

While these factors all limited Platt Brothers' ability to sell substantial quantities of metal for low-capacity fuse links, the firm nonetheless had a foothold in the fuse industry. By 1914 the company supplied rolled zinc to more than a dozen fuse producers, including several of the leaders in the field, such as Chase-Shawmut, Sprague Electric, Westinghouse, Bryant Electric, Economy Fuse and Manufacturing, D & W Fuse, and United Electrical Supply. With few exceptions these were small accounts of less than several hundred dollars a year and probably consisted primarily of metal for high-capacity fuses. The largest customer, Economy Fuse and Manufacturing, bought between $1,600 and $3,000 worth of fuse metal a year in the period 1910–1914, when Platt Brothers' total annual zinc sales probably exceeded $150,000. Significantly, several of the more prominent fuse engineers occupied key positions with Platt customers. When the company sought more fuse element work, it had access to some of the best information available.[14]

The nation's entry into the war further delayed development of Platt Brothers' fuse business. Although the rise in spelter price caused an increase in the supply of slab by bringing new producers into the field and inducing established smelters to increase capacity, the government restricted the majority of the supply to military production. Even if Platt Brothers could have obtained the metal, it would have had difficulty finding the time for fuse strip production, so busy was the plant supplying zinc for Patent Button's military-uniform and tent-button orders.[15]

The end of the war not only freed material supplies and production capacity but also brought to a close the military service of Orton Camp, Sr., and Howard P. Hart. Upon assuming charge at Platts Mills they realized that fuse zinc fit perfectly within the company's long-held strategy of small-market specialization and provided some opportunity to restore sagging nonmilitary revenues. Neither the two largest producers of rolled zinc, Ball Brothers and Matthiesson and Hegeler, which together controlled more than half of the market, nor the strongest new competitors, the fabricating operations established by the zinc mining and smelting firms, accorded high priority to the fuse business. These larger zinc fabricators all concentrated on the higher-volume, lower-precision uses: roofing, gutters, and downspouts; block zinc and some wire, used in galvanizing processes; and watertight containers used for ship-borne transport of coffee, tea, and other foodstuffs. Orders for accurately rolled fuse strip frequently called for less than a hundred pounds, a volume too small to attract competition from the larger firms. For Platt Brothers the payoff for accurate strip came in a secure market and in the higher prices than could be charged for the "commercial tolerance" strip and sheet that was more widely available. Just as the dominant button firms in nineteenth-century Waterbury had countenanced the Platts' success in the small market for zinc tent buttons, during the 1920s Platt Brothers could develop fuse strip production technology and exclusive marketing status without significant competition from the larger zinc fabricators.[16]

Orton Camp had begun calling on fuse customers before Hart's return, meticulously recording the meetings in a "call book." The key lesson from these trips was that the fuse makers did not need to know the precise metallurgical content of their zinc elements so long as the composition remained constant from order to order. Camp's notes from a meeting at Chase-Shawmut, in the summer of 1919, reflected this insight: "From their tests it didn't make much difference what kind of spelter or zinc that they used as long as it was always the same." The problem for Platt Brothers was that they could not control the composition of their incoming spelter, as the impurities could vary even within the same grade, depending on the source of the ore and the particular smelting process.[17]

Howard Hart began work on the problem as soon as he rejoined the firm. During March 1920, his first month back on the job, the new expense category of "experiment and research" appeared in the cash accounts. Hart sent samples of rolled strip as supplied to fuse makers to Yale's Hammond Laboratory to determine their composition and grain structure and to test their hardness. Once he knew the characteristics of a customer's strip, he could assure their reproduction. For customers who provided conductivity requirements, Hart cast samples using various combinations of different grades of slab, then rolled them to finish-size strip to send out for conductivity testing. Once a customer accepted a certain mix for a type of fuse, Platt Brothers could fill subsequent orders with the same metal.[18]

New output standards required a different approach to spelter purchase than had long prevailed. Rather than buying from metals brokers, Hart began to buy directly from the zinc miner-smelters, especially New Jersey Zinc Company and American Zinc, Lead and Smelting Company. Hart corresponded with metallurgists at these firms, who had detailed knowledge of their own ores and smelter output. Using his test results to determine the exact material needed, Hart then requested slabs made from certain ores, as designated by the smelters' trade names. Some fuse zinc was a mixture of different kinds of spelter, sometimes from different suppliers, and while Hart knew the chemical composition of his various fuse zinc recipes, apparently no one else did, nor did they need to. This practice prevailed for more than fifty years, as recalled by the retired vice-president for sales:[19]

Neither the customers nor Platt Brothers knew exactly what kind of zinc was being supplied for electrical fuse applications. The only thing that Platt Brothers guaranteed was that it would always be the same. They achieved that similarity by buying the zinc slabs that they used for the different zinc customers from the same supplier all the time. It was the same specifications all the time, even though we never really knew what the specifications were. We'd call American Zinc and say, "We need Granby zinc," which was their trade name, or New Jersey Zinc and [say], "We need Horsehead Zinc," which was their trade name for a different zinc. So every customer knew every time they bought it from us, they got the same stuff. And it wasn't until sometime in the 1970s that we really knew chemically and metallurgically what it was all the time.

The fuse strip business also built on the firm's long-established expertise in rolling zinc. Even though fuse engineers before 1920 distrusted the accuracy of strip rolled to less than a sixteenth of an inch thick, Hart and Camp trusted in Platt Brothers' ability to roll thin strip to tight specifications by some modification of existing equipment, construction of new equipment, and very careful finish rolling. Hart designed and oversaw the construction of all new finish-rolling machines for fuse metal. Henry Payne, who came to work as a roller hand in 1924, later remembered the contrast between the shiny new machines and the rest of the plant: "except in the fuse rolling department, equipment was quite primitive." The new finish-rolling machines for fuse strip had rolls six inches in diameter, much smaller than the standard finish rolls of at least twelve inches, and were run by one man rather than the crews that operated larger rolling mills. Hart also reduced the speed of the rolls so that the metal passed through them at the very low rate of sixty to eighty feet per minute. He had to reformulate completely the standard drive ratios, and he also began to experiment with substituting roller-chain drives for the pinion gears connecting the two rolls in each machine, apparently for smoother operation and therefore less surface variation in the metal. Waterbury-Farrel Foundry and Machine Company supplied the cast-iron rolls and roll housings, as it had done for Platt Brothers for more than seventy-five years, and Hart supervised the assembly of the machines.[20]

Accurate rolling did not demand any significant technical breakthrough. It took Hart's time and talent to develop the process, as well as willingness to devote painstaking care to running the new machines. Camp and Hart may have gained the confidence of their customers with their prestigious academic degrees, and no doubt Hart's training came into play on innumerable occasions as he equipped the fuse metal rolling department, but accurate rolling depended just as fully on the experienced, stable work force at Platts Mills.

Labor relations at Platt Brothers in the early 1920s had evolved little since the paternalistic policies put in place during the life of Alfred Platt. It would be only a slight exaggeration to describe the work force as an extended family. Kinship relationships, including many ties to Alfred Platt and his sons, abounded among the thirty-five employees. John Osborne, the superintendent, was Nirom Platt's grandson and Alfred Platt's great-grandson. Osborne's son Clayton ran the shipping room, and his nephew, Ev Wooster, succeeded him as boss roller and superintendent. Foreman Joseph Platt and roller hand Frederick Platt were distant cousins of Orton Camp and Howard Hart. Employment of multiple members of the same family was also common among those with no ties to the owners. Benjamin Peaslee ran a rolling mill, his wife ran an eyelet press, and two of their sons also worked for Platt Brothers, including Robert, who ran the annealing operation. Press hand Charles Slocum helped secure a similar job for his son Harry.[21]

Many employees owned land in the area, and Payne remembered that they saw themselves as "farmers first and then factory employees. The urge to the land was primary, but they could not make a good living farming so had to work in the factory." Despite that self-image as farmers, decades-long mill employment was typical. Though few could match Wooster's eventual tenure of fifty-three years, even production workers like Robert Peaslee (twenty-six years) commonly retired out of Platt Brothers instead of moving to other employment. Those who did not own land could rent living quarters in the boardinghouse or tenement houses, as space became available, and all were welcome to exercise their agricultural impulses by gardening on company land. Though Yankees continued as a majority in the work force, by the early 1920s at least a half dozen Polish people from Union City in Naugatuck worked at Platt. Jack Dillon, who inspected the coils of strip zinc, learned enough Polish to interpret for them and to help them participate in the informal noontime "forums . . . on how to garden and how to live."[22]

Platt Brothers nonetheless remained a part of the larger labor picture in the Naugatuck Valley and did not escape completely the region-wide strikes that took place during Orton Camp's first sixteen months at Platts Mills. At the end of the war, in late 1918, the brass plants began to lay off workers and cut wages. Tense months of protest led to an "explosive, immigrant-led strike, with meetings conducted in Russian, Lithuanian, Polish and Italian." In early June 1919, workers struck the American Brass plants in Ansonia, and in two weeks the strikes spread up the valley to Waterbury, where eight thousand people walked out of the brass mills. Within a month the brass companies increased wages to end the strike. Less than a year later, in March and April of 1920, workers in Waterbury struck again to protest another pay cut. The companies prevailed in large part because postwar contraction of the brass business vastly reduced their labor needs.[23] Platt Brothers continued working at full strength through the 1919 strike and the first month of the 1920 strike. But the payroll for April 1920 fell to nearly half of the usual wage expense, suggesting that a substantial portion of the Platt workers joined the second strike.[24] After the strikes the brass mill owners stepped up their efforts to replace the traditional power of skilled workers by increasing the scientific process control of rolling and other crucial trades.[25]

It is not surprising that some of Platt Brothers workers joined a region-wide strike organized along ethnic lines rather than according to place of employment. Perhaps more remarkable was that after the strike Orton Camp, Sr., did not impose tighter supervision on a work force that had enjoyed near-total autonomy on the shop floor. Despite an arbitrary side to Camp's personality—he did not believe in coffee breaks, and his distaste for carbonated soft drinks moved him to bar soda machines—Payne described the factory as "very informal," and the pace as "not so hurried . . .

with plenty of time to talk. . . . It was amazing how much work George McKenzie could do while commenting on everything." Another employee remembered Jack Dillon's appreciation that "nobody bothers me."[26]

Although none of the longtime employees remembered any overt negotiation, a clear understanding existed among owners, supervisors, and workers. The workers took responsibility for meeting production schedules with high-quality work and did not insist on rigid job categories: "We took our turn at the various necessary jobs and learned the business," Payne recalled. The foremen took responsibility for training workers, providing technical oversight, and coordinating among the various stages of production. And Camp kept people on the payroll once they were hired. As an employee recalled, "When things were slack, some of the men would sit on a keg and paint the white picket fence running in front of the office. The seven or eight hour day [short hours] at regular pay would be intact. Other odd jobs would be handled the same way." Richard Miller found that policy still in place when he began at Platt Brothers more than thirty years later: "They were apt to shift around. You would find a production worker in the shipping department one day, and so on." Miller attributed this flexibility to an underlying understanding: "[Orton Camp, Sr.] felt a terrific obligation to provide a place for his employees to continue to make a living . . . and generally speaking they [the shop employees] performed to the limit of their effectiveness. . . . The production workers worked." Thus, in building the fuse metal business, Camp and Hart could rely on a high degree of competence, loyalty, and responsibility from the people who had to perform the work.[27]

This approach to labor influenced Hart's design of the fuse mills. He did not utilize sophisticated machine controls for the positioning or pace of the work. He also could design machines capable of handling a wide range of work and rely on the operators to make the necessary adjustments, occasionally to the consternation of machine-part vendors who were more accustomed to very tight operating specifications that tended to remove worker skill from mechanized processes. In writing to a supplier of chain drives, Hart patiently explained that the power transmitted by the drive mechanism between the rolls differed according to the thickness of the metal, but "how much we do not definitely know." He apparently believed that was a matter for the roller hand, not the mechanical engineer. He also continued to use cast-iron rolls instead of the hardened-steel rolls that the brass mills were then adopting. Steel rolls cost more and had to be removed from the roll mill to be dressed on a grinding machine. But there was an implication for labor too, because roller hands had the critical responsibility of dressing the cast-iron rolls by hand with "a stick and emery" (without removing the rolls from the machine). Poor dressing would create imper-

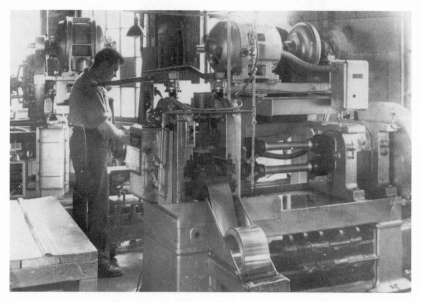

Fuse-rolling machine, c. 1950. The operator, Bill Lautenschlager, is examining the strip as it is being fed into the rolls. (Mattatuck Museum)

fections on the rolls that would show up on the strip. Finally, the fuse strip was gauged by hand, with a micrometer, as the metal came out of the rolls, placing the all-important responsibility for accuracy directly in the hands of the worker. In contrast to the deskilling of rolling mill work in the brass companies, Hart's fuse mills created a new, more highly skilled, and more highly paid labor grade. Fuse rollers, Miller recalled, became the "prima donnas of the work force" at Platt Brothers.[28]

Camp's salesmanship, Hart's metallurgical and engineering contributions, and the skilled work force enabled Platt Brothers to gain as customers every fuse manufacturer in the nation. In 1925 the company shipped almost a quarter-million pounds of fuse metal. Platt Brothers charged about $.05 a pound more for it than the strip used for lace tips. Although the slower and more accurate rolling of fuse strip cost more in labor, some of the difference in markup represented profit (it is impossible to determine the fuse metal net from the available records of this period). After steady increases in the next four years, fuse metal output exceeded 326,000 pounds. Platt Brothers dominated this market as thoroughly as its predecessor had once done in zinc tent buttons.[29]

Eyelets were the only other line to experience rising production in the early 1920s, and Camp pushed harder for eyelet sales thereafter. Expensive eyelet presses made up the bulk of the new machinery expenditures; in 1925

Eyelet department building of 1929; photograph taken in 1949. To the right is the barn erected in the early 1880s by William Platt, who lived across the street. (Mattatuck Museum)

a new eyelet press from Waterbury-Farrel cost more than $3,500. Employment in the department rose from eight workers in 1924 to more than twenty by 1929. To house the expanded production, in late 1929 the company began construction of a new one-story, sawtooth-roofed brick factory between the road and the river.[30]

Lower sales of strip for lace tips accounted for most of the falloff in zinc production. From a postwar peak in 1919 of some 600,000 pounds, shipments of tipping zinc dropped steadily to nearly half that amount in 1930. In this period all of the tipping zinc went to James H. Hill and Sons, in Rhode Island, where it was japanned, slit to width, and shipped to the lace, shoe, braid, and undergarment manufacturers who used the tips on their products. Platt Brothers and Hill had a unique financial arrangement that began in the early years of the century, when Hill fell deeply in arrears in its payments for zinc. Rather than forcing Hill to close and then having to establish direct sales to Hill's customers, Platt Brothers agreed to carry the debt in return for a mortgage on the Hill property. Hill's customers paid directly to Platt Brothers, which deducted for the zinc and debt service and sent the balance to Hill.[31]

The loss of orders in the 1920s corresponded to the growing use of celluloid (nitrate cellulose) for lace tips. With Platt Brothers holding the Hill mortgage and tipping orders falling drastically, in 1929 Camp agreed to supply Hill with celluloid strip under the same payment deal they had for zinc. Platt Brothers did not make celluloid but served as a jobber, arranging the purchases for direct shipment to Hill. In the first year Hill bought 2,000 pounds of the celluloid strip at a per-pound price more than six times higher than that of rolled zinc. By 1935 celluloid shipments grew to 30,400 pounds, for total income of $33,750; that same year, 188,900 pounds of tipping zinc brought in $30,200. Celluloid jobbing thus offset about a third of the loss in revenues from tipping-zinc sales. Camp's willingness to enter into a business so far removed from the company's established expertise indicated something of the desperation he must have felt as he watched the sales of tipping zinc slide downward.[32]

Apart from fuses and lace tips the rest of the zinc business in the 1920s consisted of strip described as "commercial tolerance," rather than accurately rolled. In the early 1920s, Platt Brothers sold a little less commercial strip than tipping zinc—in 1923, for instance, about 371,000 pounds of commercial strip versus 433,000 of tipping metal—and increasing the strip business provided the most immediate means to offset the losses in tipping sales. By far the largest use for strip was for the backs of brass- or steel-front buttons. These metals offered the desired appearance on the garments, while zinc's lower cost and corrosion resistance made it appropriate for the backs. Patent Button could be counted on for zinc orders. Orton Camp persuaded Scovill to step up the use of zinc in its extensive clothing-hardware business. He also made Platt Brothers' first aggressive effort in forty years to market zinc among the hardware manufacturers of Connecticut. Before Camp, for instance, Sargeant and Company, the New Haven producer of builders' hardware, was an intermittent customer, buying less than $100 worth of zinc a year; by 1928, Sargeant bought several hundred dollars' worth every month. Over the same period, Waterbury Buckle and the H. L. Judd Company of Wallingford moved from incidental purchases to hundreds of dollars most months and occasionally over $1,000.[33]

The eight- or ten-inch-wide commercial strip, however, sold for at least $.02 less per pound than the tipping zinc, and some of the difference represented lower profit. As commercial strip replaced tipping zinc as a percentage of output, profit would fall unless volume increased. Howard Hart addressed this problem, while also avoiding undesired expansion, by redesigning the melting and casting processes that had changed very little for at least a generation.

By elevating furnace volume and minimizing waste in casting, Hart engineered higher output without increasing the work force. Before he began this effort in the mid-1920s, the slabs of spelter were melted in small furnaces, and the metal was cast in "hand held molds, with two men pouring from small ladles." The furnaces could hold up to twenty-five slabs at a time, and temperature was monitored "by guess," aided by periodic readings with a Bristol Company pyrometer.[34] They were fired by gas, the sole improvement over the coal-based practice of the nineteenth-century. Hart designed and built an electric furnace of more than five times greater capacity, with integral temperature gauging and preset intervals for burner adjustment. He bought components, such as furnace tiles and temperature controls, and assembled them into equipment that precisely suited the firm's specialized needs. Even at the new size Platt's furnaces were small for an industrial melting operation, and they operated at a much lower temperature range than those employed for the more commonly worked metals. Hart built another furnace in 1928, this time returning to gas firing but maintaining the larger size and other improvements of the electric unit. (Thereafter, all of the melting furnaces used gas.)[35]

Molten zinc was cast into bars three to four feet long, three to ten inches wide (according to the finished width of the strip), and about three inches thick; these were the shapes that would be rolled into strip. The old method of pouring into horizontal pan molds created a casting with a shrinkage cavity, as well as "froth and scum and dross" on the top surface, even with the most careful hand pouring. The resulting strip could have many surface irregularities. Such imperfect strip might be suitable for button backs or lace tips but not for fuse metal or other more exacting uses. Rejected material could be remelted but at a loss of time and labor, and higher furnace volume made this problem more acute. To improve the quality of the cast bars Hart adapted the "book mold" developed some twenty years earlier for brass: two pieces of steel, hinged together, enclosing a cavity the size of the required casting. Filling the mold from one end ("end-pouring") meant the dross was confined to the sides of the bar, which could be trimmed off to leave the large surfaces free of imperfections. He further improved the casting process by attaching to the book mold a pan that held the exact amount of molten zinc needed to fill that mold. A motor-driven, cam-actuated trunnion tilted the pan and mold together to a vertical position, controlling the angle and the speed to minimize eddying and the capture of air bubbles in the zinc. Hart then built a turntable that rotated on a ball-bearing track set in the floor and held up to eight molds for positioning under the ladle.[36]

From the casting shop the bars went into a "soaking oven" for heating to malleable temperature, then entered the three-part process of breakdown rolling, rundown rolling, and finish rolling. The shop's capacity in rundown and finish accommodated the increased furnace output, but the soaking and breakdown rolling turned into bottlenecks. In 1923, Hart bought

TABLE 6[43]
Platt Brothers and Company, Sales of Manufactured Goods, 1923–1945
($1,000)

Year	Tip	Commercial strip	Wire	Fuse strip	Eyelets	Total	Total adjusted to base of 1926 = 100
1923	69.8	53.0	n/a	51.4	54.2	228.4	238.2
1924	39.2	47.9	n/a	48.1	43.9	179.1	178.6
1925	47.1	84.5	n/a	49.2	64.3	245.1	251.5
1926	51.1	92.5	n/a	57.4	67.3	268.3	268.3
1927	41.0	77.5	n/a	58.9	68.0	245.4	230.7
1928	41.7	77.8	n/a	46.4	59.5	225.4	209.4
1929	43.1	61.9	15.7	71.4	89.8	281.9	258.2
1930	51.1	59.3	71.9	30.7	61.8	274.8	234.1
1931	25.2	79.0	51.1	23.9	70.9	250.1	187.6
1932	18.9	63.4	30.3	13.9	47.4	173.9	122.1
1933	25.1	75.5	47.0	27.6	42.4	217.6	154.9
1934	32.3	65.3	35.0	26.7	41.5	200.8	157.4
1935	30.9	74.8	33.4	36.8	71.0	246.9	192.3
1936	23.1	82.1	47.8	49.1	84.2	286.3	227.9
1937	21.5	128.9	101.0	58.6	100.8	410.8	350.4
1938	12.0	85.8	23.9	27.8	75.1	224.6	183.5
1939	13.1	91.9	40.2	44.4	101.1	290.7	236.3
1940	15.7	106.3	66.5	53.0	111.1	352.6	292.7
1941	27.5	183.3	127.9	122.3	168.3	629.3	560.1
1942	21.5	285.5	160.4	74.2	96.3	637.9	609.2
1943	13.1	291.0	147.3	135.0	159.0	745.4	722.3
1944	18.3	306.4	124.4	93.8	164.3	707.2	696.6
1945	24.8	269.7	109.7	78.1	184.2	666.5	664.5

a new oven, offered by its maker primarily for baking japanned finishes, and specified minor modifications to equip it for Platt Brothers' purposes. The next year the firm installed another "breaking down mill."[37]

Higher furnace volume, less waste in casting, the new oven, and the additional breakdown mill propelled an increase in commercial strip production to match Camp's marketing efforts. From 1926 through 1928, Platt Brothers shipped more than 600,000 pounds per year. Increased strip production, combined with fuse zinc and celluloid jobbing, compensated for much of the decline in tipping zinc, but revenues on an adjusted-dollar basis fell (see Table 6). Only the fuse business offered the advantage of premium pricing in a noncompetitive market and the prospect for significant growth in income without multiplying the size of the plant and the work force. The continued search for further specialty lines with similar market and pricing attributes propelled Camp to start zinc wire production at Platt Brothers.[38]

Camp identified two potential markets for zinc wire or rod, in distinction to the company's flat-rolled strip. The first, an extension of the fuse strip business, was wire for elements used in large-capacity fuses that protected the components of electrical transmission systems. The second, and far more significant market, involved the spray "metallizing" process for rust-proofing: zinc wire was fed into a gun that melted the zinc, atomized it, and sprayed it onto the surface requiring protection. Developed in Switzerland, the process entered the United States in 1920 under a license held by Metallizing Engineering Company. Camp saw an opportunity to sell coarse zinc wire for redraw to smaller diameters by the wire companies that supplied finished sizes to the users of metallizing equipment. Starting in mid-1928, thousands of dollars of machinery purchases equipped the plant to roll narrow, square-section-cast bars into rod and then to draw the rod into wire. A Morgan Wire Machine performed the drawing on a series of "bull blocks," or dies through which the rod was pulled to reduce its diameter. The rod rolling was at first more of a makeshift operation, probably accomplished by fitting grooved rolls on existing mills. When the first wire order came, some five hundred pounds for Hudson Wire Company in May 1929, Platt Brothers bought a secondhand mill to "fix up for rolling wire."[39]

Hudson had to redraw the Platt wire, then await response from its own customers who used the wire for metallizing, which took almost two months. When approval came, Hudson ordered ten times the initial amount. Other wire companies began buying the zinc wire, notably the American Brass Company wire division in Ansonia, and by the end of 1929 wire sales amounted to about a third of the revenues from tipping zinc. Wire production prevented a financial disaster in the difficult year of 1930. As eyelets and fuse metal declined, and Platt Brothers achieved a small increase in commercial strip volume only by reducing the price more than 15 percent, zinc wire became the leading source of revenue (see Table 6).[40]

While the brass mills and other employers in the region laid off workers and deferred capital expenditure in the early years of the Depression, Camp and Hart persuaded their relatives on the board to expand Platt Brothers' wire-processing capability. The company liquidated securities holdings and borrowed heavily to fund the effort. Work began on a new melting furnace in May 1930, and an additional soaking oven came in July. The following January, Hart ordered a state-of-the-art "HVH" rolling mill for the last process in bringing the wire down to a size suitable for drawing; Waterbury-Farrel apologetically explained that delivery would take eight weeks due to short staffing after layoffs. The HVH mill featured a series of rolls beginning with one set on the horizontal axis, then one on the vertical, followed by another on the horizontal. By rolling around all of the sides of the rod, the HVH mill improved the formation of an oval cross-section

Morgan wire machine, c. 1950, operator unknown. The reels at the top of the machine collected the wire after it passed through successive sets of dies, which are at the front of the machine near the operator. (Mattatuck Museum)

from the square bars and speeded the process by reducing the amount of handling. In the summer the directors approved the purchase of new roll units to adapt the HVH mill for different sizes of work.[41]

Hart had to devise a means of providing the wire in the required lengths. Before rolling, the "wire bars" measured three inches square in cross-section and four feet long. Rolling and then drawing considerably elongated the piece; but in order to run their own wire-drawing machines without excessive stoppages, the customers needed wire four times longer than Platt Brothers could produce from a single bar. Along with Leaman Harvey, who succeeded Wooster as plant superintendent, Hart developed a means to weld the lengths of rod end to end. The process began by beveling the ends of the two lengths, then clamping them together and running a high electric current through the pieces. The joint then passed through a set of grooved rolls, where a stop bar knocked the clamp off before the welded section entered the rolls.[42]

After a decade of extensive marketing efforts and production innovations, Orton Camp and Howard Hart had established a new foundation for the company. The adoption of celluloid had undercut the tipping zinc that had been the firm's largest revenue producer, but by expanding eyelet and strip production and establishing a strong position in fuse zinc, by the mid-1920s Camp and Hart had restored production to the level that preceded their taking charge of the firm. The introduction of wire production and expansion of the eyelet department helped Platt Brothers achieve a near record for annual revenues in 1929, and wire offset most of the decline in other products during 1930 (Table 6).

Camp and Hart found success difficult to maintain in the economic convulsions of the 1930s, even for their newest product. Wire for metallizing attracted competition from other zinc firms, which soon cut into Platt Brothers' sales. Wire orders dropped to less than half of the prior volume.[44] By that time the owners of Platt Brothers began to place a higher priority on surviving the Depression than on any further product development. But before tracing the steps that carried the firm through that period it is necessary to outline the evolving nature of ownership in Platt Brothers and Patent Button.

The Family Fortunes: Reprise

The efforts of Orton Camp and Howard Hart during the 1920s took place against a background of contention between their two families. The central problem concerned the transition of ownership to their generation. Both the Camps and the Harts continued to favor family ownership, but the family had widened. Just as Clark and William Platt, after their father's death, had tightened their definition of family, some of their heirs found it difficult to include cousins and more distant relatives in the circle that included their own siblings and children.

The problem began soon after Thomas Porter received the last of his severance payments in 1916, when the Porter family decided to sell its interest in Patent Button. Thomas Porter's closest ally from the old board of Patent Button, Lewis A. Platt, acquired all of the Porter stock, and with it a majority of Patent Button, for the descendants of Clark Platt. Upon Lewis Platt's death in 1919, his nieces and nephews, the children of Bertha Platt and Jay Hart, inherited that controlling interest. Although direct knowledge of the events of the next five years passed away with the participants, considerable acrimony ensued, probably over the Camps' attempts to gain an equal share in Patent Button and the Harts' declining to reduce their majority. In 1924 the Harts established a family voting trust "so that the capital stock of said corporations may not be likely to be purchased or sold for speculative control." The trust would hold all of their shares in both firms and vote them as a bloc in the respective shareholders' meetings.[45]

The trust carried an ambiguous message. By preventing any of the Hart stockholders from selling out for a one-time bonanza, the trust affirmed the Harts' commitment to family ownership. But it also cemented the Harts' ability to control Patent Button, which caused resentment among some of the Camps. Roland Camp, his nephew recalled, "used to lament to me, 'Those Harts have taken almost a million dollars more than we have out of [Patent Button],' simply because they had all of the salaries." If others among the Camps objected less strenuously, it was because the Harts did not simply milk the value out of Patent Button. L. J. Hart served as president and superintendent, and Orton Camp, Sr., "thought L. J. was a superior person and a good manager." Forrest Purinton, the husband of L. J. Hart's sister Dorothy, ran the plating and finishing operations and contributed the company's most significant twentieth-century production innovations: belt-fed enamel-spraying equipment to finish button fronts and, in the 1930s, a roll-coating machine to paint linear designs on metal lipstick cases and flashlights, which Patent Button used in subcontracts for Scovill and other brass firms. The Harts also had the good sense to adopt the sales strategy of Leonard Carley.[46]

Carley, who had the title of vice president and general manager, built the new marketing system. He opened sales offices in Boston, New York, Chicago, St. Louis, Nashville, Atlanta, and Dallas, each with one or two full-time salesmen. The sales force also maintained and repaired the attaching machines that Patent Button leased to the garment makers; these service calls provided a means for salesmen to assess the level of work in a customer's plant and to identify any special need or problem. After every visit to a customer's plant their reports to Waterbury enabled Carley, L. J. Hart, and their foremen to adjust the schedule of existing work or to buy raw material in anticipation of a large order. On occasion, when reports after service calls indicated that a customer was entering a difficult period, Patent Button held up production and avoided a loss on the goods after the customer went out of business. Carley also started his own independently owned commission agency in Los Angeles, selling half-interest in it to Patent Button in 1922. That same year he established Patent Button Company Limited, a sales agency for Canada, with ownership split between the parent firm and a Canadian partner. By the mid-1920s, metal buttons from Brown Street in Waterbury held up most of the dungarees and overalls in North America. The names stamped on the button fronts included every familiar brand, including Levi-Strauss, Oshkosh, Red Ball, Sears and Roebuck, J. C. Penney, Bluebell, and Washington.[47]

Until his retirement in the early 1940s, Carley managed to log rising sales and revenues while the products and metalworking technology changed very little. Patent Button made the same metal buttons (both attached to garments with metal fasteners or sewn on), snaps, and rivets and burrs for pocket-corner reinforcement that it had before Carley arrived. The old Blake and Johnson presses, which Carley described in 1918 as "not strictly modern," formed the buttons. Many of these same machines, along with the mechanical power transmission system of overhead shafting, belts, and pulleys, were still in place until the mid-1960s, when the newly formed Occupational Safety and Health Admininstration mandated the conversion to individual motor drives on the machinery.[48]

Although Patent Button's solid earnings without substantial capital investment surely assuaged the minority owners, members of both clans continued to seek ways to eliminate the rivalry that had been solidified by the Harts' voting trust. Orton Camp, Sr., and Howard Hart, who worked together very closely at Platt Brothers, "were peacemakers and wanted to smooth out the relationship between the two families." Anticipating the next generational succession, they wanted to continue family management and to assure fruitful careers in manufacturing for their sons. By the time Orton Camp, Jr., entered Yale in 1941, he had acceded to his father's expectation that he too would work in the family enterprises. Howard Hart's son Curtiss also recalled that his father "wanted me to come to work for him." That summer of 1941 both received an initiation into some of the rigors that the workers experienced. Curtiss Hart worked in the plating room at Patent Button—"the nastiest job in the place"—and young Camp's first job was to rake the debris from the spillway at the Platt Brothers dam.[49]

Estrangement between the two clans nonetheless persisted. A telling indication was that Orton Camp, Jr., had never met L. J. Hart's son and successor at Patent Button, David Hart. After the younger Camp served in the army during World War II and finished his interrupted undergraduate program (in history) at Yale, his father introduced him to David Hart over lunch at the Waterbury Club. The younger Camp accepted the resulting offer of a job in the accounting department at Patent Button. Curtiss Hart also resumed his schooling after military service, earning a business degree from Colorado College, and began work as the Platt Brothers bookkeeper in 1948. The relationship between Orton Camp, Jr., and David Hart finally helped to bring an end to the conflict between their families, as Camp remembered: "David and I started to work well together, and we were eventually able to persuade the Harts to break up their trusts and not be afraid that the Camps were going to push them out."[50]

The rivalry between Camps and Harts played out differently at Platt Brothers, where each side held exactly half of the stock. Platt Brothers ended 1911, its first year of independent operation, with a cash account of some $437,000. While the directors understood the difficulty of expansion without active on-site management, they did not want to limit future growth by depleting the cash with dividends any higher than the substantial rates they already received. They also recognized the temptation of that balance: each of the 1,200 shares represented more than $350 in cash alone, and the larger shareholders could collect a windfall by selling. To sequester some of the money from the dividend pool, to make it less accessible to speculators, and to earn a greater return than would be available in a bank account, the directors began to buy government and corporate securities, to be held by Platt Brothers. Orton Camp, Sr., arrived to find a portfolio worth some $44,000, and while he also directed investment into new production capability, he increased the holdings to more than $82,000 in his first year. Platt Brothers bought federal, state, and municipal bonds; local stocks such as Scovill and Waterbury Gas Light Company; other Connecticut stocks, including Travelers Insurance and the New Britain hardware firm of Landers, Frary and Clark; and stock in nationally prominent firms such as United States Steel. In 1919 the portfolio yielded some $4,200 in interest, and the capital appreciated by more than $3,900; the total return of 10 percent was more than twice the rate of bank interest.[51]

In the years of antipathy leading up to the establishment of the Harts' voting trust in 1924, the securities account took on another role. Though not as stringent a constraint as the trust placed on the Harts who held stock in Platt Brothers, it encouraged any wavering Camp stockholders to keep ownership in the family and resist speculative trading of Platt Brothers shares, even in difficult periods for the firm. As long as that account kept rising, both Camps and Harts could be assured of substantial cash benefits if the company ever had to fold, as well as an ample reservoir to fund dividends. And rise it did. On continued purchases and appreciation the account value stood at more than $277,000 at the end of 1928. Interest and dividends brought in as much as $9,600 a year and never less than $2,300. After the stock market crash in 1929 knocked the account down to $195,000, it still offered sufficient cushion for the directors to award a total of $30,000 dividends for the year.[52]

The securities account also allowed a considerable degree of flexibility in the management of the firm during the early years of the Depression. As 1930 opened, Orton Camp was determined to build the wire business despite the adverse economic conditions. Judging from the declining amount of cash discounts to customers, the average age of the accounts receivable must have doubled. As cash flow dried up, equipment purchases for wire production rose, and dividends continued to be paid (at the reduced total of $18,000), Platt Brothers used the securities holdings as collateral for bank notes to support continued operations. By August, Waterbury National Bank had issued $50,000 in loans. When conditions failed to improve by October, Roland and Orton Camp began selling off securities. To override the anxiety of their relatives who had a stake in Platt Brothers, in November the directors felt compelled to reaffirm the right of the president to sell "any and all shares of stocks, bonds or other securities held by Company." At the end of 1930 the sale of securities and further decline in the stock market had driven the account down by another 35 percent, to $127,000.[53]

The securities holdings allowed Platt Brothers to solidify the wire business in its first two years, but after January 1931 the directors and managers resisted further depletion of the securities account and looked instead to economize. At their January meeting, in a coda to the ambitious policy of the prior year, the directors approved the purchase of the Waterbury-Farrel HVH wire-rolling machine and declared the usual January dividend. But as orders continued to decline for wire, fuse, and tipping zinc, they decided not to declare the customary midyear dividends; a small year-end award brought the total to half of the prior year's distribution. They devoted the saving in dividends to any necessary equipment purchases, holding those purchases to the amount saved in dividends. Platt Brothers did not economize by laying off production workers.[54]

Orders continued to fall throughout 1932 in all five areas of production, and adjusted-dollar sales slid to lowest point in a decade. For the first time in more than fifty years, Platt Brothers paid no dividend at all. In June all of the officers and salaried personnel took a 10 percent pay cut. Production workers kept their jobs, but an across-the-board reduction in hours and a wage cut brought their income down.[55]

Although the financial difficulty did not endanger continued ownership by the Camps and Harts, it did result in a complete reversal of policy by Orton Camp, Sr. He turned away from the expansive and innovative approach he had followed in the 1920s to embrace the conservative management that subsequent employees would encounter when they joined Platt Brothers. He would support investment to help the firm sustain a high level of performance and reliability in its established lines, but he disdained any further evolution.

Orton Camp, Sr.: Middle Years

Through the rest of the 1930s, Camp's guidance of Platt Brothers took advantage of the company's small size. He could monitor performance very closely: "We would sit down [at directors meetings] and he would pull his little stack of three-by-five cards out of his pocket and say, 'Well, last month we had so many dollars in sales and I estimate that the profit was such and such.' At the end of the year he would be dead right, but he was doing it in his head."[56] A firm the size of Platt Brothers could change course very quickly. Camp made rapid adjustments by raising or cutting back spending,

Platt Brothers factory, c. 1940, viewed from the southwest. The long line of brick buildings went up during the mid-1890s reconstruction. To the right, barely visible through the branches, is the Nathan Platt/Alfred Platt House. The factory complex across the river, at the upper left, is the Bristol Company. (Platt Brothers and Company)

based on this keen awareness of monthly results, particularly the amount of new orders. While never spending in anticipation of orders, he did push for higher outlays while the work was in the shop and before receiving payment for it.

The key areas of spending were wages, equipment purchases, and dividends. Hourly wages went down again before several increments restored them to nominal precrisis levels during the first half of 1934. Thereafter Camp did not use wages as a means to improve the financial picture, opting instead to juggle capital purchases, dividends, bank loans, and the securities account. He confined equipment purchases to refining existing processes, renewing some older equipment, and slowly completing the development of wire production capacity that the financial crisis had cut short. Dividends received a high priority as the finances improved. On occasion, during busy periods, short-term bank loans and sales from the securities account covered dividends, bonuses for workers, and new machinery. During slow times Camp resisted increasing indebtedness by deferring capital purchases and not giving bonuses. Despite the general policy of keeping the family happy with ample dividends, he would sacrifice dividends in favor of operating capital instead of slashing capacity to keep dividends high. The original purpose of the securities account—tying the stockholders into long-term ownership—resumed its primacy over the provision of financial backing for operating or capital expenditures, and starting in 1933 the sales of stocks or bonds required a vote of the board.[57]

Beyond Camp's hard eye for the bottom line, Hart's command of the company's technology, and the efforts and abilities of the Platt Brothers work force, the company's survival in this period also depended on the personal motivation of the principals. If Platt had folded, the liquidation of the securities account and real estate holdings, as well as income from Patent Button, would have supported very comfortable lives for the owning families. But Orton Camp and Howard Hart liked their work and wanted to continue doing it. Camp only reluctantly took vacations and "thoroughly enjoyed" running the company, according to his son. A later manager of the firm recalled that Camp never lost the joy of achievement: "Orton was very energetic and enthusiastic. If we got a new order, it would be like one of the first ones we ever got. He'd be all excited about it." The same manager recalled Hart's relish for engineering: "Howard would come in weekends. His idea of a nice Sunday would be to come in here and build some kind of mechanism, work on it and design it." Born to great wealth, raised in privileged circumstances, and educated at the finest schools, these men could not have spent their early lives more differently than Alfred Platt if they had come from another planet. Yet they displayed the same resolute determination to continue as manufacturers. Like the great-grandfather they had never met, they were producers.[58]

Their efforts in the 1920s to establish an extremely wide range of products and correspondingly diverse market base helped to stabilize Platt Brothers in the 1930s. The zinc went into shoes, garments, electrical products, and construction (metallizing and builders' hardware), and a host of customers bought brass and steel eyelets. Only twice, during the 1932 and 1938 economic troughs, did the firm experience a drop in revenues in all five lines of manufactured goods (Table 5).

The slow pace of orders that prevailed during 1932 continued into the early months of 1933. In March, Camp reduced all wages and salaries by an additional 10 percent. Eyelet sales slowed further, but by midsummer all of the zinc lines made slight advances. On that encouraging news the second pay cut was rescinded, and in August, Platt Brothers paid its first dividend in twenty-two months, a modest $2.50 per share ($3,000 total). In the fall the company made its first equipment purchase in a year, a new gear drive for the breakdown mill; Camp also started gradually to restore wages, and the directors voted another $2.50 dividend and restored half of the original pay cut to salaried employees. A small sale of stock in December, 115 shares of U.S. Steel, balanced the books for the year.[59]

Wire orders from American Brass had far outpaced those of other customers, and Howard Hart directed his work primarily toward meeting the requirements of this buyer: eighth-inch-diameter wire, which Platt Brothers had to bring down from three-inch-square cast bars. Late in 1933 Hart began experimenting with radical size reduction in wire rolling on several grades of zinc, including an alloy called 7AG. Consisting of seven slabs of Anaconda zinc (a brand name of the Anaconda Corporation) and one slab of Granby zinc (New Jersey Zinc Company), it was widely used for metallizing and was also woven into automotive brake linings. Hart determined through calculations that a size reduction of more than 65 percent was theoretically possible in a single pass, and he achieved 57 percent. Larger increments per pass meant that fewer passes would be required, affording considerable production economy when workers had to handle the wire every time through the rolls.[60]

The next three years met with mixed though generally positive results, ending in 1936 with the restoration of adjusted-dollar sales to the level last achieved in 1930. During 1934 the only significant equipment expenditure was to rebuild some of the decade-old fuse mills, and the dividend increased. In early 1935 the directors restored the pay of salaried employees to their highest previous rate, but otherwise an attitude of caution prevailed until the second half of the year. The first sign of renewed confidence came in August, when the board began to restore the securities account with an infusion of $10,000. From October through December dividends were awarded with unprecedented frequency, on a monthly basis, and Orton Camp budgeted $20,000 to rebuild the strip-rolling breakdown and rundown mills. At year's end sales were up, the securities account had grown, and total dividends had more than doubled from 1934. Camp resumed a wary posture in early 1936 until orders increased during the summer. Then he approved purchases of conveyors for the roll mills and a new eyelet press. The week of Thanksgiving he awarded a bonus to all employees, two weeks of pay for hourly wage earners and a half month's salary to the rest.[61]

As the nationwide recovery progressed through 1937, Platt Brothers set records in strip, eyelet, and wire sales as well as total adjusted-dollar revenues (Table 5). A new Waterbury-Farrel tandem mill for wire rolling, purchased in January, helped to double the rate of wire production; this machine incorporated two sets of rolls for successive stages of size reduction. Hart also replaced the finish mill for strip rolling with a new $13,000 machine, bought a new soaking oven, completed the mechanization of materials handling at the breakdown mill with more conveyors and a lifting table for the incoming bars, bought another eyelet machine, and budgeted the reconditioning of several old ones. Between March and September, Platt Brothers bought more Scovill stock and even loaned $20,000 to another local manufacturer in which the Harts and Camps had an interest.[62]

Camp changed course abruptly during the fourth quarter of 1937, when fuse strip sales and American Brass wire reorders failed to keep pace with those of the prior twelve months. He did authorize the expensive rebuilding of the breakdown rod mill and recommended that dividends stay at the same high level as the year before, but only after negotiating a short-term bank note for $10,000. Apart from a small sale of securities in mid-December, Platt Brothers repaid the note with income from orders on the books at the time of the loan. During 1938 orders fell sharply, particularly in wire (off 76 percent), fuse metal (off 53 percent), and tipping zinc (off 44 percent). Equipment purchases came to a standstill. Instead of paying dividends the company applied receipts to pay off a total of $50,000 it had borrowed through the first half of the year.[63]

Even while business slowed through the summer of 1938, Camp raised wages and benefits to keep pace with the recently unionized shops in the Naugatuck Valley. In July 1938, after decades of futile organization efforts, the first industrial union was formed in Waterbury when the employees at the American Brass north mill voted to join the International Union of Mine, Mill and Smelter Workers. Production staff at other shops quickly followed this lead. Camp had observed the protests and sitdown strikes that preceded the advent of industrial unionism in Waterbury, and he monitored the provisions of local labor contracts in order to keep wages at Platt slightly ahead (as did his counterparts at Patent Button). In 1935, Platt Brothers had increased employee medical coverage at a cost of some 40 percent more in premiums. Opposition to unionization at Platt Brothers probably motivated a wage increase in December 1937, which was achieved by a policy of paying for 50 hours while keeping the standard work week at 47.5 hours (7:00 A.M. to 4:30 P.M., five days). In June 1938, with sales down to almost half of the prior year's level, no dividends yet issued and none in sight, and a $30,000 loan taken out that month, Platt Brothers established its first paid summer vacation, the week of July 4. This action contrasted starkly with the policy at American Brass, where the union organization drive during July responded directly to the company's decision to rescind the paid vacation policy that had been established the year before. Though a traditionalist who probably disliked the idea of unions, Camp did not anger the workers through recalcitrance over wages and benefits nor embitter himself with nostalgic longing for the days of greater employer power. He had a genuine regard for employees but did not resort to transparent appeals of fellowship with them. In wage and benefit policies Camp exhibited a mixture of idealism and practicality. The ideal—assuring that Platt Brothers continue in manufacturing—had not changed. And in practical terms, he understood that production required production workers who would devote their best efforts to the task. He enhanced the firm's stability by offering compensation the workers considered fair, and he protected his own ability to exercise virtually total control over the firm by paying for the privilege.[64]

The small size of Platt Brothers and the correspondingly minimal management structure also contributed to the unusually peaceful labor relations and Camp's ability to prevent unionization at Platt Brothers during the late 1930s. After John Goss, the chief executive of Scovill, met with a committee of workers in 1938 to hear their complaints over piecework rates and favoritism on the part of foremen, one of the committee members recalled Goss's plea of ignorance during that meeting: "[Goss said] when people start squeaking, I don't know anything. I'm in the office." While Orton Camp may have been skeptical and brusque, his frequent appearances in the shop and his close attention to every detail prevented him from becoming a distant and uninvolved symbol of management. Workers at the large employers most feared favoritism in layoff and rehiring, but Platt Brothers did not lay people off. The long-held policy of avoiding precipitous growth might have cost the firm some short-term revenue windfalls, but it also prevented rapid downward adjustment by layoffs and the demoralization over lack of job security that afflicted the workers at Scovill and American Brass. The purposely small scale of operation thus played a significant role, not only in Platt Brothers' ability to thrive on small orders and small markets but also in the permanence of employment that enabled the workers to identify their own interests with that of the company.[65]

By committing Platt Brothers to survival as a manufacturer and an employer, Camp imposed rigorous discipline on the decisions that he and Hart made. To increase production he favored buying better machinery or rebuilding older equipment rather than adding a shift and then discarding the new employees when orders slowed. Although the short-term cost of briefly augmenting the work force was less than the capital cost of new equipment, and the capital expenditures took the place of dividends, upgrading the machinery not only reassured the workers but also improved efficiency and productivity for the long term. The discipline for Camp and Hart came in selecting which operations to improve and evaluating the means to improve them. Wisely choosing such expenditures demanded a close understanding of the production processes, an approach to management extending far beyond the statistical assessment of financial performance that characterized the work of managers such as Scovill's John Goss.

In 1939 and 1940, production increased for two years running in every area, for the first time since 1925–1926. Though total annual revenue did not approach the record year of 1937 (Table 5), Camp was sufficiently comforted to increase all expenditures. Dividends, wages, salaries, and vacation pay advanced. Platt Brothers bought a new rolling mill for fuse strip, built an addition to the casting shop to hold a new furnace, and completed the development of wire production to the point at which it would remain for fifteen years. Platt's largest wire customer, American Brass, had begun selling directly to Metallizing Engineering Company, a distributor, rather than to the far more segmented market of those who used the metallizing equipment. To match the potential of this larger and steadier market, Platt Brothers doubled its capacity with a new upright drawing machine from Waterbury-Farrel. With eight dies and the ability to repeat a pass through the dies, it could produce finer increments than was possible with the Morgan machine and could meet a wider range of specifications.[66]

During the most prolonged business crisis of the twentieth century Camp managed to consolidate the expansive developments begun in the 1920s. The majority of the equipment was still more than ten years old, but most of it had been reconditioned. The work force had grown slightly during the 1930s, to between forty-five and fifty employees, and they were compensated as well or slightly better than most other factory workers in Waterbury. Well poised to take part in the explosive growth of wartime production, Platt Brothers had also reached the optimum size for Orton Camp.

Platt Brothers first felt the war economy during 1941 in the orders for accurately rolled strip, which went into fuses that caused artillery shells to fire before impact. These shells were entirely a Connecticut product: Platt sold the strip to Ingraham Clock of Bristol, which made the fuses and sold them to Scovill for assembly into the brass shells. Coincidentally, as an artillery officer in Europe, Orton Camp, Jr., later put some of those fuses to use: "I directed the firing of a lot of shells and I have to assume that some of them had the zinc fuse metal in them that Platt Brothers had produced. I remember looking at the shells and looking at the fuses. A lot of them were marked SMC, Scovill Manufacturing Company." The products that had yielded high profits in prior wars—eyelets and commercial zinc strip for Patent Button's uniform and tent buttons—also surged (Table 5).[67]

Platt Brothers achieved record production in 1941, some 35 percent higher than the former peak in 1937. There were no substantial additions to plant or equipment, though the work week increased to fifty-five hours. Awash in cash, the company raised wages and vacation pay, awarded a two-week year-end bonus, and matched the $42,000 dividend yield of 1937. At the end of the year, $50,000 worth of government bonds went into the securities account.[68]

Camp grew more careful in his management despite the unprecedented levels of production. During 1942 and 1943, as output reached new highs, the firm made only one significant acquisition, a twenty-five-year-old rolling mill and slitting machine. A handful of new hires brought the work force to about fifty-five people, where it would remain for a decade thereafter (with no postwar layoffs). Camp did not trust the volatile military markets, in which sales depended on the decisions of procurement officers instead of a broad customer base; between 1941 and 1945 the line most sensitive to government purchasing—fuse metal—fluctuated sharply (Table 5). Production for military use also came under the excess profit provisions of the Defense Appropriation Act of 1942. Platt Brothers refunded to the government $18,000 out of an operating profit of $102,900 for 1943, $16,700 out of $117,900 for 1944, and $36,700 out of $178,900 for 1945. Camp traveled to Washington to negotiate these refunds, and the entire process took at least eight months after the close of each year. This uncertainty contributed to his reluctance to make capital expenditures and expand the work force, and it kept dividends low in relation to net revenues during the war years. In 1946, as the brass mills again struggled with postwar overcapacity and labor strife due to layoffs and wage cuts, Platt Brothers too faced a loss of operating profit, amounting to more than 36 percent. But with earnings retained from the war years the company raised its dividends and increased the Christmas bonus by 80 percent. This bounty amid the pain of other manufacturers' postwar contraction could only deepen Orton Camp's conviction about slow growth and long-term stability.[69]

Camp devoted increasing time to civic affairs in the 1940s. Along with the publisher of the local newspapers, in 1940 he had founded the Waterbury Tax Payers Association, which monitored municipal expenditures and argued for lower taxes. Near the end of the war the mayor appointed Camp to the Board of Finance, where he successfully opposed general-obligation bonding in favor of bond issues only for specific projects. (Later, his vociferous objection to a five-year rebuilding plan for the city cost him reappointment to the board.) In 1947, Camp helped to start the Naugatuck Valley Industrial Council, which he served as treasurer for twenty-two years. Besides lobbying on behalf of manufacturing interests, the Council compiled the annual wage and benefit surveys that both Platt Brothers and Patent Button used to set the compensation of their workers. Though still at Platts Mills every day, Camp no longer spent all of his time managing the business.[70]

The transition to peacetime required some adjustment for Camp and Platt Brothers. The least military-dependent lines, eyelets and wire, offered the best chance to compensate for falloffs in war production. Because he no longer devoted every hour to Platt Brothers, Camp hired a salesman in July 1945. Merwin Camp (no relation) came over from Scovill to concentrate on eyelets, with "an occasional sortie into a zinc customer." In 1946 he produced a 37 percent increase in eyelet orders, for gross revenue of over a quarter-million dollars. Zinc wire production rode on the marketing efforts of American Brass, surpassing wartime output in 1946 before settling back to slightly lower levels. In August 1946, Orton Camp reported to the board that further demand would require "increasing production of zinc wire," but the small decline in American Brass orders postponed any concrete plans.[71]

Camp tolerated some preliminary investigation of further applications for zinc. Platt Brothers shared the cost of Patent Button's experiments with the electrodeposition of zinc strip, which began in December 1944 and continued through the end of 1945. Howard Hart began gathering data on zinc's sacrificial protective action in rustproofing, clipping articles from trade publications and technical journals and ordering reports from research laboratories and government agencies. Rusting occurs when iron or steel comes into contact with a dilute electrolyte, such as the moisture in the air. With a lower electrical potential than iron, zinc will oxidize, or get pulled into solution with the electrolyte, more rapidly than iron. As the U.S. Bureau of Standards explained, zinc not only coats; it protects when the coating fails:

When any steel article with a metallic coating is scratched or abraded so that a small area of the steel is exposed, the two dissimilar metals, together with a small amount of moisture derived from the atmosphere, will form a tiny galvanic cell, set up a current, and start corrosion. That metal which is electronegative [lower in potential] to the other will be the one to be oxidized, while the electropositive metal will remain uncorroded. Therefore, if the coating metal is zinc, it is zinc that will be oxidized, while the iron remains bright and uncorroded.

This property of zinc, known as cathodic protection, was the basis for Platt Brothers' business in wire for metallizing, but Hart had always been more concerned with producing the base-size wire for American Brass than with exploring further applications. With the plant busy and Camp set against further development efforts, Hart's explorations did not proceed beyond collecting general data. Spectacular financial results in this period help to explain Camp's reluctance: in both 1950 and 1951 the company exceeded $1 million in sales.[72]

Eyelets accounted for more sales than the other lines, followed in order by wire, the two grades of rolled strip, celluloid, and tipping zinc. When receipts and orders for eyelets both ran high, Camp consented to add capacity, which was easy to do. In August 1950, for instance, he simply ordered two machines from Waterbury-Farrel for 1951 delivery. Wire posed a different problem. It required much more room: during breakdown rolling the rod reached 110 feet in length before reaching a diameter small enough to be coiled. And in comparison to eyelets, it required far more labor to produce. In 1953 Platt Brothers achieved record wire production and reached the limit of its capacity. During the summer Camp and Hart started discussing the continuous casting of rod. By casting a single piece of virtually any length, much of the furnace work and rolling and the irksome delay of joining short pieces could be eliminated. After analyzing all of the available technology, Hart concluded that Platt Brothers could develop a superior process and, with Camp, decided to hire an engineer to undertake the project.[73]

Since 1932, Platt Brothers had elaborated on but not advanced beyond the market and technical foundation established in the 1920s. The company had survived when the nation's economy plunged and had flourished when general industrial activity advanced. The continuous-casting project, however, departed from the strategy of Orton Camp's middle years and reflected the recognition that Platt Brothers needed the same kind of renewal that he and Hart had brought in the 1920s if it were to survive for another generation. Camp was sixty-three years old in 1953, Hart was almost sixty, and none of the younger family members had the engineering training that they, particularly Hart, had brought to the business. Though they might not have recognized the portent of the decision, when they hired an engineer to explore continuous rod-casting, they placed the firm's technological development in the hands of someone outside the family for the first time in almost a hundred years, since Ben Bristol's work on roll forming.

"You Can Really Make This?"

Milton Grele arrived in February 1954 to develop a continuous casting process. A native of the Naugatuck Valley, he had earned engineering degrees from Rensselaer Polytechnic Institute and Yale. For seven years at the National Advisory Committee for Aeronautics in Cleveland, Grele had worked on the development of a nuclear-powered airplane. Seeking relocation to his home area and a job with less administrative burden, he answered Platt Brothers' listing in the Yale Employment Bureau newsletter. Grele's first impression: "Old, staid and conservative would be a good way of describing it. . . . The machinery looked old. The building was very old. The office was definitely old; it was just an old farmhouse." He also saw "good backing, with a promise for future changes and expansion."[74]

Grele examined every patent on continuous casting, gaining "minimal" help. The Properzi process led the field at that time. Based on a water-cooled casting wheel with a peripheral groove, it produced rod at a high rate of speed but also had a tendency to produce "lapovers" that caused slivers in the wire. Grele developed a method based on passing molten

Continuous rod casting machine. (Platt Brothers and Company)

zinc through an aperture (originally seven-sixteenths-inch diameter) in a graphite die, which was cooled with water so that the metal would be solid as it exited the die. Then the rod would be fed by rollers to tandem mills for further processing. The problem came with the method of withdrawing the rod as it left the die, and the solution, in the spring of 1955, came from trial and error:

We tried repeatedly to withdraw the metal out at a constant rate and we were very unsuccessful. One day we brought it out in a discontinuous motion by starting it and stopping it, moving a half inch or so in a fraction of a second, and it started going successfully. We didn't have a very sophisticated feed roll, in fact it was hand-operated. But we were casting and [the wire] started heading down toward Union City! We didn't want to stop. Everyone was so excited.

Grele then devised a powered withdrawal roll and refined the process toward starting production.[75]

In May and June 1955, Camp and Hart obtained cost estimates for building an addition to the north mill and equipping it with the new process. They projected a cost saving of $.015 a pound in labor and overhead, compared with the old methods of casting and breakdown rolling to produce seven-sixteenths rod. In July the directors approved a budget of $75,000 to install continuous casting, a decision of some magnitude because that amount exceeded the entire profit of the prior year. Platt Brothers let the construction contract and started work on the casting machine.[76]

Grele and Hart scheduled a meeting for August 19, 1955, with Waterbury-Farrel engineers to discuss the tandem rolling equipment that would process the rod as it left the continuous caster. That day, after a wet summer and three days of rain, the Naugatuck River overflowed its banks, gathered momentum and volume by breaching dams in the upper-valley communities, and bore down on Waterbury with devastating force. Curtiss Hart recalled the scene as he reached the west bank, opposite the plant: "I stood on the railroad tracks by the Bristol Company and took some pictures. While I was there one of the main buildings washed into the river. When I walked back up to Bristol Street, the tracks washed out. I could see that some of the high buildings that were still standing on the other side of the river had the water eight, ten feet up the side of them." Merwin Camp described the plant when he arrived, after the flood subsided:

The only thing left standing on the mill floor was the large breaking-down roll. That did not move. The brick building housing the Eyelet Department was left intact, minus windows, but with at least two feet of mud around each eyelet machine, plus half a telephone pole and debris of all kinds inside. The road between the office and the mill was a wide, long and deep hole. I found a man's body wedged in an apple tree in back of the office, and another body on a newly formed debris island in the river. Very hot weather followed, and [noxious] smell was everywhere. The office had no first-floor windows left and there must have been eighteen inches of mud on that floor, plus turned over desks, files and chairs in the wet mud.

Platt Brothers had washed down the river.[77]

The following Monday, Orton Camp had the surviving files moved to his personal office in a downtown office building and "the girls that were in the office were on duty and the phones were ringing." Camp and Hart immediately decided to rebuild. "There was no question," said Curtiss Hart. Orton Camp, Jr., by then a director of the firm, remembered the emergency directors' meeting five days after the flood: "Some of the stockholders felt that the company should fold. The company had a substantial portfolio of common stock . . . and that stock should be distributed to the stockholders and say goodbye. . . . My father was not going to let the flood defeat him. Against some of the stockholders' wishes, he went ahead." The majority decided to "spend a minimum amount on the present site and make plans for a new building on a new site," east of the old plant, on land the company owned that was forty feet higher.[78]

Camp's son recalled him "working like the devil trying to figure out where the money was going to come from." He began negotiating with the Small Business Administration (SBA) for a $500,000 loan, which came through in March 1956. The loan, technically a "participation note," required that private sources carry 25 percent of the debt. Camp negotiated

Salvage work after the 1955 flood. The riverbank is strewn with zinc strip and wire. (Platt Brothers and Company)

with two local banks, Waterbury National and Colonial Trust, to secure that part of the package. At the end of the year he sold securities the company owned for a profit of $70,000, which reduced Platt Brothers' losses for 1955 to a little under $100,000.[79]

In resuming production, fuse metal received the highest priority because the fuse makers could not get the accurate strip anywhere else. After erecting a temporary structure around the remaining furnaces, the furnace crew started casting zinc bars. Scovill Manufacturing Company let Hart and Grele adapt an unused rolling mill for breaking down zinc. They fished two fuse mills out of the river, renovated them, and set them up in the old shipping room, which had withstood the flood. The eyelet crew cleaned and rewired their machines one at a time. By December, Camp reported that sales and production of fuse metal and eyelets were "better than average." Two weeks after the flood Grele had also resumed the development of the continuous-casting process by ordering the tandem rolling mill from Waterbury-Farrel. The following summer the continuous-casting line went into operation in the new building.[80]

In January 1956, Camp hired a civil engineer to help build the new factory. Richard Miller, a Waterbury native trained as an engineer at the University of Toronto, had worked for ten years in plant engineering and construction and for five years in a variety of other industrial jobs. After the flood hit Waterbury, he started looking for a job helping someone to rebuild. Through his acquaintance with plant superintendent Leaman Harvey, Miller obtained an interview with Orton Camp, Sr., beginning an often awkward but long-lasting and ultimately fruitful relationship: "The main memory I have of that [interview] was [Camp saying] that "We are only a small company and we can't pay much money." . . . His relationship with me was very typical as to his modesty, his unassuming and deliberate pattern of living, not to let anybody know his worth. . . . It took me several months, at least, before I realized that he owned half the town." Orton Camp, Jr., recalled that "[Miller] was aggressive, and I think he rubbed my father the wrong way because he was, but he did a good job." When the plant was built, Orton Camp, Sr., offered to keep Miller on the payroll, as Miller recalled, "if I could find a job to do. . . . I gradually got involved in the correspondence and the sales that were happening in the office. It wasn't long before it was obvious to me that if I was going to contribute anything to the company it had to be in sales." In consenting, Orton Camp, Sr., acknowledged that his own efforts in securing financing and rebuilding the company had left the zinc customers unattended, and he had to overcome his preference for family involvement in such matters.[81]

The four years following the flood demanded the same kind of juggling that Camp had employed to guide the firm through the Depression, with the additional constraints that Platt Brothers had to mortgage all of its assets to secure the SBA note, and the private lenders asked for representation on the board. The directors amended the bylaws in order to seat Harlan Griswold, the president of Waterbury National Bank. A new, college-trained superintendent, John Aldrich, took over the plant management after Harvey retired, but the lenders requested a more formal approach to financial reporting than Camp's three-by-five cards. Platt Brothers then set up the new post of general manager and hired Norman Greist, a Harvard Business School graduate. Greist's cost-accounting systems may have comforted the lenders, but the results they showed did not: net losses of more than $116,000 in 1956 and some $65,000 in 1958, low profits of $12,450 for 1957 and $3,200 for 1959. Besides the added burden of debt service, the company incurred some $3,000 greater monthly operating costs in the new plant. (Much of the added cost came from the loss of waterpower that had directly driven selected rolling processes and powered generators that furnished a portion of the electricity; the new plant ran entirely on purchased electric power.) For the stockholders, dividends were only a fond memory.[82]

Orton Camp, Sr., submitted to the management changes but would not compromise what he believed to be the fundamental strength of the firm—its way of doing business rather than its account balances, although in the long term the reputation did help the finances. Miller recalled some frustration over Camp's view:

In the beginning, it seemed to me that if a sales effort could with reasonable assurance increase the profits, you could justify that sales effort by the probability of additional profits. Mr. Camp would practically never agree that that was reason enough to change a process or a product or anything else. . . . He would never have been happy losing money . . . . but still, making money was never a primary objective in my observation. . . . The objectives were to establish a quality product without worrying about the price, and to make certain that Platt's reputation with every customer for product quality and fair dealing was never impugned.

Miller adjusted to those objectives, aided by the fact that they applied to his performance as well: "I was never brought to task for not selling enough." Particularly in fuse metal, a reputation for integrity was crucially important:

These sixteen fuse companies were intensely competitive and did everything they could to get an advantage over each other. Yet they were all bound to one [zinc strip] supplier. When I got to know all of these fuse customers, to tour all of their plants and see all of their equipment and techniques . . . it was obvious to me that I could make or break any fuse company if I were willing to divulge what I knew. We made a very strong thing of having every fuse manufacturer trust us implicitly not to give away any secret, any product, any information, any sales figures, and having established that reputation we suffered very little from competition.

He also began to see the value of occasionally holding back in such a specialized business as zinc: "Every fuse had a metal cap which was an eyelet-machine product of copper or some alloy. . . . While we all knew that every fuse [strip] customer was a potential eyelet customer too, we made no attempt to compete for those eyelet products. There was reluctance to test our reputation in a highly competitive line with these same customers who bought the strip, which was noncompetitive." Even while struggling out of the debt from rebuilding, Camp preferred to defer some eyelet business in favor of protecting Platt Brothers' long-standing position in accurate strip.[83]

In 1958, which began with Camp's report to the board that "business does not look good," American Brass lost its contract with Metallizing Engineering Company. Overnight, Platt Brothers lost some thirty thousand pounds a month in wire business, and Miller started to work on recapturing some of it. He compiled a list of every company in the metallizing business—"it turned out that in every big city there are two or three"—and concentrated on the larger users who did not depend on Metallizing En-

Zinc furnaces, 1957, in the rebuilt plant. Caster Joe Ketrys (right) and an unknown helper are using a conveyor cart to charge the furnace with a load of slabs. (Mattatuck Museum)

gineering for technical data. Grele, who became superintendent in early 1959, started working on a production line that took zinc from the continuous-casting process through the final redrawing operations to the sizes that American Brass had been supplying. He also developed coiling and packaging for smaller lots, instead of the bulk shipments that American Brass had received. Miller started sending sample coils to the firms on his list, and "pretty soon those who were interested in saving a few cents a pound started buying from us direct." The orders started slowly, and the production and packaging processes developed along with them. By 1960 these efforts had restored the wire business to prior volume, although the single customer had been replaced by more than a hundred. After debt service and the costs of developing slightly expanded manufacturing capability, the company still showed a loss for most months.[84]

In restoring the wire business Miller gained a familiarity with most of the nation's zinc users. Though he initially targeted the metallizing market, he began to receive inquiries regarding other products. Platt Brothers broke into the building materials business by casting and rolling a zinc-copper-titanium alloy used for roofing and flashing. Beginning in 1959, Grele adapted the continuous-casting line to produce the rectangular divider strip used in terrazzo floors. With different tooling the same process also produced the heavy D-shaped zinc wire, known as "skid wire," that electrical manufacturers wrapped around insulated cables to protect them when pulled through conduits. The fuse strip business expanded to other non-ferrous alloys (copper, brass, bronze, and phosphor bronze), which Platt would buy, then reroll and slit to the accurate dimensions required in fuses.[85]

One of Miller's new contacts, American Smelting and Refining Company (ASARCO), developed and sold cathodic-protection products utilizing zinc's sacrificial quality in relation to iron. Most of the applications required zinc anodes in the form of large slabs, which did not fit Platt Brothers' intent of making more precise products with a higher value added in manufacturing. During one of his occasional visits Miller learned of a zinc anode that ASARCO had devised but could not obtain: "a long, skinny piece [of zinc] with a [steel] wire in it so that you could weld it" to the steel being protected. When Miller took the idea back to Waterbury, Orton Camp, Sr., told him "there wasn't any point in working on such a product." But Grele was intrigued: "One Saturday afternoon Milt Grele was fooling around in the plant and he made some short pieces by experimentally continuously casting a zinc rod around some lengths of straight steel wire. . . . We left the pieces lying around the plant. Eventually Orton Camp [Sr.] saw one of them and said, 'You can really make this?' Milt said yes." In 1963, Platt Brothers signed a development contract with ASARCO; Platt would work on producing the "cored rod," and ASARCO would market it.[86]

ASARCO wanted longer pieces than could be cast by the conventional pouring methods. Once again the continuous-casting line supported a new venture, although Grele had to address chemical and metallurgical issues beyond the more mechanically oriented problems of prior work. The rod would not function properly if the zinc had more than the slightest trace of iron in it—"a very difficult trick," Miller recalled, because the iron dissolved slightly in the molten bath of zinc. Passing the wire through the zinc bath as quickly as possible helped, as did starting with galvanized wire. The rolling that reduced the diameter and elongated the rod also elongated the embedded steel wire, which could harden from the tension and increase its tendency to crack. At this time Grele began improving the firm's laboratory capability to conduct the necessary tests on the cored rod, in part to assure that the core remained intact after rolling. At first Platt Brothers made hundred-foot lengths, and ASARCO "thought that was great." ASARCO named it "Diamond Line," after the shape imparted by the grooved rolls, and sold it to protect underwater electrical conduits, the holds of oil tankers, pipelines, and above-ground water tanks.[87]

Added to the business in eyelets, zinc strip, and zinc wire, these new lines helped Platt Brothers break even for the first six months of 1961, the longest period without an operating loss since the flood. At the end of the year the net operating profit stood at $38,900. As annual profits rose through 1964, Platt Brothers began prepaying the SBA note and started to install another continuous-casting production line. In the first half of 1965, with the new continuous-casting line operating, the steady operating profits convinced the directors to pay the remaining SBA balance on August 19, 1965, the ten-year anniversary of the flood and ten years before it was due. In December the stockholders received their first dividends since the flood.[88]

Over the next two years, as they had done during the 1920s and early 1950s, when rising production and sales coincided with healthy cash balances, Orton Camp, Sr., and Howard Hart raised the shop wages and benefits and renewed and slightly expanded the production capability: new eyelet machines, an addition to the rolling department, and the development of a new wire-drawing machine. This time, however, Norman Greist set the wages, and Milton Grele specified the purchases and designed the new machine. On March 1, 1968, Camp and Hart retired. Orton Camp, Jr., became the president, although his primary duties remained at Patent Button, where he had become vice-president. Two years later, Norman Greist became the first nonfamily president of Platt Brothers.[89]

At Patent Button the postwar performance fluctuations ran opposite to those of Platt Brothers. During the war high military demand had brought splendid results. But while Platt Brothers enjoyed steady profits in the late 1940s and early 1950s, Patent Button "was in trouble," according to Orton Camp, Jr.: "They had lost a lot of money right after the war, were heavily in debt, and borrowed a lot of money from the Reconstruction Finance Corp., but was only given the money by the government if the stockholders put up some more money on their own. Business was very good, we were very busy most of the time, and we didn't lay off people, [but] we had serious cash problems at Patent Button Company in those years." Since the two firms shared substantially the same list of stockholders, the high Platt Brothers dividends in the early 1950s assisted the family members in weathering the down years at Patent Button.[90]

While Platt Brothers suspended dividends during its recovery from the flood, Patent Button managed to pull out of its difficulties. As Platt Brothers always rose or fell according to its technical abilities, the button business performed according to its success at marketing, and a new sales manager had restored high sales and profits. By the mid-1960s, David Hart and Orton Camp, Jr., decided it was "time to get out," as Camp described: "It's got a good track record, it's making good money. We don't have anyone in the family interested, quite frankly anyone capable of coming along in the company, and we said let's sell it." They offered the firm to a competitor, which was itself acquired by the conglomerate TRW before the sale went through in 1968. Camp ran the plant for TRW until, disillusioned with corporate oversight, he retired in 1974.[91]

For the first time in over a century, the holdings of Alfred Platt's descendants did not include buttonmaking. Any regret was quickly tempered, however, as one of Platt Brothers' newer products achieved unexpected and unprecedented success. In 1973, ten years after the original cored-rod development contract, ASARCO delivered the stirring news to Richard Miller that the Alyeska Pipeline Service Company wanted to use Diamond Line for cathodic protection of some four hundred miles of the Alaska oil pipeline that ran underground. With protection on both sides, the pipeline would need more than eight hundred miles of cored rod. Grele readied coiling and packaging systems to handle much longer pieces. In January 1975, Platt started shipping eighty thousand pounds (about 160,000 feet) a month. Then, as Grele recalled: "They said they needed more, and we went to 160,000 pounds a month. They needed more, and we were shipping it by air. Then it went to 240,000 pounds a month. Finally it went to 320,000 pounds a month. We really felt our oats! We felt, hey, we really know how to do this now!" Two continuous-casting lines, running around-the-clock, turned out 2.8 million pounds of the cored rod, invoiced at some $2 million. Extra dividends in March, August, and December brought the year's total to $96,000. The directors required scant deliberation to appoint Milton Grele president in June 1975 and to approve his recommendation that Richard Miller be appointed to the new position of vice president for sales. The new management immediately applied one of Orton Camp, Sr.'s favored tactics of spending most heavily when the plant was busy and the backlog high: $100,000 to purchase a continuous-casting machine for strip; $200,000 for new melting furnaces, rolling mills, and slitting mills to accompany the new strip machine; $200,000 for an addition to house all of the new equipment; and a 6 percent increase in all wages and salaries.[92]

Successful transition to nonfamily management depended on the character of the firm as well as the abilities of the new officers. Orton Camp, Sr., continued as board chairman, considerably easing the transfer. Having worked closely with Grele and Miller for twenty years, Camp could entrust them with the firm because he knew that they had absorbed his own approach to manufacturing, which he had in turn derived from key features of the company he inherited. Though the Camps and Harts, who owned all of the stock, appreciated the substantial dividends, the owners did not measure performance solely on the basis of short-term financial results. As chairman, Camp assessed the new management as he had assessed himself. He looked for long-term stability based on continued expansion of selected technological capabilities and the development of new products for specialized, and profitable, niche markets. Unlike the custodial oversight of

Orton P. Camp, Sr., and Howard P. Hart, at the time of their retirement. (Platt Brothers and Company)

nonfamily managers in the early twentieth century, or the devotion to marketing that the Porters had contributed, the management that took over in 1975 accepted responsibility for the entire range of concerns that had previously been handled on a comprehensive basis only by family members.

Grele and Miller relished the opportunity. During the pipeline contract Grele remembered thinking, "We can do anything!" Miller appreciated the excitement of developing new business: "There always seemed to be something, either a new eyelet project or special zinc wire or new zinc alloy that we were working on, something that we'd develop to take the place of one we'd lost." These explorations expanded on established product lines and customer relationships. Among the products that achieved regular production and yielded steady profits were the elements for a new type of automobile fuse, a series of cored-rod products for the cathodic protection of steel structures such as bridges, and a heavy, continuously cast anode for batteries.[93]

In the most spectacular instance, automotive fuses, the company's long-established characteristics of specialized technical facility, agile response to niche markets, and a priority on premium pricing in noncompetitive lines all came into play. A longtime fuse strip customer, Littel Fuse (based outside Chicago), sought Platt Brothers' aid in making a radically redesigned fuse. The new fuse featured a molded plastic body with a bent link cut from zinc strip that was plated along its edges and had an exposed zinc surface down the middle. The unplated surface was also thinner than the edges, and the entire strip had to meet stringent dimensional specifications. Littel Fuse had bought Platt fuse strip as the base material but had failed to produce suitable plated and machined strip for the new links. Miller brought the problem to Grele, who solved it in "a month or so." The Littel Fuse engineers had milled out the center of the base strip, then tried to mask the center while plating the edges. In the kind of insight that seems simpler in retrospect than during development, Grele instead plated the entire base strip and then made the central groove, leaving "fresh mill zinc" down the center of the strip. Grele described the means of making that groove as "Rube Goldberg machines," and Miller identified long experience with zinc as a critical aspect of the innovation: "[Grele] had been in the zinc business forever, and zinc is not like other metals. It lends itself to different techniques." After viewing a sample, the president of Littel Fuse visited Grele and Miller in Waterbury. According to Miller, a familiar exhange ensued: "'I understand you can make this.' Milt said yes." Littel Fuse offered $1 a pound for as much as Platt could supply. A week later Miller visited Chicago with the counterproposal of $5 a pound, which Littel Fuse accepted.[94]

As all of the domestic automakers adopted the new fuses, Littel Fuse grew uncomfortable with having only a single source for the strip and persuaded Platt Brothers to sell it the technology. In the early 1980s, when Japanese auto producers also began to use the innovative fuses, Platt Brothers sold its strip manufacturing methods to the Littel Fuse licensee in Japan. Platt Brothers continued to profit by selling the base strip to the recipients of the production method. Though this reversal in the typical direction for technology transfer was remarkable by itself in light of recent history— "You don't usually sell know-how to the Japanese," asserted Grele—another long-term aspect of Platt Brothers' approach to manufacturing proved critical in the arrangement. Platt Brothers sought to understand fully its customer's requirements and never hesitated to guarantee the quality of its product: "They sent their engineers over here and we worked out all the details. We got to know them pretty well. If we shipped them anything they couldn't use, all they had to do was tell us and we'd give them full credit, and they would scrap it in Japan." Platt Brothers did not extend itself to make this guarantee but simply continued the same policy it had always followed.[95]

The most significant change under nonfamily management was a more structured approach to labor relations. Informal, paternalistic policies could not survive when workers no longer had frequent access to the owners. An employee handbook codified job posting and bidding for newly opened positions, job descriptions and labor grades, a problem-solving procedure, and other regulations. Grele instituted a policy of monthly meetings with groups of employees to inform them as to the state of the business and answer their questions or complaints. In 1972, Norman Greist and Orton Camp, Jr., had established an incentive plan that awarded bonuses to management based on annual profit. Under Grele the company extended profit-sharing to all employees.[96]

Money inevitably measures success in business, but as Platt Brothers has unabashedly sought profit, it has also pursued other goals. The most basic goal has been simply to survive, evident in reinvestment of revenues as well as the willingness to continue operations during periods of low revenue and even through catastrophe. Though many point to the flood of 1955 as the stimulus for plant renewal that enabled subsequent success, the flood offers insufficient explanation for what followed. Many other local companies suffered severe damage, but most took it as a reason to limit further investment. Furthermore, the post-1955 success in the zinc business depended on the continuous-casting process that Orton Camp, Sr., and Howard Hart had committed Platt Brothers to develop more than a year before the flood.

A policy of survival, or at least favoring long-term stability over short-term gain, also dictated restraint in pursuing some obvious sales opportunities. In the early twentieth century, for instance, the children of William and Clark Platt objected strongly to Thomas Porter's moving Patent Button into buckles and loops, general hardware lines that were dominated by much larger firms. Fearing competition against such powerful adversaries, the family members eventually dismissed Porter. Fifty years later, a similar policy of protecting the company's role in small, less competitive markets motivated refusal by Orton Camp, Sr., to offer eyelets for fuse caps to the same customers that bought fuse element strip from Platt Brothers. In these actions, and throughout the history of the Platt enterprises, owners and managers kept alive the strategy of survival through small-market specialization first employed by Alfred, William, and Clark Platt in the 1840s.

Another goal has been to act responsibly. Platt Brothers did not subordinate every decision to the question of profit. In the words of the most recent president, "The number one item is not making money. We have a tradition to uphold." Preeminently, that tradition represents an approach to manufacturing that always adhered to certain core values: "Our customers and our suppliers like to do business with us because we're fair, we're honest and we want to do a good job for them."[97] Platt Brothers never had to rediscover quality.

Three compelling moments stand out in the long and eventful history of Platt Brothers and its predecessors, when old men refused to limit their vision by conserving the gains from a lifetime of work. At the age of eighty, Alfred Platt supervised the construction of the first brick factory at Platts Mills. He spent much of his Civil War profit on the factory and built it to last, knowing that he would not long benefit from its operation himself. In 1895, at the age of seventy-one, Clark Platt picked through the rubble of the burned-out rolling mill to recover any fragments that he could use to re-build. Then, in his role as the firm's dominant owner-manager, he depleted the ample cash reserves to build a much larger mill that served as the heart of the zinc business until the flood of 1955 destroyed it. The final image is of the sixty-five-year-old Orton Camp, Sr., presiding over the board meet-ing after the flood and overriding the dissent of his relatives to devote all of the firm's assets to another extensive rebuilding program. The recurring episodes of aggressive marketing and innovative technological development that sustained Platt Brothers were largely the work of younger people. They owed every success, however, to the aged predecessors who unquestion-ingly invested in an uncertain future.

Epilogue

CONCLUDING his pathbreaking work on batch production, Philip Scranton set forth a series of tasks to be accomplished: documenting batch manufacturing "without presuming it to be a failed effort to achieve bulk or mass production"; locating it within the more general framework of American industrial enterprise; elaborating on the "differing constructions of rationality in business, especially as they bear on the tradeoff between flexibility and routinization"; and attempting to make "more intelligible the present mix of dilemmas and opportunities while highlighting the diversity of business institutions, values, and practices."[1]

The preceding narrative has addressed the first three of those tasks and part of the fourth. The basic goal of documenting the experience of batch production took place within the larger framework of non-ferrous metal production. In the history of Platt Brothers the family-based partnership and the family-controlled corporation present an institutional alternative to the Chandler model of more widely dispersed and less emotionally involved ownership in companies run by managerial elites. The Platts, Camps, and Harts clearly favored survival as a family-owned firm rather than growth. Their story therefore demonstrates how personal and family values determined business practice, how small family firms managed generational transitions, how business families coped with the perils of success, and how family firms incorporated managerial participation by those outside the family. Yet to be addressed is whether this story can contribute any understanding of the dilemmas and opportunities encountered by manufacturers in the late twentieth century.

It is important to emphasize that batch manufacturing has always been a part of industry in the United States; its recent articulation as flexible production reflects the effort to comprehend industrial decline in the late twentieth century. The history of the Naugatuck Valley metals industries indicates that small-scale batch manufacturing characterized the origin of industrial production in entire sectors of the United States economy. Batch manufacturing as practiced by Platt Brothers and its competitors during the Second Industrial Revolution emerged directly from the characteristics of earlier production. Platt Brothers differed from the more general experience in its original, more modest goals, signified primarily by the adoption of zinc as the material of specialty. From that beginning, the firm's course diverged ever more widely from common practice as its owners and managers practiced selective expansion rather than zealously pursuing growth.

Platt Brothers' enormous array of adaptations throughout its history tend to dilute any specific insight that might be drawn from the company's experience into present dilemmas of the manufacturing sector as a whole. The firm's survival and success are a triumph of substance over structure. No method or organizing scheme proved inherently more effective than any other except as an approach to a specific set of evolving circumstances. Attention to changing markets and technology sustained the firm, but there is meager instruction to be drawn from that experience beyond the admonition that manufacturers should listen very closely to their customers and potential customers to find out what is wanted, then produce it cheaply and well.

This study can help unravel more recent industrial history by way of contrast with more general experience rather than as an object lesson for others to follow. Platt Brothers' continuing ability to win profitable niches as larger forces transformed the economic environment goes far toward explaining the company's enviable record. How did other firms and other sectors meet that challenge?

In Scranton's case studies, producers of jewelry and machine tools "both suffered reverses in the 1920s that became far more severe in the Great Depression. Yet machine tool builders held their ground until recovery dawned, whereas jewelers slid toward a lasting demoralization." Scranton applied four operational factors—price management, distinctive machine products versus easily copied jewelry designs, technical cumulation, and the direct sales of machinery versus the series of brokered transactions separating jeweler from end user—to explain the different courses of these sectors.[2] Beyond these factors, it is difficult to overlook the impact of the vast market for machinery created by the expansion of automobile production in the 1920s. In Detroit alone, dozens of major car plants opened between 1917 and 1930. Ford's vast River Rouge facility was the largest industrial complex in the world, and even the less stupendous car factories dwarfed the previous scale of manufacturing; the Fisher Body Company Fleetwood

Plant, completed in 1922, held 600,000 square feet of production space. Even during the 1930s the car companies continued to expand. The press shop at River Rouge opened in 1939, and the Lincoln plant added capacity during the Depression.[3] These factories required thousands of machine tools that represented considerable benefit to the machinery industry but had little impact on the jewelers.

A similar phenomenon occurred within sectors. Firms that sold to carmakers sustained or increased revenues and profits, while others that did not renew their customer and product base succumbed to more aggressive competitors in other regions and other nations, demoralization of leadership, and defensive financial tactics that protected personal fortunes but ultimately depleted company assets. In eastern Connecticut, a textile industry that employed tens of thousands of people in the 1880s shrank to less than a tenth that size by the 1930s. Among the integrated producers of staple goods, the largest survivor was a plant that made the cotton duck used as laminating material in rubber tires. In nineteenth-century New Haven, dozens of shops produced carriages and carriage parts. All had perished by 1930, except the one factory that had turned its capacity in stamped metal goods to the production of doorlocks, ashtrays, and decorative moldings for automobiles.[4]

If, as Scranton suggests, the 1920s represent a dividing line between industrial eras, it was the automobile industry that drew the line. The ability of long-established manufacturers in older industrial regions such as the Naugatuck Valley to build fruitful relationships with auto production, and the nature of those relationships, therefore deserve further examination as critical determinants of the course of American manufacturing enterprise during the twentieth century.

Platt Brothers' niche in fuse elements connected the firm to the rapidly growing automotive sector. Of equal importance, the company maintained diverse capability and equally diverse customers, and did not come to depend solely on the enormous automotive market. Thus, during the recent contraction in the United States auto industry, when no less a pillar of American enterprise than Ford Motor Company lost half its employees in ten years,[5] Platt Brothers' mix of products limited its exposure in the event of collapse in the car business. Furthermore, consistent attention to product quality and customer satisfaction enabled Platt Brothers to sell automotive fuse technology to the Japanese producers that competed with carmakers in the United States. Platt Brothers capitalized on the opportunities afforded by car production without becoming captive to the auto industry or any single part of it.

The role of military production in the twentieth century offers a similarly worthwhile means of examining manufacturers, particularly in light of that field's diminished prospects in the 1990s. Throughout Connecticut's metal-working region, manufacturing firms achieved their peak employment and output during the two world wars, but postwar adaptation to civilian markets eluded all but the most agile and tenacious enterprises. After World War I, debilitating levels of debt and vastly overbuilt production capacity afflicted even the most successful producers, most of which had gambled on the war lasting longer than it did. World War II brought temporary salvation from the lingering effects of postwar contraction twenty years earlier. But those producers that relied completely on the military windfall suffered disconnection from civilian customers and markets, which handicapped post–World War II performance. Ingraham Clock, for instance, which made the artillery fuses that used Platt zinc, never resumed clock production at previous levels after World War II. Instead, Ingraham concentrated on fuse production for military applications. The company had a single major customer, and marketing became a political process as a succession of Congressional representatives from Connecticut influenced the Pentagon to order Ingraham fuses. Absolute reliance on military work replaced prior broad-based sales efforts, and when the conglomerate that acquired Ingraham reduced local capacity there were no market-based alternatives to bolster production and employment levels.[6]

Conversion of defense plants to civilian production, according to a leading critic of the garrison economy, requires that defense-plant employees "unlearn the habits of work that have been appropriate for the Pentagon and learn the standards of civilian design, managing, production, and selling."[7] Military contractors design to extremely tight specifications for narrowly defined tactical functions rather than moving a rapidly designed product through the plant, then adjusting on the run according to customer response. Nor can the Pentagon's captive fabricators draw on any breadth of market awareness. An electronics firm that developed a sophisticated cardiac monitor for military aerospace use tried to sell the device to physicians. Doctors asked if the American Medical Association had approved the monitor, and if the manufacturer would indemnify users, as was standard among producers of medical equipment. These questions had not occurred to the manufacturer, which abandoned the effort rather than learn how to satisfy a demanding group of customers.[8]

This failed effort to sell an innovative product might recall the Platts' experience with zinc pipe in the 1850s. Since then, however, for over four generations, Platt Brothers cultivated an acute sense of potential niche markets as well as the ability to produce for them. If flexible production offers a solution to the predicament of overcapacity in the nation's defense plants, a similar learning process must be undertaken with unprecedented speed.

Perhaps the most important perspective that the history of Platt Brothers can offer in considering our present mix of dilemmas and opportunities lies in the depth of commitment that Alfred Platt and his successors brought to the task. It was a simple goal to survive as manufacturers, if endlessly complicated in the execution. It resulted in otherwise inexplicable actions, such as an eighty-year-old man building a new and larger factory; or, in the 1920s, the creation of a new type of highly skilled labor in fuse rolling at a time when the rest of the metal-rolling firms were accelerating efforts to isolate skill from that process. To the owners and managers of Platt Brothers, survival was a worthy goal, against which they weighed their more immediate decisions. It widened the range of possibilities from which they could choose, unbound by purely short-term considerations. That commitment cannot be imposed or enforced, but without it our dilemmas deepen and our opportunities recede.

Appendix A

Platt, Camp, and Hart Families

(Italics indicate people who played a significant management role in the family enterprises.)

GENERATION 1
Alfred PLATT (1789–1872) and Irene Blackman (1791–1863)
    Nirom Blackman Platt (1818–1863)
    Charles Sanford Platt (1820–1896)
    William Smith Platt (1822–1886)
    Clark Murray Platt (1824–1900)
    Alfred LeGrand Platt (1825–1896)
    Seabury Blackman Platt (1828–1895)

GENERATION 2
William Smith PLATT and Caroline Elizabeth Orton (1822–1901)
    Orton William Platt (1847–1847)
    Helen Irene Platt (1849–1932)
    Caroline Amelia ("Carrie") Platt (1853–1935)
    William Hubert Platt (1856–1862)
    Irving Gibbs Platt (1860–1896)

Clark Murray PLATT and Amelia Maria Lewis (1826–1916)
    Bertha Louise Platt (1851–1930)
    Lewis Alfred Platt (1854–1919)
    Edward LeGrand Platt (1857–1862)

GENERATION 3
Helen Irene Platt and *Wallace Henry CAMP* (1850–1924)
    Roland Heaton Camp (1879–1948)
    Edith Caroline Camp (1881–1942)
    Hilda Mary Camp (1888–1981)
    Orton Platt Camp (1890–1976)

Bertha Louise Platt and *Jay Hiscox HART* (1847–1918)
    Amy Louise Hart (1874–?)
    Bertha Murray Hart (1876–1930)
    Lewis Jay ("L.J.") Hart (1878–1946)
    Alfred Lucius Hart (1880–1958)
    Ruth Spencer Hart (1882–?)
    Dorothy Hart (1889–1950)
    Howard Platt Hart (1891–1970)

GENERATION 4

Orton Platt CAMP and Miriam Noble (1900–)
    Orton Platt Camp, Jr. (1922–)
    Miriam Camp (1926–)
    Nancy Camp (1931–)

Howard Platt HART and Doris Marion Variell (1897–1991)
    Curtis Variell Hart (1921–)
    Howard Spencer Hart (1924–)
    Nelson Platt Hart (1931–)

Appendix B

Statement of Orton P. Camp, Jr. Chairman of the Board, Platt Brothers and Company

Several years ago Platt family members and Platt Brothers management started to discuss the writing of the company's history. We believed Platt Brothers had an unusual and interesting story—how interesting we did not know until we saw the early drafts of this book.

Unfortunately, by the time this project got underway none of the grandchildren of William and Clark Platt—the original Platt brothers—were living. The members of that generation were at many family gatherings where they overheard or participated in discussions about the company. They took with them a great deal of anecdotal and factual information. It was also unfortunate that the 1955 flood destroyed so many of the old records.

Nevertheless, Matt Roth was enthusiastic about the project. He, and we, wanted an objective work that included everything pertinent, whether or not it was favorable to the company or the family. We think that has been achieved and we are pleased with this book.

Dick Miller, who joined the company soon after the flood and had recently retired as vice president for sales, served as the company's liaison for the project. He has served with great skill and patience, as well as contributing a wealth of information acquired during his working years.

We are proud of the Platts' integrity, tenacity and ingenuity in building the company. Their goals were modest, their determination great, and their success long lasting. Their humility and generosity did not allow them to be consumed by ambition.

While Alfred Platt's descendants are no longer involved in daily management, four of his great-great-grandchildren serve on the board of directors and are pleased to be working with the excellent staff that Milt Grele has assembled.

Orton Platt Camp, Jr.
Chairman of the Board

Notes

Introduction (pp. 1–20)

1. Caroline Ware, *The Early New England Cotton Manufacturers: A Study of Industrial Beginnings* (Boston, 1931), 3; Judith A. McGaw, *Most Wonderful Machine: Mechanization and Social Change in Berkshire Paper Making, 1801–1885* (Princeton, N.J., 1987), 8. Brooke Hindle, *Technology in Early America: Needs and Opportunities for Study* (Chapel Hill, N.C., 1966), and Thomas C. Cochran, *Frontiers of Change: Early Industrialism in America* (New York, 1981) identify many of the previously overlooked aspects of the nation's transformation to an industrial economy. In Steven Hahn and Jonathan Prude, eds., *The Countryside in the Age of Capitalist Transformation: Essays in the Social History of Rural America* (Chapel Hill, N.C., 1985), Section One (The Northeast) examines at close range some of the issues connected with incremental industrial growth. Bruce Clouette and Matthew Roth, *Bristol, Connecticut, 1785–1985* (Canaan, N.H., 1985), Section Two, surveys the small-scale enterprises of the early clock industry.

2. The foolish literature on Yankee peddling would fill a trunk. Even the reliable works, such as Richardson Wright, *Hawkers and Walkers in Early America* (Philadelphia, 1927), and J. R. Dolan, *The Yankee Peddlers of Early America* (New York, 1964), concentrate on peddlers' work in the field rather than their relationship with merchants in the producing towns. Priscilla Carrington Kline, "New Light on the Yankee Peddler," *New England Quarterly* 11 (March 1939): 80–98, highlights that relationship with extended excerpts from a peddler's reports to his storekeeper-employer. In Clouette and Roth, *Bristol*, 49–54, the relationships among peddlers, merchants, and manufacturers in the clock trade are tracked through storekeepers' accounts, which were the central documents in this web of commerce.

3. The converted shop was Potter and Snell of Deep River; interview with proprietor Charles Messerschmitt, May 1984.

4. Alfred D. Chandler, Jr., *The Visible Hand: The Managerial Revolution in American Business* (Cambridge, Mass., 1977), 1–12, 484–88.

5. Small Business Administration, *State of Small Business: A Report to the President* (Washington, D.C., 1987), is a compendium of the statistical measures used to define

small business by various government agencies and private analysts. Philip Scranton, "Diversity in Diversity: Flexible Production and American Industrialization, 1880–1930," *Business History Review* 65 (Spring 1991): 30–32, 89, questions the validity of quantitative definitions.

6. Mansel G. Blackford, "Small Business in America: An Historiographic Survey," *Business History Review* 65 (Spring 1991), 2–4.

7. Clouette and Roth, *Bristol*, 260–61.

8. Harold G. Vatter, "The Position of Small Business in the Structure of American Manufacturing, 1870–1970," in Stuart Bruchey, ed., *Small Business in American Life* (New York, 1980), 142–68 and Carson Deane, ed., *The Vital Majority: Small Business in the American Economy* (Washington, D.C., 1973). David L. Birch, *Job Creation in America: How Our Smallest Companies Put the Most People to Work* (New York, 1987) claims, for a recent period, that as many as two-thirds of new jobs were in small firms, which seems excessive.

9. Blackford, "Small Business," 4–10.

10. Rowland Berthoff, "Independence and Entrepreneurship: Small Business in the American Dream," in Stuart Bruchey, ed., *Small Business in American Life* (New York, 1980), 28–48; William Letwin, *Law and Economic Policy: The Sherman Antitrust Act* (New York, 1965). The cost, quality, and convenience advantages offered to consumers by large-scale food merchandising are thoroughly presented in M. M. Zimmerman, *The Super Market: A Revolution in Distribution* (New York, 1955).

11. McGaw, *Most Wonderful Machine*; Anthony F. C. Lewis, *Rockdale: The Growth of an American Village in the Early Industrial Revolution* (New York, 1978).

12. James H. Soltow, "Origins of Small Business and the Relationship between Large and Small Firms: Metal Fabricating and Machinery Making in New England," in Stuart Bruchey, ed.,*Small Business in American Life* (New York, 1980), 192–211.

13. *Proprietary Capitalism: The Textile Manufacture at Philadelphia, 1800–1885* (Philadelphia, 1983), and *Figured Tapestry: Production, Markets and Power in Philadelphia Textiles, 1885–1941* (Cambridge, Mass., 1989).

14. Scranton, "Diversity in Diversity," 27–90.

15. Ibid., 30–33.

16. Ibid., 35–36.

17. Ibid., 33–38.

18. Alfred D. Chandler, Jr., *Scale and Scope: The Dynamics of Industrial Capitalism* (Cambridge, Mass., 1990), 602–28.

19. Cecelia F. Bucki,*Metal, Minds and Machines: Waterbury at Work* (Waterbury, Conn., 1980), 10–14, 22–26; Matthew Roth, *Connecticut: An Inventory of Historic Engineering and Industrial Sites* (Washington, D.C., 1981), iii, 154–57.

20. The clockmaker Samuel Terry, for instance, ended his industrial career in prosperous middle age after exploiting a series of market niches; Clouette and Roth, *Bristol*, 71.

21. Kevin C. Seymour, "Inter-generational Relationships in the Family Firm: The Effect on Leadership Succession," (Ph.D. diss., California School of Professional Psychology, 1992), 1–4.

22. Chandler, *Visible Hand*, 19.

23. For instance, Daniel Bell, *The End of Ideology* (New York, 1962), chap. 2.

24. Among many examples, Barbara M. Tucker, *Samuel Slater and the Origins of the American Textile Industry, 1790–1860* (Ithaca, N.Y., 1984), discussed the early manufacturing experience; Robert G. Cleland, *A History of Phelps Dodge, 1834–1950* (New York, 1952), examined a long-lived enterprise in commerce and mining; and Peter C. Wensberg, *Land's Polaroid: A Company and the Man Who Founded It* (Boston, 1987),

considered a firm based in the new technology and consumer markets of the mid-twentieth century.

25. C. Roland Christensen, *Management Succession in Small and Growing Enterprises* (Boston, 1953), used a case study of Cole Hardware Co. to address the issue of balancing company needs and family commitments.

26. B.S. Hollander and N. S. Elman, "Family-owned Business: An Emerging Field of Inquiry," *Family Business Review* 1 (Fall 1988): 145–64.

27. Seymour, "Inter-generational Relationships," 9–13; Harry Levinson, "Conflicts That Plague Family Busineses," *Harvard Business Review* 49 (April 1971), 90–98; Grant H. Calder, "The Peculiar Problems of a Family Business," *Business Horizons* 4 (June 1961), 93–102; Herbert A. Simon, *Administrative Behavior: A Study of Decision-Making Processes in Administrative Organization* (New York, 1957), notes the lack of complete rationality under any circumstances of business ownership.

28. Manfred F. R. Kets de Vries, *The Neurotic Organization* (San Francisco, 1984), attributed the strategy of the firm to the founder's personality. Orvis F. Collins, David G. Moore, and Darab Unwalla, "The Enterprising Man and the Business Executive," *Business Topics* 12 (Winter 1964): 19–34, and Donald K. Clifford, Jr., "The Case of the Floundering Founder," *Organizational Dynamics* (Fall 1975): 21–31, contrasted the founder's total absorption in the business with the delegation and gradual withdrawal necessary for successful management transition. Louis B. Barnes and Simon A. Hershon, "Transferring Power in the Family Business," *Harvard Business Review* 54 (July–August 1976): 105–14, argued that the founder is the chief obstacle to successful transition. The long-term impact of the founder is addressed in Edgar H. Schein, "The Role of the Founder in Creating Organizational Culture," *Organizational Dynamics* (Summer 1983): 13–28.

29. Seymour, "Inter-generational Relationships," 36–55; Elaine Kepner, "The Family and the Firm: A Co-Evolutionary Perspective," *Organizational Dynamics* (Summer 1983): 26–32; Richard B. Peiser and Leland M. Wooten, "Life-cycle Changes in Small Family Businesses," *Business Horizons* (May–June 1983): 58–65; J. L. Ward, *Keeping the Family Business Healthy* (San Francisco, 1985).

30. Lawrence L. Steinmetz, "Critical Stages of Small Business Growth: When They Occur and How to Survive Them," *Business Horizons* 12 (February 1969): 29–36; Eric G. Flamholtz, *Growing Pains: How to Make the Transition from Entrepreneurship to a Professionally Managed Firm* (San Francisco, 1990); L. A. Danco, *Inside the Family Business* (Cleveland, 1980); Seymour, "Inter-generational Relationships," 21–36; Ronald E. Berenbeim, "How Business Owners Manage the Transition from Owner to Professional Management," *Family Business Review* 1 (Spring 1990): 69–111.

31. Seymour, "Inter-generational Relationships," 53–55.

32. Neil C. Churchill and Virginia L. Lewis, "The Five Stages of Small Business Growth," *Harvard Business Review* 61 (May–June 1983): 30–52.

33. Seymour, "Inter-generational Relationships," 72–87, 123–30; Ronald E. Berenbeim, *From Owner to Professional Management: Problems in Transition* (New York, 1984).

34. Philip Scranton, "Learning Manufacture: Education and Shop-Floor Schooling in the Family Firm," *Technology and Culture* 27 (January 1986): 40–62; William H. Mulligan, Jr., "The Transmission of Skill in the Shoe Industry: Family to Factory Training in Lynn, Massachusetts," in Ian M. G. Quimby, ed., *The Craftsman in Early America* (New York, 1984), 234–46.

35. Basic brass products statistics in William G. Lathrop, *The Brass Industry in the United States* (Mt. Carmel, Conn., 1926), 122–31; other statistics in United States

Census, 13th Census, *Manufactures, 1909: General Report and Analysis* (Washington, D.C., 1913), 8:124–26.

36. Henry Bronson, *The History of Waterbury, Connecticut* (Waterbury, Conn., 1858).

37. Joseph Anderson, ed., *The Town and City of Waterbury, Connecticut, from the Aboriginal Period to the Year Eighteen Hundred and Ninety-Five* (New Haven, Conn., 1896).

38. William J. Pape, *History of Waterbury and the Naugatuck Valley, Connecticut* (Chicago, 1918).

39. Theodore Marburg, *Small Business in Brass Fabricating: The Smith & Griggs Manufacturing Co. of Waterbury* (New York, 1956).

40. Bucki, *Metal, Minds and Machines,* 22–34, 38–43; Roth, *Connecticut,* 154, 169–70; Scranton, "Diversity in Diversity," 34.

41. Bucki, *Metal, Minds and Machines*; Jeremy Brecher, Jerry Lombardi, and Jan Stackhouse, *Brass Valley: The Story of Working People's Lives and Struggles in an American Industrial Region* (Philadelphia, 1982).

42. For instance, Michael J. Piore and Charles F. Sabel, *The Second Industrial Divide: Possibilities for Prosperity* (New York, 1984).

1. "A Sett of Rolls for Hard Metal" (pp. 21–49)

1. The intergenerational rhythm of land hunger in colonial Connecticut and its role in the expansion of settlement in Bruce C. Daniels, *The Connecticut Town: Growth and Development, 1635–1790* (Middletown, Conn., 1979); see also Stewart H. Holbrook, *The Yankee Exodus: An Account of Migration from New England* (Seattle, 1950), and Lois K. M. Rosenberry, *Migrations from Connecticut Prior to 1800,* Tercentenary Pamphlet no. 43 (Hartford, Conn., 1934). Platt family history in G. Lewis Platt, *The Platt Lineage* (New York, 1891), 66–71, 185–88; *The Warren, Little, Lothrop, Park, Dix, Whitman, Fairchild, Platt, Wheeler, Land and Avery Pedigrees of Samuel Putnam Avery* (New York, 1925), 125; and manuscript notes in the Platt Brothers Archive at Mattatuck Museum, MSS 33, Box 1, Folder I (this archive will subsequently be cited as PBA, followed by a number designating the box and a letter for the folder). For Josiah III's Waterbury land grant, deed in Waterbury Land Records, Town Clerk's Vault, vol. 1, 903 (1729); 1740 land donations in Henry Bronson, *The History of Waterbury, Connecticut* (Waterbury, Conn., 1858), 67. All Waterbury deeds will hereafter be cited as WLR, vol:page (year).

2. Bronson, *History of Waterbury,* 516–18, and Joseph Anderson, ed., *The Town and City of Waterbury, Connecticut, from the Aboriginal Period to the Year Eighteen Hundred and Ninety-five,* (New Haven, Conn., 1896), 2:263, discuss Leavenworth's apprenticeship; also see Cecelia Bucki, *Metal, Minds and Machines: Waterbury at Work* (Waterbury, Conn., 1980), 9–10, and Chris H. Bailey, "Mr. Terry's Waterbury Competitors: The Leavenworths and Their Associates," *Bulletin of the National Association of Watch and Clock Collectors* 20 (June 1979): 3–43. WLR, 25:212 (1797); in the deeds examined for this study the first use of the name Naugatuck River instead of Great River occurred in 1801.

3. Anderson, *Town and City,* 1:579; in WLR, 25:440 (1796), the nailworks is used as a boundary reference.

4. Connecticut Archives, Industry, 2nd Series (1747–1820), vol. 2, document 73 (petition) and 74 (affidavit).

5. Hopkins and Byington petition.

6. Hopkins and Byington petition.

7. Hopkins and Byington petition. For a detailed treatment of the account book system of exchange in Connecticut during the early national period, see Bruce Clouette and Matthew Roth, *Bristol, Connecticut, 1785–1985* (Canaan, N.H., 1985), 16–17.

8. WLR, 25:212 (1797), sale and mortgage to Platt; WLR, 27:120 (1798), mortgage to Benedict. Nathan Platt probably got the cash by selling his share of the family's land in Newtown.

9. WLR, 27:197 (1801), sale to Gideon Platt; WLR, 27:321 (1802), mortgage to church; WLR, 27:458 (1802), settlement of Hopkins–Nathan Platt mortgage; WLR, 28:370 (1805), settlement of Benedict mortgage; Platt, *Platt Lineage*, 66, Nathan's father's estate.

10. Platt, *Platt Lineage*, 66–71. On Levi, see U.S. Census of Population, manuscript returns, Connecticut State Library (hereafter CSL), 1810, 2:1366; 1820, 2:1705.

11. On mandatory childhood education in Connecticut, see Samuel Hart, "The Common Schools of Connecticut," in William L. Davis, ed., *The New England States* (Boston, 1897), and Henry Barnard, *History of the Legislation of Connecticut Respecting Common Schools down to 1838* (Hartford, Conn., 1853). Alfred's certificate of examination for district schoolteacher, PBA, Box 1, Folder A; Morris school, Anderson, *Town and City*, 2:394; Leonard's wages, Day Book of J. M. L. and W. H. Scovill (1831–32), Mattatuck Museum Archives, M-5, Series III (Ledgers), Item no. 42, n.p.

12. Floods of 1801 and 1803, Bronson, *History of Waterbury*, 112. Millwrighting, Louis C. Hunter, *Waterpower: A History of Industrial Power in the United States, 1780–1930* (Charlottesville, Va., 1979), vol. 1, *Waterpower in the Age of the Steam Engine*, 91–94 (quoted words on p. 91), and William Fairbairn, *Treatise on Mills and Millwork* (London, 1861–1863), pt. 1, ix–xi.

13. Reminiscences in "Platts Mills Named After Nathan Platt Explains 'XYZ,'" *Waterbury American*, 1 January 1936, and typescript chronology of Platt businesses, PBA, 2, A. Leonard was definitely a skilled metalworker, later serving as an inside contractor with the Scovills, and Almon worked there too: Day Book of J. M. L. and W. H. Scovill (1831–32), Mattatuck Museum Archives, M-5, Series III (Ledgers), Item no. 42, n.p. Wooster and Judd were definitely on the scene in this period. David Wooster's brother Jesse had a short-lived business venture with Alfred Platt in 1821: Mattatuck Museum Archives, M-5, Series II, Box 4, Folder DDD. Lucian Judd was Nathan Platt's nephew, son of his sister Martha and her husband Asahel Judd (Platt, *Platt Lineage*, 69–70). Platt and Wooster button shop in U.S. Census of Manufactures, 1820, schedule no. 72, microfilm of manuscript at CSL.

14. Teaching certificate, PBA, 1, A; marriage in Platt, *Platt Lineage*, 185. Distributions of Irene's father's estate in 1814 (the $250 land) and 1816, both PBA, 1, B; in the later distribution she received personal property worth $165. WLR, 34:250 (1815), deed to third of house.

15. Alfred's carding venture in the 1816 Mechanic's Assessment List of the Second Turnpike Company as "Alfred Platt & Company, Carding Mill," Anderson, *Town and City*, 1:596; saw- and gristmilling in Anderson, *Town and City*, 2:394–95; clock peddling in Bronson, *History of Waterbury*, 322. Nathan's mortgage in WLR, 36:150 (1818). Henry Bronson's history is a reliable source on Alfred's peddling because the book was based on the notes and manuscripts of Henry's father, Bennet Bronson, who had kept the accounts for Leavenworth's peddlers. Even though the surviving fragments of these accounts do not cover 1819, the year of Platt's reported peddling, the Bronsons would have known if he had peddled; see Bennet Bronson Record

Books, Connecticut Historical Society, Manuscript no. 85574, vol. 2, 1817–1818, 18–21. Platt and Wooster 1821 mercantile license in Mattatuck Museum Archives, M-5, Series II, Box 4, Folder DDD.

16. *Waterbury American*, 19 and 26 October 1855.

17. "Master Miller" in 1860 Census Manuscript, CSL, 4:56 (paginated by town).

18. Sawmill in Anderson, *Town and City*, 2:394–95. In WLR, 37:320 (1822), the deed by which Alfred bought seven rods of land from his father, "Alfred's Button Shop" is mentioned as a boundary reference; the parcel is further identified as "the same land on which said Alfred is now erecting a barn." In deeds cited below, the button shop is described as occupying the old nailworks.

19. The earliest positive data on Alfred's buttonmaking and metalworking capability comes from three 1842 deeds, WLR, 49:388; WLR, 49:549; and WLR, 49:551. The equipment in these deeds depicts a well-equipped operation with casting, rolling, fabricating, finishing, and toolmaking capabilities. Given the earlier presence of nail making on the site and the presence in 1820 of some sort of button shop, it seems certain that Alfred had some range of metalworking capacity in 1822. Even clearer is the need to view cautiously the later accounts that have telescoped several decades' worth of activity into a few short years after 1820 and retroactively attributed a scale of production that could not have been reached until near mid-century. If all of the assertions from seventy-five or more years later were true, before 1829 Alfred Platt made all of the wire and at least half of the rolled brass to supply the town's two largest button firms—an impossible scenario; see, for instance, Anderson, *Town and City*, 2:394, and "Recollections of Charles S. Miller," c. 1936, typescript in PBA, 9, G.

20. "Statement of debts due from [Benedict and Coe's] Button Company," 2:26, in Bennet Bronson Record Books, manuscript at Connecticut Historical Society, Hartford; Anderson, *Town and City*, 2:315.

21. For the most complete list of operations used to make a button in Waterbury during this period, see Kenneth T. Howell, comp., "History of Abel Porter and Co.," 1952, 12–16; typescript at Connecticut Historical Society.

22. William G. McLoughlin, *New England Dissent, 1630–1833: The Baptists and the Separation of Church and State* (Cambridge, Mass., 1971); esp. see "Disestablishment in Connecticut, 1776–1818," 2:912–1084.

23. Ibid., 2:919; Bronson, *History of Waterbury*, 55; Anderson, *Town and City*, 3:671–76; the Second Baptist Church of Wallingford was in the part set off as the town of Meriden in 1806.

24. Bronson, *History of Waterbury*, 553; Anderson, *Town and City*, 3: 674; Jarvis Means Morse, *A Neglected Period of Connecticut History, 1818–1850* (New Haven, Conn., 1933), 133.

25. Bronson, *History of Waterbury*, 554; Anderson, *Town and City*, 3:673.

26. McLoughlin, *New England Dissent*, 2:919, 1021–22.

27. Richard M. Purcell, *Connecticut in Transition, 1775–1818* (Washington, D.C., 1918), 332–419.

28. Clark's pew rent, 1 May 1865, PBA, 1, LL; William S. Platt to A. Legrand Platt, 30 July 1856, PBA, 1, R.

29. Anderson, *Town and City*, 3:680.

30. Ibid., 3:672, 680; Platt-Wooster partnership in Mattatuck Museum Archives, M-5, Series II, Box 4, Folder DDD.

31. Platt, *Platt Lineage*, 185–87. The fifth son's full name was Alfred Legrand Platt. This study refers to him as Legrand (as his own family did) to avoid confusion with his father.

32. J. D. Van Slyck, *New England Manufacturers and Manufactories* (Boston, 1879), 1:81.

33. On the role of merchants and credit in the birth of Connecticut manufactures see Clouette and Roth, *Bristol*, 49–54, 62–69.

34. Van Slyck, *New England Manufacturers*, 1:81–84; Anderson, *Town and City*, 2:296; Bronson, *History of Waterbury*, 448. Abel Porter was a distant relation to the Baptist Timothy Porter, though Abel's family was Episcopalian.

35. Van Slyck, *New England Manufacturers*, 1:81–82; Bronson Record Books, 2:28.

36. Smith to Benedict, 8 December 1817, Mattatuck Museum Archives, Record Group M-12, Box 2, Folder A.

37. On the general quality of Connecticut consumer-hardware products, see Shirley Spaulding Devoe, *The Tinsmiths of Connecticut* (Middletown, Conn., 1968), 4; "dandelion water" in Anderson, *Town and City*, 2:296; Benedict's inventory in Bronson Record Books, 2:28.

38. Van Slyck, *New England Manufacturers*, 1:85; Smith and Curtis in Bronson Record Books, 2:28; Burnham's partnership in WLR, 44:489–90 (1834).

39. Anderson, *Town and City*, 2:296–97; Van Slyck, *New England Manufacturers*, 1:82; inventory in Bronson Record Books, 2:28.

40. Van Slyck, *New England Manufacturers*, 1:82. WLR, 38:89 (1823); WLR, 38:291 (1823); WLR, 38:268 (1825); WLR, 42:121 (1831).

41. Benedict and Coe partnership in WLR, 39:534 (1829).

42. The 1834 partnership agreement in WLR, 44:489–90 (1834). That the firm valued Platt's shop is evident in subsequent dealings treated later in the text, in which Benedict and his associates lent substantial sums so that Platt could keep his shop going.

43. The 1838 and 1840 partnership agreements and 1843 Certificate of Incorporation are in WLR, 46:513–15 (1838); WLR, 47:445–46 (1840); and WLR, 48:552 (1843).

44. Benedict's store is evident in Alfred Platt's Day Book No. 6, PBA, covering the years after 1842; among many entries see pp. 7, 20, 29, 40. On Benedict financing his manufacturing partnership through land sales, see WLR, 42:169 (1832); 42:311 (1832); 43:434 (1834).

45. Van Slyck, *New England Manufacturers*, 1:83, and Matthew Roth, *Connecticut: An Inventory of Historic Engineering and Industrial Sites* (Washington, D.C., 1981), 156.

46. WLR, 38:89 (1823). Since 1823 the area has been known as Platts Mill, Platts Mills, Plattsville, and several other close variations.

47. WLR, 38:291 (1823); WLR, 38:368 (1825).

48. WLR, 38:291 (1823) describes the carding shop as "standing on the East bank of the Waterbury [Naugatuck] river . . . and over the mouth of the ditch leading from our Grist Mill."

49. WLR, 38:368 (1825), contains the first simultaneous reference to both the old Hoadley gristmill and the "Grist Mill now standing a little Eastward, on another ditch." WLR, 42:121 (1831), uses the "Breastwork Gates" as a boundary marker.

50. WLR, 42:121 (1831).

51. As early as 1818, deeds bearing Gideon's name give his residence as Middlebury, e.g., WLR, 36:150 (1818). Nathan's second marriage in Waterbury Vital Records, 3:49 (1829).

52. Nathan's sale in WLR, 44:74 (1835); Alfred's note for $2,200 to Nathan in WLR, 44:75 (1835); Gideon's heirs' sale to Alfred in WLR, 45:154 (1836).

53. WLR, 45:251 (1836).

54. The system of mills and races in the late 1830s after Alfred attained control is inferred from the deeds from 1823 to 1836, plus subsequent deeds that use the races as boundary references; see WLR, 53:504 (1848) and WLR, 54:130 (1849). The number of houses is inferred from the above-cited deeds prior to 1836. U.S. Population Census, 1830, 8:672–73, and 1840, 8:749–50, both CSL, provide only the name of the household head and the number of other people living in the household, so the identities of all of the residents cannot be precisely determined. It is certain that Alfred, Irene, and their children lived in the enclave. In 1830, Alfred's unmarried sister Anner probably lived there too, as did Nathan. Other likely residents include Asahel and Martha (Platt) Judd and their four children and one or two boarders who may or may not have been relatives.

55. Diet inferred from numerous entries in Alfred's Day Book No. 6, passim., PBA, 1842–1873; household possessions in WLR, 49:552 (1842). Both of these sources are from a decade later than the period being discussed, but they probably reflect the Platts' material circumstances in the 1830s; the eight silver spoons, for instance, corresponded to the parents and six sons, but in 1842 at least two of the sons lived elsewhere.

56. Legrand Platt to Charles Platt, 23 December 1856, in PBA, 1, Q; Clark to Legrand, 27 July 1856, in PBA, 1, S.

57. Platt, *Platt Lineage*, 185–87; Anderson, *Town and City*, 2:394–97, 3:827.

58. Scovill Store Day Book, 1831–32, n.p., lists numerous transactions with Leonard and Almon that are consistent with the use of store accounts in employer-employee relationships in this period. Both appear to have served as inside contractors, responsible for hiring, supervising, and paying employees; the contractors received credit for these wages in their accounts with the proprietors. See, for instance, Almon's "labor account" for 3 January 1832, which includes credit for wages paid to Anner. Anderson, *Town and City*, 1:584–85; Bucki, *Metals, Minds, and Machines*, 19.

59. In WLR, 44:200 (1835), WLR, 44:395 (1835), factory and water privilege; WLR, 45:290 (1836), WLR, 45:357 (1836), house and barn; Anderson, *Town and City*, 1:585.

60. Bronson, *History of Waterbury*, 554; Anderson, *Town and City*, 1:674–75.

61. WLR, 44:236 (1835); WLR, 49:212 (1842); Bronson, *History of Waterbury*, 555; *A Century of History in the First Baptist Church in Waterbury, Connecticut* (Hartford, Conn., 1904), engraving of church facing p. 152.

62. Bronson, *History of Waterbury*, 555; Anderson, *Town and City*, 1:675–76; *A Century of History*, 151–55; WLR, 49:212 (1842), execution of the 1836 guarantee by Platt, Porter, Hall, and Frost.

63. Bronson, *History of Waterbury*, 555; Anderson, *Town and City*, 3:675–76; *A Century of History*, 152–55.

64. WLR, 49:164 (1842); WLR, 49:270 (1842); WLR, 46:203 (1838).

65. WLR, 48:73 (1840), Bronson mortgage; WLR, 48:74 (1840), Leonard Platt mortgage.

66. WLR, 47:1 (1839); WLR, 47:2 (1839); WLR, 47:3 (1839); WLR, 47:4 (1839).

67. WLR, 48:222 (1841); WLR, 49:5 (1841); WLR, 49:6 (1841).

68. WLR, 49:552 (1842); WLR, 49:164 (1842); WLR, 49:175 (1842); WLR, 49:388 (1842); WLR, 49:551 (1842); WLR, 49:212 (1842); note co-signed by Nathan in Inventory of Nathan Platt Estate, Wallingford Probate District, File No. 1360, CSL.

69. WLR, 49:549 (1842); WLR, 49:552 (1842); WLR, 49:432 (1842).

70. "Act Incorporating the Baptist Church of Waterbury," in *Resolves and Private Laws of the State of Connecticut* (New Haven, Conn., 1857), vol 3 (1836–1857), 501; *A Century of History,* 154, 156; Bronson, *History of Waterbury,* 555; Alfred Platt Ledger No. 2, p. 46.

71. WLR, 49:388 (1842); WLR, 49:549 (1842); WLR, 49:551 (1842).

72. On the grocery partnership, see *Waterbury Directory,* 1873, 105. Nirom's important role as a supplier of groceries and sundries to the family is evident in Alfred Platt Ledger No. 2, pp. 49, 55. On the source of Nirom's credit, see WLR, 49:388 (1842).

73. Charles's lease in WLR, 49:551 (1842). Platt's lack of nonfamily employees in the early 1840s is evident in his Day Book No. 5, Mattatuck Museum Archives, Record Group M-5, Series II, Box 3, Folder MM; Day Book No. 6 and Ledger No. 2, both PBA; the labor accounts for nonfamily members all begin no earlier than 1847. On retiring the loan from the Congregational Church, see WLR, 49:492 (1843).

74. "Industries of Newtown," in Jane E. Johnson, comp., *Newtown History* (Newtown, Conn., 1917), 6; *Connecticut Business Directory,* 1851, 270.

75. Alfred Platt Ledger No. 2, 26; Day Book No. 6, pp. 7, 20, 29, 40.

76. WLR, 52:27 (1845); WLR, 52:42 (1845); Platt, *Platt Lineage,* 185.

77. Nathan Platt Estate Inventory and Will, Probate File No. 1360, Wallingford Probate District, CSL. Alfred's assignment of five acres to family members is indicated in WLR, 65:123 (1856), and WLR, 65:129 (1856) and in U.S. Population Census, manuscript returns, 1850, 4:850–51; the assignment occurred sometime between 1845 and 1850, and Alfred Platt's obligation to Benedict and Burnham was still for the full forty-two acres.

2. *"You Are Now Lucrative in Business" (pp. 50–82)*

1. Population Census, 1840, 8:747–50, and 1850, 4:851, manuscript returns at CSL; Daybook No. 6, pp. 18–20, 91; Ledger No. 2, p. 52; letter from William to Legrand Platt, 7 July 1856, PBA, 1, R.

2. Farm and household work by Platt women is inferred from the numerous entries for processed foods, traded by Alfred, that lack corresponding entries for processing work (e.g., butter, salt pork) in Daybook No. 6, pp. 22, 25, 35, 45.

3. "Industries of Newtown," in Jane E. Johnson, comp., *Newtown's History* (Newtown, Conn., 1917), 6, paginated by chapter; Alfred Platt Ledger No. 2, p. 16; L. L. Platt and Co. Bankruptcy Inventory, 1855, Newtown District Probate File No. 1566, CSL.

4. The most definitive recounting of the various Platt partnerships is on p. 332 of the state supreme court decision that ultimately settled Alfred Platt's estate; see "Platt v. Platt" in John Hooker, ed., *Connecticut Reports: Cases Argued and Determined in the Supreme Court of Errors of the State of Connecticut* (Hartford, Conn., 1876), 330–47 (hereafter cited as *Platt v. Platt*). Also see L. L. Platt and Co. Bankruptcy Inventory, 1855; Legrand to Clark Platt, 5 November 1855 and 8 August 1856, both PBA, 1, Q; crockery receipt (1848), PBA, 6, J.

5. Charles's family in West Stockbridge and Platt and Barnes in *A Century of History in the First Baptist Church of Waterbury, Connecticut* (Hartford, Conn., 1904),

153 and G. Lewis Platt, *The Platt Lineage* (New York, 1891), 185–86; equipment in Daybook No. 6, pp. 47, 65, 69; buckwheat-fanning process in patent number 8,659, awarded 13 January 1852, "Report of the Commissioner of Patents," U.S. Senate Documents, 32nd Cong., 2nd sess., vol. 9, no. 55, 132–33.

6. Platt, *Platt Lineage,* 185–87; Henry Bronson, *The History of Waterbury, Connecticut* (Waterbury, Conn., 1858), 522; U.S. Population Census, 1850, 4:850–51, CSL; A. Budington and R. Whiteford, *Map of the County of New Haven, Connecticut* (New Haven, Conn., 1852). In Alfred Platt Day Book No. 5, of which unpaginated fragments survive (Mattatuck Museum Archives, M-5, Series II, Box 3, Folder MM), Alfred posted debits to William and Clark for rent and board; WLR, 54:130 (1849), William's land purchase; WLR, 56:331 (1851), Clark's land purchase; Clark's receipts for labor and materials to build his house in PBA, 1, FF and GG.

7. Connecticut Secretary of State, *State of Connecticut Register and Manual* (Hartford, Conn., 1977), 592–93; Cecelia Bucki, *Metals, Minds and Machines: Waterbury at Work* (Waterbury, Conn., 1980), 84.

8. Bucki, *Metals, Minds and Machines,* 13–14, 17, 22–24; U.S. Census, "Products of Industry for the Year 1850," 287–90, manuscript returns at CSL. German silver consisted of copper, zinc, and nickel.

9. 1850 Manufacturing Census, 287–90.

10. Ibid.; Matthew Roth, *Connecticut: An Inventory of Historic Engineering and Industrial Sites* (Washington, D.C., 1981), 165, 170; Bronson, *History of Waterbury,* 561–63. For late-1840s casting purchases, see Alfred Platt Day Book No. 5, n.p. ("Press castings") and accounts in Ledger No. 2, pp. 29, 38 (Waterbury Iron Foundry Co.), 30, 96 (The Foundry Co.) and 39 (Naugatuck Machine Co.). Among many examples of Platt's buying the more sophisticated parts of the machines he made are "2 Gears and one Ratchet" and several lead screws in his itemized account with Naugatuck Machine Co., 1855, PBA, 6, K.

11. Bucki, *Metals, Minds and Machines,* 19, 60; Naugatuck Railroad Company, *Annual Report* (Bridgeport, 1853), 7. The availability of banking services in New Haven delayed the opening of Waterbury's first bank.

12. Bucki, *Metals, Minds and Machines,* 15–16; Budington and Whiteford, *Map*; freight receipts, 1848, Mattatuck Museum Archives, M-5 (Manufacturing and Business—Small Collections), Series III, Box 3, Folder HH; shipping arrangements noted on receipts from Hendricks and Brothers and from Stokes and Brothers, 1854, PBA, 6, J.

13. On the ties between metals brokers and Waterbury manufacturers, see Robert G. Cleland, *A History of Phelps Dodge, 1834–1950* (New York, 1952), 31; Maxwell Whiteman, *Copper for America: The Hendricks Family and a National Industry, 1755–1939* (New Brunswick, N.J., 1971), 167; Elva Tooker, *Nathan Trotter: Philadelphia Merchant, 1787–1853* (Cambridge, Mass., 1955), 94, 137–38. The Platts' direct relationship with Phelps, Dodge and Co. by 1847 is found in two receipts for zinc, Mattatuck Museum Archives, M-5, Series III, Box 3, Folder HH. Other receipts show that by the mid-1850s the Platts were making extensive spelter purchases from both Phelps, Dodge (PBA, 6, J) and Hendricks and Bros. (PBA, 6, K). The 1850 Manufacturing Census does not list zinc or zinc products under the output for any Waterbury firm other than Alfred Platt's, even though it lists outputs as small as $500 (pp. 287–90).

14. Tooker, *Nathan Trotter,* 207; *Metal Industry* 2 (February 1904): 21, 27; *Metal Industry* 2 (September 1904): 150; Ernest W. Horvick, "Zinc and Zinc Alloys," in Frank W. Wilson, ed., *Tool Engineers Handbook,* 2nd ed. (New York, 1959), chap. 14, 60–65.

15. Joseph Anderson, ed., *The Town and City of Waterbury, Connecticut from the*

Aboriginal Period to the Year Eighteen Hundred and Ninety-five New Haven, Conn., 1896), 2:395.

16. Spelter receipts, Mattatuck Museum Archives, M-5, Series III, Box 3, Folder HH. There is no direct mention of a new rolling mill in any of the documents from the late 1840s, but rolling metal always involved a sequence of machines imparting smaller thicknesses; some of the unspecified foundry purchases and unspecified charges for the labor of Alfred, William, and Clark likely represent material and work that went into some additional capital equipment in this period; see Alfred Platt Ledger No. 2, pp. 29, 35, 38, 39, 56, 92, 98.

17. 1850 Manufacturing Census, p. 287; PBA 3, HH (Warren, Wheeler and Woodruff), and PBA 4, K (W. R. Hitchcock); Bronson, *History of Waterbury,* 562.

18. A. Platt and Co. account with Eli Curtis, 1847–1849, PBA, 4, F; letter from J. C. Welton and Co., 31 September 1847, PBA, 3, HH; letter from L. B. Norton and Co., 2 August 1850, PBA, 6, J; material receipts from Phelps, Dodge (M-5, Series III, Box 3, Folder HH). Richard Miller owns a pair of early Platt wire-eye buttons made of 95 percent tin and 5 percent copper, or Britannia metal; x-ray fluorescence analysis courtesy of Nancy Wilson and Mark Tveskov, Department of Anthropology, University of Connecticut.

19. Equipment in 1842 from Alfred Platt's leases to his sons, WLR, 49:388; WLR, 49:549, and WLR, 49:551, all 1842. Accounts with various selling agents note the later two-hole and four-hole varieties; PBA, 4, W. Early buttons courtesy of Richard Miller.

20. Japanning: Edward H. Knight, *American Mechanical Dictionary* (Boston, 1881), 2:1211, 3:2693. Recipes in Alfred Platt Ledger No. 2, unnumbered page second from back cover; receipts and statements from Apothecaries Hall and from Baker and Brother, New York City, in PBA, 6, J, which also includes a receipt for the scale and weights used in measuring out the ingredients.

21. Surviving fragments of Alfred Platt Day Book No. 5, n.p., and Ledger No. 2, p. 26, include sales of finished products to the button firms of F. Hayden and Sons, Mattatuck Manufacturing Co., and Benedict and Burnham, among others, and japanning hundreds of great gross for others. A Scovill sales agent who handled about 10 percent of Platts' buttons in 1849 may have been acting for Scovill or on his own behalf; see Eli Curtis account book, 1849, PBA, 4, F.

22. Legrand Platt to Clark Platt, 31 December 1856, PBA, 1, Q. The standard wholesale unit for buttons was the "great gross," or one dozen gross (1,728 buttons). Legrand must have been writing about great gross.

23. J. D. Van Slyck, *New England Manufacturers and Manufactories* (Boston, 1899), 2:85–86; Anderson, *Town and City,* 2:251–53, 304–5, 337; Eli Curtis correspondence, 1850, PBA, 4, E.

24. Curtis account book, with 1848 missing, PBA, 4, F.

25. Anderson, *Town and City,* 2:337–38. Alfred recorded the placement of his will in his Ledger No. 2, inside the back cover.

26. J. C. Welton and Co. account of sales for July–December 1849, PBA, 4, W.; J. C. Welton to A. Platt and Co., 27 December 1849, PBA, 4, W.

27. J. C. Welton to A. Platt and Co., 31 September 1847, PBA, 3, HH.

28. 1850 Manufacturing Census, 287; in 1849 Welton sold a total of 842 great gross, per Welton accounts of sales for January–June 1849 and July–December 1849, PBA, 4, W; J. C. Welton to A. Platt and Co., 19 January 1850, PBA, 4, W.

29. J. C. Welton and Co. to A. Platt and Co., 10 January, 19 January, 25 February 1850; all in PBA, 4, W.

30. J. C. Welton and Co. to A. Platt and Co., 20 June 1850, 31 July 1851; Clark M. Platt to J. C. Welton, 15 January 1851; all in PBA, 4, W.

31. J. C. Welton to A. Platt and Co., 27 December 1849, 10 January 1850 (emphasis in original); Clark Platt to J. C. Welton and Co., 31 December 1849; all in PBA, 4, W. "B. Platt" was probably D. Baldwin Platt; see Platt, *Platt Lineage,* 69–70, and Legrand Platt to Clark Platt, 5 November 1855.

32. J. C. Welton to A. Platt and Co., 5 May, 7 June, 28 June 1850; all in PBA, 4, W; L. B. Norton and Co. to A. Platt and Co., 13 July 1850, PBA, 6, J.

33. Alfred Platt Ledger No. 2, pp. 75, 94. On the calculations of dividends, see *Platt v. Platt,* 332.

34. J. C. Welton and Co. statement of account with A. Platt and Co., January–June 1849, and letters from Clark Platt to J. C. Welton and Co., 15 and 29 January 1851; all in PBA, 4, W. Variation in average price for the two months is accounted for by the mix of straps versus suspenders, order sizes, and different finishes.

35. J. C. Welton to A. Platt and Co., 18 January 1853, PBA, 4, W.

36. Dividends in Ledger No. 2, p. 94; Welton investments in Anderson, *Town and City,* 2:337; J. C. Welton to A. Platt and Co., 10 February 1853, PBA, 4, W.

37. Alfred Platt Daybook No. 5, n.p. The entries include items for parts made elsewhere, such as "Press castings," as well as metal stock intended for use on these new machines but apparently cut to shape after arrival, such as "Iron for Press" and "steel for slitting machines."

38. U.S. Census, "Products of Agriculture for the Year 1850," 2:169, manuscript returns at CSL; *Waterbury American,* 29 January 1848.

39. Day-by-day records of Platt's dealings begin in 1850 with Daybook No. 6. The surviving fragments of Daybook No. 5 are concerned with the button shop, not farming or the other processing enterprises. Ledger No. 2, in which daybook entries were posted for settlement, includes references to both Daybooks No. 5 and No. 6, but usually just gives amounts, not the goods or services that underlay the transactions. Some reconstruction of events prior to 1850 is possible by using the ledger accounts that include earlier postings and assuming some continuity before and after 1850. (Ledger No. 2 also has postings from Platt's "Mill Book" or "Mill Ledger" and his "Sawmill Ledger," but these volumes have not come down to the present.)

40. Ledger No. 2, p. 77; Daybook No. 6, pp. 16, 23, 25, 31, 42, 64, 87, 88, 110–12, 116, 129, 130, 142, 146, 149, 156; Population Census Mss., 1840, 8:749–50 and 1850, 4:852.

41. Ledger No. 2, p. 22; Daybook No. 6, pp. 9, 12, 14–16, 18, 20, 21, 23, 26, 28, 42, 45, 46, 54, 64, 66, 71, 74, 80–82, 86, 94, 108, 115; 1850 Population Census Mss., 4:848.

42. Ledger No. 2, pp. 40, 113; Daybook No. 5, n.p. (Benjamin rolling zinc); Daybook No. 6, pp. 5, 11, 30, 41, 42, 47, 50, 54, 61, 62, 64–66, 71, 72, 76, 77, 88, 91, 94, 95, 98, 99, 104, 107, 121, 124, 128, 130, 132, 133, 142, 143, 146, 162; 1840 Population Census Mss., 8:749–50.

43. Ledger No. 2, pp. 10, 23; Daybook No. 6, pp. 19–22, 26–29, 32, 46, 50, 70, 91, 93, 95, 98, 101, 113, 125, 131, 132, 143, 146, 153, 157, 158, 162, 164, 173; 1850 Population Census Mss., 4:848.

44. Thanks to Patricia Haefs for counting the number of transactions made each day in Daybook No. 6.

45. In the Budington and Whiteford (1852) and the Smith (1856) maps, the nearest competing flour and lumber suppliers were about a mile to the south in the village of Union City and two miles to the north in the built-up area of Waterbury.

In the 1850 Population Census, 8:846–54, the forty households to either side of Alfred Platt, extending about halfway to the clusters to north and south, held 368 people; assuming that some of these families had other sources, Platt was the principal supplier of lumber and flour for some fifty households containing over two hundred people. See cash accounts for mill products in Daybook No. 6, pp. 4, 5, 7–10, and real estate valuations in 1850 Population Census, 8:848, 851.

46. Ledger No. 2, pp. 37, 49, 51, 61; Daybook No. 6, pp. 1, 3, 10, 12, 17–19, 26–29, 51, 57, 68, 82–84, 92–94, 100, 127–30, 141–47, 165–68, 180–83, 201, 206, 207, 216–18, 221–29, 234, 239, 245–47, 250–55.

47. Ledger No. 2, pp. 52, 73; Daybook No. 6, p. 91. "Bergan" is the most common of the numerous spellings (Bergin, Berrigan, Berigan, Berrigin) given for the miller's name in census reports and Platt's accounts.

48. E. R. R. Green, "The Great Famine (1845–1850)," in T. W. Moody and F. X. Martin, eds., *The Course of Irish History* (Cork, Ireland, 1967), 263–74; Bucki, *Metals, Minds and Machines,* 70–71. In the 1850 Population Census, 8:846–54, the eighty-one households including Alfred Platt's and forty to either side contained a total of 374 people of whom 77, or 20.58 percent, were born in Ireland; there were also a half-dozen young children born in the United States to Irish parents.

49. 1850 Population Census Mss., 8:849, 854; Daybook No. 6, p. 59.

50. 1850 Population Census Mss., 8:851; Daybook No. 2, p. 289.

51. William Platt to Legrand Platt, 30 July 1856, PBA, 1, R.

52. Daybook No. 6, pp. 35, 39, 46.

53. Daybook No. 5, n.p. (Foundry Co., Thomas, F. Judd); Ledger No. 2, pp. 38, 64 (Foundry Co.); 1850 Population Census Mss., 8:851 (T. Judd); Daybook No. 6, p. 81 (F. Judd).

54. Daybook No. 5, n.p.

55. Daybook No. 5, n.p. (Lorraine Lawrence); Ledger No. 2, p. 21 ("Syntha" Lawrence) and 35 ("Mother making boxes"). Though button packing appears to have been compensated on a piecework basis initially, Daybook No. 5 gives only the numbers packed, not the rate of pay; Ledger No. 2 provides the total pay.

56. Daybook No. 5, n.p.; Ledger No. 2, p. 34; 1850 Population Census Mss., 8:848, 850.

57. Daybook No. 5, n.p.; Daybook No. 6, p. 59; Ledger No. 2, p. 82.

58. Medicinal notations on back flyleaf of Daybook No. 6. Clark subscribed to *The Maine Law Advocate,* a periodical favoring local licensing for alcohol distribution to limit its availability, a system that Connecticut adopted in 1850; receipt in PBA, 1, EE.

59. Dividends in Ledger No. 2, p. 94; Wheeler statements, PBA, 6, J; Horton statements, PBA, 4, L.

60. L. B. Horton and Co. to A. Platt and Co., 7 February and 23 December 1853; A. Platt and Co. to L. B. Horton and Co., 27 December 1953; all in PBA, 4, L.

61. A. Platt and Co. to L. B. Horton and Co., 27 December 1853; Horton, Boon and Frost, the successor firm, to A. Platt and Co., 4 April 1855; both in PBA, 4, L.

62. This handwriting transition is evident in the correspondence with J. C. Welton, Wheeler, and Horton, all cited above.

63. Daybook No. 5, n.p.

64. W. S. Platt, "Improvement in Making Seamless Tubes," U.S. patent no. 16,630, 10 February 1857, in House Documents, 35th Cong., 1st Session, "Report of the Commissioner of Patents," 2:501–2 (description) and 3:101 (illustration).

65. A. Platt and Co. accounts with The Foundry Co., 1855–1856; Naugatuck Ma-

chine Co., 1854–1856 (and receipts from 1856); and Scovill Manufacturing Co., 1855–1856; materials from 1854 and 1855 in PBA, 6, J, and from 1856 in PBA, 6, K. The reason for the new press's unprecedented size is not known; it may have incorporated more than one ram or simply have run faster than prior presses.

66. Receipt for new saw frame, 22 January 1856, PBA, 6, K; Clark Platt to Legrand Platt, 30 July 1856 ("water shut out"), 28 August 1856 and 19 December 1856 (turbine), all PBA, 1, S; 10th Census, *Report on Water Power,* 150.

67. John Tyler to Alfred Platt, 3 and 10 November 1856 and receipt for purchase, 26 November 1856, all PBA, 6, K; Louis C. Hunter, *Waterpower: A History of Industrial Power in the United States, 1780–1930* (Charlottesville, Va., 1979), vol. 1, *Waterpower in the Age of the Steam Engine,* 292–318; and Arthur T. Safford and Edward P. Hamilton, "The American Mixed-Flow Turbine and Its Setting," *Transactions of the American Society of Civil Engineers* 85 (1922): 1270 ff.

68. John Tyler to Alfred Platt, 3 and 17 November 1856; both PBA, 6, K.

69. Turbine receipt, 26 November 1856, PBA, 6, K.

70. Ledger No. 2, pp. 38, 65.

71. Day Book No. 6, pp. 282–85 (Nirom), and p. 39 (Alfred's $500 loan).

72. WLR, 65:123 (1856), 65:129–31 (1856), 66:68 (1856), 66:69 (1856).

73. WLR, 65:129–31 (1856), the bank loan, specified semiannual interest payment but gives no rate of interest; the typical 5 percent for transactions in this period would yield annual interest of $400, or $200 semiannually. Buckwheat fan patent sale in Clark Platt to Legrand Platt, 4 April 1857, PBA, 1, S.

74. Clark Platt to Legrand Platt, 4 April 1857 (first quotation) and 19 December 1856 (second quotation), both in PBA, 1, S.

75. William Platt to Legrand Platt, 30 July 1856, PBA, 1, R.

76. Daybook No. 5, n.p.; Daybook No. 6, pp. 59, 123; Ledger No. 2, p. 82.

77. Ledger No. 2, p. 82; Daybook No. 6, pp. 4, 6, 11, 14–31, 59 ("sick and absent"), 61–75, 123; William Platt to Legrand Platt, 30 July 1856, PBA, 1, R.

78. At age fifty in 1850, Fitzpatrick was ten years older than the other Irish males in the vicinity, 1850 Population Census, 8:846–54; Daybook No. 6, pp. 4, 59, 123.

79. Ledger No. 2, p. 23 (Upson account), accounts of Irish workers on pp. 45, 46, 49, 72 (Falen), 101, 108; Daybook No. 6, pp. 81 (Judd), 112 (Yankee machinist), 160 (Irish male factory worker). In the 1860 Connecticut Manufacturing Census Mss., the button shop reported four male and three female employees, in addition to the proprietors (p. 363).

80. Daybook No. 6, p. 116, for instance, has credit postings from the "timebook," which has not itself survived; Ledger No. 2, pp. 72 (Falen), 79 (Christmas).

81. 1860 Population Census Mss., 4:52–60; Alfred Platt's household and the forty to either side yielded a total of 345 people, of whom 105 were born in Ireland and 183 in Connecticut. The samples used herein from the 1850 and 1860 censuses are similarly drawn selections of eighty-one households, but new construction during the intervening decade had made for denser settlement so that the 1860 sample covers a smaller geographic area; in both cases the samples represent those people living closest to the Platts. See *Atlas of New Haven County, Connecticut* (New York, 1865), plate 55.

82. Ledger No. 2, p. 106, shows 1855 to be the only year in the 1850s when A. Platt and Co. paid no dividend to the partners. All quotations in Clark Platt to Legrand Platt, 6 April 1857, PBA, 1, S.

83. E. S. Wheeler statements for 1857 and 1858, PBA, 6, L; R. Hitchcock orders for 1856–1858, PBA, 4, K.

84. Expenses for Alfred's trips in Day Book No. 6, pp. 97, 105; Anderson, *Town and City*, 2:252.

85. A. W. Welton and Porters to A. Platt and Sons, 29 May 1856, PBA, 4, W.

86. Clark Platt to Legrand Platt, 6 April 1857, PBA, 1, S; orders from Armstrong and Blacklin, 1859–1861, PBA, 4, B.

87. Thomas Porter to A. Platt and Sons, 11 February 1858, PBA, 4, W.

3. *"Taking Down the Whole U.S."* (pp. 83–109)

1. Henry Bronson, *The History of Waterbury, Connecticut* (Waterbury, Conn., 1858), 522.

2. *Platt v. Platt*, 332. Pipe correspondence, 1859–1861, PBA, 4, B; William's time charged to A. and C. M. Platt in Alfred Platt Ledger No. 2, p. 111. In general, it was impossible to apply lawyerly precision to Alfred Platt's informal conduct of his ventures; for instance, he used the name A. Platt and Sons in some of his accounts for 1859 and A. and C. M. Platt for others. Among the more egregiously misleading "facts" established in *Platt v. Platt* was that Alfred had no part in conducting the metalworking business after 1861; Ledger No. 2, pp. 106, 131, 132, and corresponding entries in Daybook No. 6, however, indicate his near-constant involvement.

3. Legrand Platt to Clark Platt, 4 November 1855 ("crumbs"), 27 March 1857 ("money"), and 23 December 1856, all PBA, 1, Q.

4. Ledger No. 2, pp. 68, 69; Daybook No. 6, pp. 180, 200, 214.

5. Sales statements, 1 July and 20 December 1858; Samuel Porter to A. and C. M. Platt, 7 October and 6 November 1858; all in PBA, 4, W.

6. Quotation in A. W. Welton and Porters to A. and C. M. Platt, 20 December 1858; A. W. Welton and Porters sales statements, 22 June, 13 and 31 December 1859; order for New Orleans in Porter letter of 2 September 1859; all PBA, 4, W. Later letters from the Porters—10 October 1859, 16 August 1862, and 23 November 1863 (all PBA, 4, W) revealed that local manufacturer Anson Bronson made the Naugatuck button and that E. S. Wheeler sold it.

7. Letter from J. L. Lawrence, 4 September 1859, PBA, 4, N.

8. E. S. Wheeler and Co. sales statements, August and December, 1859, and 1860–1865; all in PBA, 5, D. Quotations in Nathan Porter to William Platt, 10 October 1859, PBA, 4, W.

9. Letter from A. W. Welton and Porters, 1 September 1859, PBA, 4, W.

10. Letters from A. W. Welton and Porters, 29 March and 10 August 1860, PBA, 4, W.

11. A. W. Welton and Porters sales statement, 31 December 1860, PBA, 4, W.

12. Letter from A. W. Welton and Porters, 10 August 1860, PBA, 4, W.

13. Examples of orders, delivery problems, stock notices, and other routine business in letters from A. W. Welton and Porters, 9 March, 7 May, 8, 11, 29 June, 26 July, and 7 August 1860; sales statements, January–June and July–December 1860; all in PBA, 4, W. Dividend in Ledger No. 2, p. 122.

14. Bray Hammond, "The North's Empty Purse," *American Historical Review* 67, no. 1 (October 1961): 8–11; Milton Friedman and Anna Jacobson Schwartz, *A Monetary History of the United States* (Princeton, N.J., 1963), 18, 20.

15. Letter from A. W. Welton and Porters, 23 July 1861, PBA, 4, W.

16. John Hatch, "Button," U.S. patent No. 3915, issued 20 February 1845, mi-

crofilm at CSL, Patents, Reel 1845–1. Hatch also figured out how to make the burrs raised inside the stamped holes so that they mated solidly when the button halves were assembled.

17. Letter from A. W. Welton and Porters, 23 July 1861, PBA, 4, W.

18. Letter from A. W. Welton and Porters, 1 August 1861, PBA, 4, W.

19. Letter from A. W. Welton and Porters, 10 August 1861, PBA, 4, W.

20. Letters from A. W. Welton and Porters, 15 and 29 August 1861, PBA, 4, W.

21. Letters from A. W. Welton and Porters, 20 September and 15 October 1861, PBA, 4, W.

22. Letter from A. W. Welton and Porters, 8 November 1861, PBA, 4, W.

23. Letters from A. W. Welton and Porters, 11, 12, 20, 21, and 23 November and 11 December 1861 (summary of orders), PBA, 4, W.

24. Letters from A. W. Welton and Porters, 9 and 11 November 1861, PBA, 4, W.

25. Letters from A. W. Welton and Porters, 11 November 1861 (money); 16, 20, and 21 November (tin scraps); and statement of tin purchases, 21 December 1861; all in PBA, 4, W. Since the Platts seem to have stamped button parts out of the unused portions of tinplated sheet-iron strip, their stamping machine must have been hand-fed, the only way to position correctly such irregular stock under the ram of the press. This method is consistent with the assignment of only the most experienced and trusted personnel to operate the stamp—Frank Judd and the Platts themselves.

26. Letters from A. W. Welton and Porters, 21 and 23 November 1861, PBA, 4, W.

27. Letter from A. W. Welton and Porters, 11 November 1861, PBA, 4, W. Candle expenses in A. Platt and Co./A. Platt and Sons Bank Book, 1855–1864, Mattatuck Museum Archives, Manufacturing and Business, Series II, Box 3, Folder NN, not paginated.

28. Letter from Milo Peck and Co., 23 November 1861, PBA, 5, N. Bank Book, 1855–1864, includes entries from December 1861 through February 1862 for castings, screws, and labor on a press; the 1861 statement from Farrel Foundry and Machine (PBA, 6, O) has December charges for castings and day work that indicate a major new machine. Bank Book, 1855–1864, shows a new male employee and likely stamp operator in February 1862—Henry Roberts, the son of neighbor George Roberts. Letter from A. W. Welton and Porters, 11 December 1861 ("another machine"), PBA, 4, W.

29. A. W. Welton and Porters, statement of sales, July–December 1861, PBA, 4, W.

30. Bank Book, 1855–1864, n.p. Some of the overall increase in monthly labor cost may have come from increased rates of pay, but the Platts did not raise wages by 50 percent.

31. Ledger No. 2, pp. 122–24; Bank Book, 1855–1864, n.p.

32. Statements of Porter sales (1862 total of 6,052 great gross), January–June and July–December 1862; individual orders in separate letters from A. W. Welton and Porters; all PBA, 4, W. Dividends, salaries, and total annual output of 6,862 great gross in Ledger No. 2, pp. 122–24. Request for guarantee in letter from Clark Platt to Hitchcock and Castle, PBA, 5, N.

33. Statements from A. W. Welton and Porters, January–June and July–December 1862; letter from A. W. Welton and Porters, 13 March 1862; all PBA, 4, W.

34. Letters from A. W. Welton and Porters, 4 April, 16 May, and 4, 10, and 16 June 1862, PBA, 4, W.

35. Letters from A. W. Welton and Porters, August 7 (pricing) and 16 August (Naugatuck button), 1862, PBA, 4, W. The new great gross prices were $1.125 for fronts versus the 1861 average of $1.24; for suspenders, $1.375 versus $1.46.

36. Letters from A. W. Welton and Porters, 14 August (2), and 16, 21, 23, and 25 August 1862, PBA, 4, W.

37. Letter from A. W. Welton and Porters, 5 September 1862, PBA, 4, W; Bank Book, 1855–1864, n.p. Henry Roberts was the son of George, Alfred's livestock expert.

38. Letter from A. W. Welton and Porters confirming telegraph order, 3 October 1862, PBA, 4, W.

39. Zinc orders in letters from A. W. Welton and Porters, 1, 8, and 18 February 1862, PBA, 4, W. Total wartime zinc output is unknown, but the estimate is inferred from correspondence between A. Platt and Sons and various purchasers, most of whom made cloth buttons: Merrill and Co., PBA, 4, O; E. Robinson and Sons (of Waterbury, *not* the Attleboro producer of Hatch buttons), PBA, 4, S; Newell Bros. and its successor D. Chandler and Co., PBA, 4, Q; Geiershofer, Leowi and Co., PBA, 4, I; Goddard and Brother, PBA, 4, J; G. H. Smith and Co., PBA, 4, V; Beardsley and Richard, PBA, 5, P; and John D. Wood (quotation), PBA, 5, P.

40. Letters from A. W. Welton and Porters, 12 November and 3 and 17 December (quotation) 1862, all PBA, 4, W.

41. A. W. Welton and Porters sales statements, January–June and July–December 1863, PBA, 4, W; total output, dividend and shop rent in Ledger No. 2, p. 131; sons' salaries in Bank Book, 1855–1864, n.p.

42. A. W. Welton and Porters sales statements, January–June and July–December 1863; letters from A. W. Welton and Porters, August 18 (Brooks Brothers), 24 February and 18 May ("French"), 1863; PBA, 4, W.

43. A. W. Welton and Porters sales statements, January–June and July–December 1863; letters from A. W. Welton and Porters, 18 February and 23 November 1863; PBA, 4, W. "Low brass" had a greater proportion of copper and lower proportion of zinc than other grades, yielding a deeper, more goldlike color than those grades with more zinc.

44. Letters from A. W. Welton and Porters, 23 May and 13 August 1863, PBA, 4, W; diemaking cost in Bank Book, 1855–1864, n.p.

45. Letters from A. W. Welton and Porters, 31 March ("look as well"), 4 May ("Cheshire Co."), 4 June ("costs too much"), 3 July ("double button"), and 17 August (Nathan's advice), 1863, PBA, 4, W. On taggers tin and taggers iron, see, *A New English Dictionary on Historical Principles* (Oxford, 1919), s.v. "taggers tin." Cheshire Manufacturing Co. specialized in shirt and coat buttons, so its line complemented the Platts' rather than competing with it.

46. Letter from A. W. Welton and Porters, 10 February 1864, PBA, 5, A.

47. Letters from A. W. Welton and Porters, 26 and 31 March, 3 July, 13 and 8 August 1863, PBA, 4, W. Zinc's cost advantage over brass generally follows from the observation that zinc was only one of the components used in making brass, along with higher proportions of expensive copper. This observation is borne out when surviving data for a fairly tight period allow direct comparison. In one such period, July and August 1864, brass strip cost the Platts between $.30 and $.32 per pound; zinc slabs, between $.095 and $.105 per pound (receipts, PBA, 6, R). The Platts rolled the zinc slabs into strip, which they sold for $.24 a pound (invoice, PBA, 4, J). Though their processing cost cannot be determined from available records, it is safe to assume that they did not sell the strip at a loss, and their own cost for the strip they used in buttons was no more than $.24 a pound, or about 80

percent of what they paid for brass. Tinplated taggers iron cost around $.33 a pound in the same period (A. W. Welton and Porters statement, July–December 1864, PBA, 4, X).

48. Letters from A. W. Welton and Porters, 8 and 14 April 1863, PBA, 4, W.

49. Letter from A. W. Welton and Porters, 19 November 1863, PBA, 4, W.

50. Letters from A. W. Welton and Porters: market forecasts and production planning, 27 February, 21 March, 9 June, and 21 September 1863; stock orders, 4 and 9 June, 3 and 8 August, 1, 7, 9, and 11 September 1863; quotation, 15 September 1863; all PBA, 4, W.

51. Letter from George Lincoln Co., Hartford, acknowledging order for a "17 in[ch] Screw Lathe," PBA, 5, P; Naugatuck Machine Co. bill for "3 lever presses," PBA, 6, Q; payments for press castings and freight on lathe, Bank Book, 1855–1864, n.p.; letter from A. W. Welton and Porters, 21 May 1863, PBA, 4, W.

52. *Connecticut State Register and Manual*, 592; U.S. Manufacturing Census, 1860, 363–68, and 1870, 643–50. City population during the 1860s rose by 31 percent, 10,004 to 13,106, and brass mill employment by 62 percent, 683 to 1,105; button shop jobs declined by 30 percent, 324 to 225. Mortgage retirement in WLR, 77:64 (1865).

53. Bank Book, 1855–1864, n.p.

54. Ibid.

55. Ibid.; monthly bills from Griggs Brothers were as little as $39 in May, as much as $189 in March, and the annual total was $1,062. Griggs Brothers was probably one of the side ventures opened during the war by Henry Griggs, of Smith and Griggs; see Theodore Marburg, *Small Business in Brass Fabricating: The Smith & Griggs Manufacturing Co. of Waterbury* (New York, 1956), 6–7, 85–86.

56. Starting in late 1863, freight instructions specify stopping at the bridge rather than Union City; a typical notation on a zinc order reads "Naugatuck RR to Platts Bridge," PBA, 6, R. Lumber receipts in PBA, 6, R, and 6, S.

57. Letter from J. A. Brooks, attorney, 3 September 1863, PBA, 7, M; letter from A. W. Welton and Porters, 23 November 1863, PBA, 4, W. It is possible that the threat of an infringement lawsuit was empty because the seventeen-year duration of Hatch's 1845 patent would have expired in 1862; there is no record of a renewal.

58. Letters from A. W. Welton and Porters, 26 and 28 March, 16 June, and 30 September 1864; all in PBA, 5, A.

59. Porters' debit statement and receipts for 1864, PBA, 4, X. Platt correspondence with metals brokers in PBA, 4, R, and 6, R.

60. Letters to zinc strip customers, as in PBA, 4, Q, and 4, V; "peculiar treatment" in letter to Beardsley and Richmond, 9 March 1863, PBA, 5, P.

61. Letters from A. W. Welton and Porters, 16 January, 10 February, 5 and 13 April, and 21 December 1864; all in PBA, 5, A.

62. A. W. Welton and Porters sales statement, January–June 1864; letters from A. W. Welton and Porters, 22 January, 19 February, and 26 March 1864; all PBA, 5, A.

63. Letters from A. W. Welton and Porters, 26 February and 2 March 1864, PBA, 5, A.

64. Letters from A. W. Welton and Porters, 18 January, 26 February, 15 March ("Tell Ben"), 19 March, 30 March ("not advise"), and 5 April 1864; all in PBA, 5, A.

65. Letters from A. W. Welton and Porters, 5 and 13 May 1864, PBA, 5, A.

66. *Atlas of New Haven County*, 1869; lease in WLR, 74:432–33 (1864); letter from A. W. Welton and Porters, 10 June 1864, PBA, 5, A. Center Square is known today as Waterbury Green.

67. Statements for 1864 from Farrel Foundry and Machine Co., PBA, 6, S (press castings, shafting and pulleys, oven castings, and furnace frame), Naugatuck Machine Co., PBA, 6, R (lever presses, press castings and die beds, pulleys, and clutches); and carpenter Charles Perkins, PBA, 6, R. No employment records survive for the period between March 1864 and January 1868, but the labor force must have doubled too, to judge from the number of machines installed in the new shop and the subsequent surge in production.

68. Letters from A. W. Welton and Porters, 5, 17, and 24 August, 6, 16 September (quotation), 20, 21, and 30 September 1864; all in PBA, 5, A.

69. Letters from A. W. Welton and Porters, 7, 8, and 30 October, 6, 12, 16, 22, and 29 December (telegram and letter), 1864; all in PBA, 5, A.

70. A. W. Welton and Porters, statement of sales, July–December 1864, PBA, 5, A.

71. Letter from A. W. Welton and Porters, 23 January 1865, PBA, 5, B.

72. Letter from E. Ivins Co., 5 January 1865; letters from A. W. Welton and Porters, 7 January (two short quotations) and 11 January (three long quotations) 1865, PBA, 5, B. Ivins's letter admitted that he wanted the zinc for buttons, but apparently in an afterthought, he inserted the word *suspender* (using a caret) before the word *buttons.*

73. Copy of letter from A. Platt and Sons to E. Ivins, 14 January 1865, PBA, 5, B. Filed with this copy, there is also a draft of another letter to Ivins that was not sent, including the following passage: "Our rolling works failed but we have the rolls going again today." It demonstrates something of the anguish Clark must have felt in claiming a breakdown—he could not do it without adding that they had corrected the problem. Realizing that by hedging he defeated the purpose of the claim, he wrote the letter that was then sent. Shop output in "Account of Tent Buttons Shipped," January 1865, PBA, 4, Y.

74. Letters from A. W. Welton and Porters, 8, 11 February (telegram and letter), 22 February, 8 and 15 March, 18 April, and 24 May 1865; all in PBA, 5, B; "Account of Tent Buttons Shipped," 1865, and A. W. Welton and Porters, statement of sales, January–June 1865, PBA, 4, Y.

75. Letter from A. W. Welton and Porters, 24 May 1865, PBA, 5, B. Benedict tax returns in Mattatuck Museum Archives, Series M-12, Box 2, Folder C.

4. *"For Purposes of Experiment" (pp. 110–131)*

1. Joseph Anderson, ed., *The Town and City of Waterbury, Connecticut, from the Aboriginal Period to the Year Eighteen Hundred and Ninety-five* (New Haven, Conn., 1896), 2:246; Mattatuck Museum Archives, Personal Papers, Box 1, Folder D.

2. Letters from A. W. Welton and Porters, 21 and 23 March 1865, PBA, 5, B.

3. Letters from A. W. Welton and Porters, 20 February, 17 and 23 March, 25 May, 12 June 1865; all in PBA, 5, B.

4. Letters from A. W. Welton and Porters, 2, 6, 18, and 26 May ("night work"), 31 May 1865; all in PBA, 5, B.

5. Letters from A. W. Welton and Porters, 18 May, 28 June, 8, 10, 13–18, 20, and 29 July, 2, 8, 21, and 23–24 August, 2 and 16 September, 13–14, 19, and 24–27 October, 3, 11, 20, and 25 November 1865, PBA, 5, B. A. W. Welton and Porters, statement of account, 31 December 1865, PBA, 4, Y.

6. The Porters reported on three new competitors in postwar 1865: Goddard Brothers of New York, and Maltby and Norton and U.S. Button Co., both of Waterbury; letters of 31 May, 24 August, and 22 September 1865; PBA, 5, B. Prior zinc orders from all three or their direct predecessors in PBA, 4, J; 4, S; 5, R.

7. Dwight Porter, ed., "The Water Power of the Region Tributary to Long Island Sound," in 10th Census, *Reports on the Water Power of the United States,* pt. 1 (Washington, D.C., 1885), 150; new press, bill from Edward Brown (successor to Waterbury Mach. Co., 27 October 1865, PBA 5, R; small presses, bill from John Whitlock for shafting and 12 pulleys, 16 November 1865, PBA, 5, R.

8. Receipt for dial press from Edward Brown, 27 October 1865, PBA, 5, R. The full details of the Platts' change in processes are not available. In general, the extraordinary innovations in metal forming made in the Naugatuck Valley during the last third of the nineteenth century remain substantially undocumented. Joseph Wickham Roe in his *English and American Tool Builders* (New Haven, Conn., 1916), 231–37, noted: "Much of this machinery has never been made public." This proprietary approach is evident in advertisements of the machine-building shops, such as Waterbury's Blake and Johnson: "Builders of Machinery from Drawings or Models When Requested, *In Strict Confidence,*" in *Waterbury Directory,* 1882, ix. The Platts patented their product designs, as will be seen below, but kept their production innovations to themselves, resulting in this intriguing entry in the appraisal of Alfred's estate: "improvements in machinery kept secret and not patented." See *Platt v. Platt,* supplementary documentation, 19.

9. Diemaking receipts in PBA, 5, C, and charges in Porter Brothers semiannual account with A. Platt and Sons, PBA, 5, B; delays due to lack of machinist in letters from Porter Brothers, 14, 16, 23 September and 19 October 1865, PBA, 5, B.

10. Letter from Porter Brothers, 26 June 1865, PBA, 5, R. The Reed button is an ancestor of the riveted buttons found today on most blue jeans.

11. Letter from Porter Brothers, 26 June 1865, PBA, 5, R.

12. Letters from William H. Reed, 12 and 19 July and 20 August 1865; PBA, 5, R. The Porters expressed their lack of concern with direct ordering by Reed in a letter of 5 February 1866; PBA, 5, C.

13. Letters from Lemuel Serrell, 6 and 28 October 1865, Mattatuck Museum Archives, Series M-5, Box 3, Folder MM. Patent No. 56,261, *Annual Report of the Commissioner of Patents, 1866* (Washington, D.C., 1867) 1:944; engraving on 3:574.

14. Letters from William H. Reed, 26 and 28 June, 7, 13, 14, and 23–25 July 1866, Mattatuck Museum Archives, Series II, Box 3, Folder LL; subsequent hub adjustments in letters from Reed, 31 December 1866, 19 January and 16 February 1866, PBA, 10, B.

15. Letter from William H. Reed, 28 June 1866, Mattatuck Museum Archives, Series II, Box 3, Folder LL.

16. Letters from Porter Brothers, 1 November 1865 (PBA, 5, B) and 5 February 1866 (quoted words), (PBA, 5, C).

17. License for use of Charles Johnson's patent on four new presses, 29 March 1866, PBA, 7, O; Blake and Johnson's accomplishments in the mechanization of precision metal-forming included furnishing equipment to the U.S. Mint and the Royal Mint of Great Britain and providing seventy presses and other machines to the U.S. Arsenal at Frankford, Pennsylvania, for the first large-scale production of brass rifle cartridges, see Anderson, *Town and City,* 2:406–7. Letter from Porter Brothers on use of scrap, 5 May 1866, PBA, 5, C. To make room for the Blake and Johnson presses, in February 1866 the Platts sold an old "drop press" to F. W. Willard Co. of New York, PBA, 5, S.

18. Letter from William H. Reed, 2 September 1866, PBA, 10, B.

19. Letters and monthly account statements from Porter Brothers, 7, 10, and 17 February, 3, 5, 19, and 31 March, 4, 21, and 24 April, 7, 12, 14, 18, and 30 May, 4, 6, and 16 June, 3 July, and 31 December 1866; 3 and 9 January and 7 February 1867; all in PBA, 5, C. The last-cited letter is the latest surviving piece of correspondence from Porter Brothers; the rest either perished in the 1955 flood or were discarded when a new ledger system began in 1868. U.S. Patent Button sales for December 1866 in account letters from William H. Reed, 25 January and 5 February 1867, PBA, 10, B. Receipts for shells from Thomas Manufacturing, 1866–1867, in PBA, 5, T, and 6, U; Lane account in A. Platt and Sons Ledger, 1868–1877, 16.

20. A. Platt and Sons Ledger, 1868–1877, 16, 48; receipt for Pratt and Whitney lathe and chuck, PBA, 6, U. The Kirk and Welton account notes only some $200 paid for "presses," which would have bought five to ten of these simple machines, depending on attachments. On power transmission equipment, John Whitlock of Birmingham, Connecticut, billed $183.72 for shafting, hangers, oilers, and pulleys to power six machines; PBA, 7, O.

21. WLR, 79:61 (1866), and 76:462–64 (1867). The other fast-growing industrial district was around Benedict and Burnham's plant in the south end, where South Main Street crossed the Mad River.

22. Letter from Porter Brothers, 13 January 1866, PBA, 5, C; description of Lane's property in WLR, 80:426–29 (1869).

23. WLR, 82:301 (1869), Library Fund loan to Lane; WLR, 74:423–30 (1864), Lane's purchase of property (sale price, p. 424).

24. Factory purchase, including Kirk lease, in WLR, 80:426–29 (1869). Though there is no mention of cash payment to Lane in the deed, it seems unlikely that Lane would accept only $10,000 for property he paid $15,000 for five years earlier; perhaps duress did force him to discount the property, but the whole story died with the principals to this transaction. Lane's assignment of notes to Library Fund in WLR, 92:356 (1874); power lease in WLR, 80:430–32 (1869); rents in A. Platt and Sons Ledger, 1868–1877, 16, 48. On Lane's subsequent career see Anderson, *Town and City*, 2:373–74.

25. Retirement of the 1856 mortgage in WLR, 77:64 (1865); account of brick shop construction in Alfred Platt Ledger No. 2, p. 132.

26. Letters from William H. Reed, 21 February 1867 and 4 August 1868; A. Platt and Sons Ledger, 1868–1877, 14, 34, 35.

27. A. Platt and Sons Ledger, 1868–1877, 30, 44 (Porter Brothers), 34–35 (U.S. Patent Button); Clark Platt to U.S. Patent Button, 13 January 1870, Mattatuck Museum Archives, Series II, Box 3, Folder NN.

28. Patent nos. 118,640 (rivet) and 118,743 (machine), in *Annual Report of the Commissioner of Patents, 1871* (Washington, D.C., 1876), vol. 3, unpaginated (patents are listed in numerical order). A. Platt and Sons Ledger, 1868–1877: quoted words on p. 30 and reduced commissions (calculated by the author) on pp. 63, 70, 71, 92, 93, 104.

29. A. Platt and Sons Ledger, 1868–1877, 48, 79 (Kirk); 30, 38, 44, 45 (Porter Brothers); 39, 115 (Benedict and Burnham); 41, 131 (Brown and Brothers); 3, 50, 67 (Waterbury Brass). Press "for making Patent Buttons" from 1876 inventory of equipment held by Clark and William, the surviving partners of A. Platt and Sons, PBA, 2, K.

30. A. Platt and Sons Ledger, 1868–1877, 79 (Kirk), and 63, 70, 71, 92, 93, 104 (Porter Brothers, with capital investment calculated by the author).

31. A. Platt and Sons Ledger, 1868–1877, 63, 70, 71, 92, 93, 104.

32. It is impossible to determine with any precision how much rolled zinc went into the firm's own buttons because the Platts kept no comprehensive financial records before 1876. The court decision on the distribution of Alfred's estate included an estimate that the rolling mill produced about $10,000 worth of metal annually, which substantially exceeded the total sales to external customers; see *Platt v. Platt*, 333. External sales have been reconstructed to the extent possible from the customers' letters to the Platts and their accounts in A. Platt and Sons Ledger, 1868–1877, as follows. Goddard Brothers: letters, 1860–1864, PBA, 4, J, and 5, R; Ledger, 19. G. H. Smith: letters, 1855–1866, PBA, 4, V; letters from Smith's New York agent, Merrill and Co., 1862–1866, PBA, 4, O; Ledger, 22, 54. Newell Brothers (and its predecessor D. Chandler and Co.): letters, 1856–1866, PBA, 4, Q; Ledger, 11, 40, 56, 73, 88, 106, 120, 150. Giershofer, Leowi and Co.: letters, 1857–1866, PBA, 4, I; Ledger, 17, 76. Bridgeport Button Co., letters, 1866–1867, PBA, 5, R; Ledger, 24, 103, 143. U.S. Button Co. (and its predecessor E. Robinson and Sons): letters, 1858–1865, PBA, 4, S; Ledger, 36, 37, 130.

33. General makeup of the zinc supply in letter from Porter Brothers, 11 October 1865, PBA, 5, B; "Tough metal" in letter to customer, Beardsley and Richmond, 9 March 1863, PBA, 5, P.

34. A. Platt and Sons Ledger, 1868–1877, 44, 49, 55, 64, 116, 139 (Carrington); 37, 51, 52, 65, 72, 84, 95, 112, 157 (American Ring); Anderson, *Town and City*, 2:436. 438; Henry Bronson, *The History of Waterbury, Connecticut* (Waterbury, Conn., 1858), 562.

35. A. Platt and Sons Ledger, 1868–1877, 37, 51, 52, 65, 72, 84, 95, 112, 157 (American Ring); 119 (American Suspender); 58, 97, 132 (Matthews and Stanley). *Shells* originally referred to button fronts. *Eyelets* originally referred to parts made, like shells, by a sequence of press operations, but eyelets generally had a concentric hole. The two terms became synonymous by the end of the nineteenth century, united by their manufacture on an "eyelet machine," on which more below.

36. Total net income from *Platt v. Platt*, supplementary documentation, 18; dividends and dates in Alfred Platt Ledger No. 2, pp. 131–32. It is not possible to determine total net before 1868, when the firm unified its accounting.

37. The pattern of entries Daybook No. 6 indicates that Platt stayed very busy overseeing farm chores until a year before his death in 1872, if not hard at work himself. The hat, the size of which indicates Platt's diminutive stature, is in the possession of Platt's great-great-grandson, Orton P. Camp, Jr.

38. On west-bank land and who worked it, see WLR, 89:634–37 (1876), partial distribution of Platt's estate to Charles and Fannie Platt Russell and to Wilson and Margaret Platt Osborn. On what Platt did with his money, see his Estate Inventory in Administrative Account, Waterbury Probate Records, 30:270, 277–80.

39. Letters from Porter Brothers, 1865–1867, PBA, 1, PP; 4, W; and 5, B; William Platt probate inventory, 1886, in Waterbury Probate Records, 44:567–70; mortgages in WLR, 78:413 (1866), 82:258 (1869), 81:408 (1869), 81:409 (1869), 81:58 (1869), 86:543 (1872), 83:562 (1872), 87:581 (1872).

40. Clark's Meadow Street purchase in WLR, 79:225 (1867), and his change of address from Platts Mills to Meadow Street in *Waterbury Directory*, 1868, 82. William's purchase of Clark's house in WLR, 79:334 (1867), and his lease of old house in A. Platt and Sons Ledger, 1868–1877, 154. Purchase of Matthews farm in WLR, 79:461 (1867).

41. WLR, 81:332 (1869).

42. Legrand Platt Daybook, 1862–1869, PBA, 3–20, 66, 99, 128, 145–51, 182, 184,

243–47, 266, 270–73, 288; A. Platt and Sons Ledger, 6, 81; 1870 Manufacturing Census Mss., 643 (net income for gristmill).

43. Alfred Platt Will, Waterbury Probate Records, file no. 6500, microfilm at CSL.

44. All of the petitions, briefs, and decisions regarding settlement of the estate are in *Platt v. Platt,* 330–47, and the accompanying supplementary documentation, which is separately paginated as 1–28; quotation in supplementary documentation, 15.

45. Appraisals in *Platt v. Platt,* 331 (total estate), 334 (A. Platt and Sons); dividends in A. Platt and Sons Ledger, 1868–1877, 154–55; estate distribution in WLR, 89:634–37 (1876).

46. WLR, 89:634–37 (1876); WLR, 109:323–26 (1884); *Waterbury Directory,* 1882–1895, passim.; Anderson, *Town and City,* 2:397.

47. Anderson, *Town and City,* 2:396.

48. Ibid.; William J. Pape, *History of Waterbury and the Naugatuck Valley, Connecticut* (New York, 1918), 2:90, 3:390. Helen's reminiscence was reported by her grandson, Orton P. Camp, Jr., interview with the author, 7 July 1987.

49. *Waterbury Directory,* 1873, 41 (Camp), 70 (Hart), 105 (Porter); Pape, *History of Waterbury,* 3:376 (Hart); Anderson, *Town and City,* 2:293–94 (Camp).

50. Articles of Incorporation and Bylaws for The Platt Brothers and Co., PBA, 2, J; for Patent Button Co., PBA, 10, C. Original stock issues in Platt Brothers and Co. Daybook, 1876–1880, 1, and Patent Button Co. Daybook, 1876–1886, 1. All of the shares of both companies had a nominal value of $25 and the stockholders all gave the respective companies demand notes in return for the value of their holdings; these notes were never collected.

5. Small Business in the Gilded Age (pp. 132–164)

1. Minute Book of Patent Button Co., Directors' Meetings, 1876–1913, 17–18. Patent Button Co. Journal, 1876–1886, 33, III, 127.

2. On the changes in the garment industry in the late nineteenth century, see David Montgomery, *The Fall of the House of Labor* (Cambridge, 1987), 117–23.

3. Platt Brothers and Co. Ledger, 1876–1884, 187, 208, 210; 1884–1897, 430–36; 1898–1902, 376–78.

4. Machinery appraisal in *Platt v. Platt,* supplementary documentation, 25–27. For a full technical description of eyelet machines, see Frank W. Wilson, ed., *Tool Engineers Handbook,* 2nd ed. (New York, 1959), secs. 56–15 and 57–31.

5. Platt Brothers and Co. Ledger, 1876–1882, 156; Platt Brothers and Co. Journal, 1876–1880, 8–11, 13–15, 18–20, 24–27, 30–32, 36, 38, 40, 41, 43, 44, 47, 50, 51, 55, 61, 63, 67, 68, 71. In sharing the cost of insurance on the machinery (Journal, 9), twelve twenty-sevenths went to Patent Button and fifteen twenty-sevenths to Platt Brothers.

6. Patent Button Co. Journal, 1876–1886, 28, 30; Platt Brothers and Co. Journal, 1876–1880, 67.

7. Platt Brothers and Co. Ledger, 1876–1882, 41, 85, 86, 197, 260; Journal, 1876–1880, 348; Ledger, 1884–1897, 120–22. On the products of Waterbury machine-builders, see Matthew Roth, *Connecticut: An Inventory of Historic Engineering and Industrial Sites* (Washington, D.C., 1981), 170.

8. Platt Brothers and Co., Ledger, 1876–1882, 41, 85, 86, 197, 260; Journal, 1876–1880, 348; Ledger, 1884–1897, 120–22; Ledger, 1909–1912, 6; Directors' Minutes, 1:169–81.

9. 1880 Manufacturing Census Mss., 457; *Waterbury Directory, 1886,* passim.

10. Wages in 1880 Manufacturing Census, 457–61; *Waterbury Directory, 1886,* passim; job passing among Irish employees in interview with Orton P. Camp, Jr., transcript in PBA.

11. Rivet and burr patents in *Report of the Commissioner of Patents,* 1880, no. 229,459; 1881, no. 249,255; and 1886, no. 343,848. On Patent Button's metal consumption in this period: Platt Brothers and Co. Ledger, 1876–1882, 156–59, 176.

12. Platt Brothers Ledger, 1876–1882, 237; Platt Brothers Journal, 1876–1880, 2; Patent Button Journal, 1876–1886, 2–3. The estate valuation of the partnership appears reliable, as the appraisers were machine builders William Brown (Edward Brown and Co.), Franklin Farrel (Farrel Foundry and Machine), and John Isbell (Naugatuck Machine Co.), all of whom had provided equipment to the business during Alfred's lifetime (*Platt. v. Platt,* supplementary documentation, 28). Nor does it seem likely that Clark and William would have countenanced an inaccurately high appraisal because it would have cost them money in the distribution of the estate. William Platt's discounted valuation for asset transfer in PBA, 2, K.

13. Platt Brothers Ledger, 1876–1882, 2; Platt Brothers Journal, 1876–1880, 7–11, 13, 14, 18, 20–22, 27, 36, 40, 45, 51, 64, 68, 71, 72, 74, 76, 80, 81; Platt Brothers Inventory Book, 1876–1900, 3–5.

14. Platt Brothers and Co. Ledger, 1876–1882, 25–26 (cash account) and 156–59, 176 (Patent Button account); 1880 Manufacturing Census Mss., 457.

15. Platt Brothers and Co. Ledger, 1876–1882, and Journal, 1876–1880.

16. The percentages in Table 3 are based on several calculations. First, from the total annual dollar value of purchases for each metal were subtracted the year-end inventory value of metal not worked and the value of resales to Patent Button; the resulting figure thus included the value of metal in manufactured goods shipped and invoiced as well as the value of metal in the inventory of manufactured goods unshipped or shipped but not yet invoiced. This calculation gives the value of metal actually worked, excluding stockpiles the company built up to take advantage of fluctuations in raw material cost. Second, for each year an average cost per pound of each metal was derived, using the first purchase for each quarter that exceeded $100. Third, the average cost per pound was divided into the value of metal worked to arrive at the number of pounds of each metal that went through the shop. The percentages in the table are based on these weights. See Platt Brothers and Co. Ledger, 1876–1882, 13–15, 44, 67 (brass account), 96–100, 125–26 (tinplate), and 46–49, 143, 145 (zinc).

17. Platt Brothers and Co. Ledger, 1876–1882, 23, 122, 160, 162, 165, 198, 200, 224, 239, 252; Platt Brothers and Co. Journal, 1876–1880, 4, 6, 11, 18, 28, 37, 47, 56, 94, 106, 109, 119, 124, 132, 134, 153, 160, 179, 186, 195, 212, 229, 236, 242, 254, 268, 273, 276, 277, 281, 282, 287, 292, 304, 310, 311, 327, 337, 345, 346; zinc prices to Patent Button in Journal, 153–59. Patent Button paid $0.11 in 1878 (all others paid $0.12) and received $.06 for scrap.

18. Platt Brothers and Co. Ledger, 1876–1882, 238, 256; Journal, 1876–1880, 14, 47, 69, 105, 119, 154, 168, 176, 181, 220. On India Rubber Glove, see Roth, *Connecticut,* 163–64.

19. E. A. Anderson, "Physical Metallurgy of Zinc," in C. H. Mathewson, ed., *Zinc: The Science and Technology of the Metal, Its Alloys and Compounds* (New York, 1959), 411–12.

20. On Fletcher Manufacturing, see Lisa C. Fink, *Providence Industrial Sites,* Rhode Island Historic Preservation Commission Report No. P-P-6 (Providence, R.I., 1981), 47; Platt Brothers and Co. Ledger, 1876–1882, 132–33, 135–38; Journal, 1876–1880, 124–26, 129, 131–32, 292–93; Ledger, 1884–1897, 320–24.

21. Platt Brothers and Co. Ledger, 1876–1882, 65, 128, 190, 261; Ledger, 1884–1897, 364–69, 490–91; Adah Hill, James H. Hill & Sons, to Richard Miller, Platt Brothers, 23 March 1981, in Platt Brothers History Notebook No. 3.

22. Platt Brothers and Co. Ledger, 1876–1882, 258, 273; Journal, 1876–1880, 248, 252, 264, 276, 278, 292, 293; *Annual Report of the Commissioner of Patents,* 1882, no. 278,598; 1884, nos. 313,615, 313,616, and 320,684. The customer was Galvano-Faradic Manufacturing Co. of New York, which made machines that treated various afflictions by giving mild shocks to the patient; see *Asher & Adams' Pictorial Album of American Industry* (New York, 1876), 172.

23. Platt Brothers and Co. Ledger, 1876–1882, 214, 220, 222, 259; Journal, 1876–1880, 201, 274.

24. Theodore Marburg, *Small Business in Brass Fabricating: The Smith & Griggs Manufacturing Co. of Waterbury* (New York, 1956), 9; Roth, *Connecticut,* 154–57.

25. Platt Brothers and Co. Ledger, 1876–1882, 217, 241, 243, 250, 255, 256; Platt Brothers and Co. Ledger, 1884–1897, 259, 425, 468, 483.

26. Platt Brothers Ledger, 1876–1882, 185–86, 244; Journal, 1876–1882, 19, 62, 73–74, 80, 100, 117, 122, 164, 173, 184, 186–88, 191–94, 197–99, 200–201, 204, 206–7, 210, 212, 214, 216, 220, 225, 228, 237, 245, 246, 259, 266, 272, 274, 276, 279, 290, 297, 308, 315, 325, 349; Ledger, 1884–1897, 230–31. On Ammidon, *Polk's Baltimore City Directory,* 1884–1910; courtesy of Ann Steele, Assistant Director and Curator, Baltimore Museum of Industry.

27. *Waterbury Directory,* 1886. Also see Reminiscences of Clayton L. Osborne, typescript, 1934, Platt Brothers and Co. Historical Notebook No. 3 (Richard Miller, Vice President—Sales, retired, compiled four notebooks of material from the company vault and miscellaneous files.)

28. Platt Brothers and Co. Journal, 1876–1880, 76, 141, 203.

29. Table 4 is calculated from the Profit and Loss Account for each year in Platt Brothers and Co. Ledger, 1876–1883, 108–9, and Ledger, 1884–1897, 128–31. After 1897 the Profit and Loss Account was kept in a separate ledger that is not part of the Platt Brothers Archive.

30. Patent Button Co., Minute Book of Directors' Meetings, 1876–1913, 23–67.

31. Joseph Anderson, ed. *Town and City of Waterbury, Connecticut, from the Aboriginal Period to the Year Eighteen Hundred and Ninety-five* (New Haven, Conn., 1896), 2: 251–53, quoted words on p. 252.

32. Platt Brothers and Co. Ledger, 1876–1883, 230, 232; Ledger, 1884–1897, 260–61; Journal, 1876–1880, 303; sale of farm in WLR, 110:320 (1884). On the Bristol Co., see Constance McL. Green, *History of Naugatuck, Connecticut* (Naugatuck, Conn., 1948), 217–20, and *Waterbury Directory, 1897,* xxii.

33. WLR, 88:519 (1873), 92:653 (1875), 98:136 (1878), 98:633 (1879), 99:183 (1878), 99:224 (1878), 107:342 (1884), 107:343 (1884), 107:344 (1884); William J. Pape, *History of Waterbury and the Naugatuck Valley, Connecticut* (Chicago, 1918), 2:46, 3:376, 390, 465, 484–86; Anderson, *Town and City,* 2:100.

34. WLR: 101:402 (1880), 103:40 (1881), 103:217 (1881), 104:357 (1884), 105:364 (1882), 105:584 (1882), 105:632 (1883), 114:91 (1885), 114:516 (1886), 115:394 (1887), 115:667 (1887), 118:75 (1887), 118:196 (1887), 118:332 (1887), 118:528 (1888), 118:639 (1888), 120:555 (1888), 123:267 (1889), 124:563 (1890), 128:155 (1890), 128:488 (1892), 129:469

(1892). Malone signed his mortgage deed, WLR, 123:371 (1889), with an *X*; occupations of mortgage borrowers in *Waterbury Directory*, 1876–1899.

35. *National Cyclopedia of American Biography*, s.v. "Lewis Platt."

36. *Waterbury Daily Index*, 30 March 1886; Directors' Minutes, 1:41; factory purchase in WLR, 102:603 (1886).

37. Irving Platt obituary, *Waterbury Republican*, 7 December 1896; *National Cyclopedia of American Biography*, s.v. "Irving Gibbs Platt." Patent Button Director's Minutes, vol. 1, p. 56.

38. *Annual Report of the Commissioner of Patents*, patent nos. 296,216 (1883), 329,336 (1884), 420,828 (1889), 446,466 (1890), 449,698 (1890), and 450,828 (1890).

39. William G. Lathrop, *The Brass Industry in the United States* (Mt. Carmel, Conn., 1926), 122–31; Cecelia F. Bucki, *Metal, Minds and Machines: Waterbury at Work* (Waterbury, Conn., 1980), 22–24, 81; Theodore Marburg, *Small Business in Brass Fabricating: The Smith & Griggs Manufacturing Co. of Waterbury* (New York, 1956), 13, 31.

40. Platt Brothers and Co. Ledger, 1876–1882, 192–95; Journal, 1876–1880, 12, 19, 22, 24, 33, 48, 83, 92, 111, 125, 231, 255, 284, 312, 332; Ledger, 1884–1897, 400–402; Roth, *Connecticut*, 169; WLR, 116:395 (1887). This firm was also known as Matthews and Willard during the 1880s.

41. Patent Button Co., Directors Minutes, 1:70–72.

42. Patent Button Co., Directors Minutes, 1:73–82; quotations on pp. 73, 80.

43. Patent Button Co., Directors Minutes, 1:83–86.

44. U.S. Census, *Bulletin 42: Census of Manufactures, 1905, Connecticut* (Washington, D.C., 1906), 36–37. The other two button firms were Steele & Johnson and Waterbury Button.

45. Platt Brothers and Co. Ledger, 1884–1897, 450, 452, 480.

46. James D. Norris, *AZn: A History of the American Zinc Company* (Madison, Wis., 1968), 3–15; H. D. Carus, "Historical Background," in Champion H. Mathewson, *Zinc: The Science and Technology of the Metal, Its Alloys and Compounds* (New York, 1959), 1–8; Walter R. Ingalls, "The Joplin District," *Engineering and Mining Journal*, 67 (7 January 1899): 20.

47. Norris, *AZn*, 35; Fredric A. Birmingham, *Ball Corporation: The First Century* (Muncie, Ind., 1980), 78.

48. 1879 *Atlas*, plate 11; *Sanborn Map of Waterbury*, 1890, plate 11.

49. WLR, 132:291–94 (1892), 134:213 (1892); Platt Brothers and Co. Ledger, 1884–1897, 156.

50. Bucki, *Metal, Minds and Machines*, 63; Directors' Minutes, 1:39–45.

51. WLR, 134:78 (1892); Platt Brothers and Co. Ledger, 1884–1897, 120.

52. Anderson, *Town and City*, 2:397; Platt Brothers and Co., Directors' Minutes, 1:53; Ledger, 1884–1897, 77.

53. "Plan of Land of The Platt Brothers and Co.," 1905, PBA; Ledger, 1884–1897, 368, 496 ("New Rolling Mill Expense"), 326 (Fletcher); Reminiscences of Howard Hart, Platt Brothers History Notebook No. 1; Westcott and Mapes, Consulting Engineers, "Appraisal of the Water Power Plant of Platt Bros. & Company," 1928, PBA, 3, B. The turbines were all made by Holyoke Machine Co.

54. "Plan of Land of The Platt Brothers and Co.," 1905, PBA; Ledger, 1884–1897, 31 (new fabricating building), 392 (Pratt and Whitney); Reminiscences of Howard Hart, Platt Brothers History Notebook No. 1; Westcott and Mapes, PBA, 3, B.

55. Robert A. Cairns, "Sewage Disposal at Waterbury," *Proceedings of the Connecticut Society of Civil Engineers* (1906), 1–10; Connecticut Superior Court, 3rd Dis-

trict, *Report of the January Term, 1900,* "Platt Brothers v. The City of Waterbury," 1–57, quotations on p. 2; paginated by case.

56. "Platt Brothers v. The City of Waterbury," 10–15, quotations on pp. 13, 14.

57. Cairns, "Sewage Disposal," 7; *Annual Report of the City Engineer of Waterbury,* 1952, 21–25. The sewage case caused Platt Brothers to set another legal precedent by successfully opposing the Internal Revenue Service's claim that the proceeds from the lawsuit were taxable income; see ruling from U.S. Board of Tax Appeals, 1933, PBA, 3, L.

58. Pape, *History of Waterbury,* 3:372, 390; *Waterbury Republican,* obituaries of Jay Hart (3 December 1918) and Wallace Camp (6 June 1924).

59. Patent Button Co., Directors' Minute Book, 1:94.

60. Patent Button Co., Directors' Minutes, 1:95, 119, 192–93; Bucki, *Metal, Minds and Machines,* 28–29; Marburg, *Small Business,* 31–35.

61. Platt Brothers and Co. Ledger, 1909–1912, index to customer accounts; Directors' Minutes, 1:126, 130.

62. Platt Brothers and Co. Directors' Minutes, 1:155–56, and appended typescript report by Wallace Camp, 11 January 1910.

63. Platt Brothers and Co. Directors' Minutes, 1:161–81; Patent Button Co. Directors' Minutes, 1:122–37.

64. Platt Brothers and Co. Directors' Minutes, 1:181; Patent Button Co. Directors' Minutes, 1:123.

65. Patent Button Co. Directors' Minutes, 1:145.

66. Ibid., 156–78.

67. Ibid., 179–80.

68. Ibid., 184–94, quotation on p. 184.

6. "A Pleasant Little Operation" (pp. 165–209)

1. Interview with Orton P. Camp, Jr., 11 May 1989; Platt Brothers and Co. Ledger, 1898–1902, 175–77; "Process of Printing from Zinc Plates," *Metal Industry* 1 (February 1903): 22.

2. Platt Brothers and Co. Cash Book, 1909–1914, 87; Camp interview; Directors Minutes, 2:25–41; Carrie Platt received $18,000 in Platt Brothers dividends for the year 1914.

3. Directors Minutes, 2:44, 64–108; "Trade News," *Metal Industry* 13 (March 1915): 127.

4. Camp interview; interview with Richard Miller, Vice President for Sales (retired), Platt Brothers, 11 May 1989; interview with Milton Grele, President, Platt Brothers, 10 April 1989.

5. Grele interview; Camp interview.

6. L. E. DeForest, ed., *History of the Class of 1912, Yale College, Volume 2: Decennial Record* (Albany, N.Y. 1924), 78–79; *MIT: Alumni/ae Register* (Minneapolis, 1989), 1078; Charles H. Snyder, ed., *Class of 1914-S[heffield], 25 Year Record* (New Haven, Conn., 1940), 60.

7. Camp interview.

8. L. W. Downes, "Electric Fuse Testing," *Electrical World* 61, 8 (22 February 1913): 413; "Important Code Change Suggested," *Electrical World* 61 (15 March 1913): 553–54.

9. The periodical *Electrical World* (hereafter *EW*) provided a regular forum for the lively debate over fuse elements among electricity users, academic researchers, government regulators, insurers, and fuse producers. Besides publishing many technical articles, *EW* weighed in with its own editorials and granted ample space for argument in its letters section. Following are the articles and letters on which this discussion is based, listed chronologically: A. A. Somerville, "Electric Fuse Testing," *EW* 61 (18 January 1913): 123 ff; L. W. Downes, "Letter: Electric Fuse Testing," *EW* 61 (22 February 1913): 413; "Important Code Change Suggested," *EW* 61 (15 March 1913): 553–54; L. B. Buchanan, "Letter: Electric-Fuse Construction," *EW* 61 (15 March 1913): 578–79; Harvey S. Pardee, "Letter: Fuse Economy," *EW* 61 (17 May 1913): 1044–45; C. T. McDonald, (Chief Engineer, Chicago Fuse Manufacturing Company), "Change in the National Electrical Code," *EW* 61 (22 March 1913): 630; "Controversy over Refillable Fuses," *EW* 66 (17 July 1915): 126; Walter Arthur, "Characteristics of Standard Inclosed Fuses," *EW* 69 (10 March 1917): 456–58; Walter Arthur, "Characteristics of Standard Inclosed Fuses—II," *EW* 69 (19 May 1917): 962–63; A. B. Eason, "Open and Inclosed Type Fuses," *EW* 70 (15 September 1917): 533–34; "Assuring Satisfactory Fuse Operation," *EW* 71 (13 April 1918): 763–65; "Improved Renewable Fuse," *EW* 72 (13 July 1918): 90; "Selection of Fuses for Motor-Driven Machines," *EW* 72 (3 August 1918): 208.

10. "Peace vs. War," *Metal Industry* 12 (May 1914): 210.

11. "Spelter—Its Manufacture and Properties," *Metal Industry* 13 (September 1915): 370–71.

12. "The Kinds of Spelter," *Engineering and Mining Journal* (hereafter *E&MJ*) 99 (6 February 1915): 292–93; Platt Brothers and Co., Directors' Minutes, 2:57. The designations of zinc grades have changed since 1915; currently, Special High Grade tops the list, at 99.99 percent pure zinc.

13. James D. Norris, *AZn: A History of the American Zinc Company* (Madison, Wis., 1968), 38, 73; Richard J. Lund, "Review of the Mineral Industry," in U.S. Bureau of Mines, *Minerals Yearbook, 1937* (Washington, D.C., 1937), 14–17; "The Rise in Spelter," *E&MJ* 99 (6 February 1915): 293; untitled editorial ("orgy in spelter") in *E&MJ* 100 (21 August 1915): 326; Platt Brothers and Co., Directors' Minutes, 2:58.

14. Platt Brothers and Co., Ledger, 1909–1914, 178, 186, 202, 228, 251, 322, 349, 393, 436, 441, 445, 445, 451. The uncertainty over total zinc sales in this period is due to the incomplete survival of Platt Brothers and Co., Ledger, 1914–1923, n.p., which was damaged in the flood of 1955. (Starting in 1914 the ledgers consisted of ruled pages in three-ring binders, replacing the bound volumes used previously; from this time forward, only fragments of ledgers survive, though some are substantial if not complete. Subsequent references to ledgers will cite them as "fragments.") Among the Platt customers who published technical articles on fuses were L. W. Downes of D & W Fuse, who wrote one of the most comprehensive treatments of fuse testing in *Transactions of the American Institute of Electrical Engineers*, 28 (1909): 947 ff; and H. E. Clifford of Economy Fuse, who campaigned for rigorous standards of fuse operation, as in "Controversy over Refillable Fuses," *EW* 66 (17 July 1915): 126.

15. E. H. Wolff (General Manager., Illinois Zinc Co.), "The American Sheet-Zinc Industry," *E&MJ* 106 (17 August 1918): 304; Platt Brothers and Co., Directors Minutes, 2:64–108.

16. "Zinc and Its Uses," *E&MJ* 106 (19 October 1918): 705–6; George S. Harney (American Zinc Products Co., Greencastle, Ind.), "New Uses for Zinc," *E&MJ* 108 (19 July 1919): 100–101.

17. Orton P. Camp, Sr., Call Book, 1919, n.p.

18. Platt Brothers and Co., Cash Book, 1918–1923, 75; letters from Hammond Laboratory, 7 September, 15 October 1921, and Bridgeport Brass (conductivity testing), 15 September 1928, PBA, 8, W.

19. Zinc technology correspondence files, 1921–1937, PBA, 8, W; Miller interview.

20. Reminiscences of F. Henry Payne, in letter to Milton Grele, 28 December 1979, Platt Brothers History Notebook No. 2; Grele interview; letters from Whitney Manufacturing Co. (chain drives), 31 December 1928, PBA, 8, C; letter from Waterbury-Farrel re reorder of fuse rolls, 2 February 1937, PBA, 8, D.

21. Payne reminiscences and reminiscences of Clayton Osborne, both in Platt Brothers History Notebook No. 2; *Waterbury Directory*, 1915, 1920, passim.

22. Payne and Osborne reminiscences; Platt Brothers History Notebook No. 2; Directors Minutes, 2:186 (Peaslee).

23. Cecelia F. Bucki, *Metal, Minds and Machines: Waterbury at Work* (Waterbury, Conn., 1980), 77–79 (quotation, p. 78); Jeremy Brecher, Jerry Lombardi, and Ian Stackhouse, *Brass Valley: The Story of Working People's Lives and Struggles in an American Industrial Region* (Philadelphia, 1982), 78–89.

24. Platt Brothers and Co., Cash Book, 1919–1923, 6, 40–44. Though company records and reminiscences yield no direct statement of involvement in the strike of 1920, the drop in payroll for April 1920 was completely anomolous; it was not a seasonal phenomenon, it did not correspond to a fall in orders, and it did not come during any major renovation or installation of new equipment that could have caused short-term production interruptions. Absent any other explanation, the coincidence of the region-wide strike and the falloff in wages at Platt Brothers is too compelling to ignore.

25. "Metal Melting in Electric Furnaces," *Metal Industry* 17 (May 1919): 221–24; "The Manufacture of Brass Sheets and Coils," *Metal Industry* 18 (March 1920): 113–15; William Reuben Webster, "Notes on the History, Manufacture and Properties of Wrought Brass," *Transactions of the Institute of Mining and Metallurgical Engineers: Institute of Metals Division* 147 (1942): 13–27.

26. Miller interview; Payne reminiscences; reminiscences of Merwin Camp (no relation), who later worked in eyelet sales, in Platt Brothers History Notebook No. 2.

27. Payne and Merwin Camp reminiscences, Platt Brothers History Notebook No. 2; Miller interview.

28. Carbon copy of letter from Howard Hart to Diamond Chain and Manufacturing Co., 3 November 1928, PBA, 8, C; Payne reminiscences, Platt Brothers History Notebook No. 2; Grele interview; Miller interview.

29. Orton Camp, Sr., "Fuse Metal Sales Summaries," 1923–1945, copy of manuscript in Platt Brothers History Notebook No. 1; Ledger fragments, 1914–1932.

30. Camp, "Fuse Metal Sales Summaries"; Cash Book, 1923–1929, 66, 100, 133, 161, 194; Payne and Merwin Camp reminiscences; Platt Brothers History Notebook No. 2; Directors Minutes, 2:179, 212.

31. Camp, "Sales Summaries, Japanned Zinc, 1919–1946"; Adah Hill, "James H. Hill and Sons," typescript, 1981, in Platt Brothers History Notebook No. 1; Cash Book, 1918–1923, 133, passim. Hill finally paid off the mortgage in 1944, as noted in Directors Minutes, 3:147.

32. Camp, "Sales Summaries"; Adah Hill. The popularity of celluloid in spite of its higher price can be attributed to the ability to heat-seal it onto the lace with equipment far simpler and less expensive than that used to apply zinc tips; Miller interview.

33. Camp, "Sales Summaries, Zinc Strip Commercial Tolerance," 1921–1945; Ledger 1909–1914, 286, 412; Cash Book, 1923–1929, passim.

34. Payne reminiscence; Platt Bothers History Notebook No. 2; "Slab Zinc Used in Furnaces," record card for daily furnace operation, 5 December 1927, PBA 8, J.

35. Carbon copy of letter from Howard Hart to George P. Reintjes Co. (fire brick), 16 April 1928, PBA, 8, J; Directors Minutes, 2:212.

36. Eugene S. Smith, Jr. (Assistant Superintendent), "Report on the Platt Brothers and Co.," 11 March 1948, 3–4; Grele interview; "The Casting of Zinc Plates," *Metal Industry* 1 (March 1903): 34; carbon copy of letter from Howard Hart to Easton Car and Construction Co. (ball-bearing track), 27 July 1926, PBA, 8, T; calculations and records of experiments for cam and mold angles, October 1934, manuscripts in PBA, 8, S.

37. Young Brothers Co., Detroit, sales order for heating oven, 25 January 1923, and letters from Young Brothers, 12 March and 7 April 1924, all PBA, 8, L; Platt Brothers and Co. Directors Minutes, 14 October 1924, 2:175.

38. "Sales Summaries, Zinc Strip Commercial Tolerance," 1921–1945.

39. Orton P. Camp, Sr., Call Book, n.p.; "Notes on Wire Manufacturing," in Platt Brothers History Notebook No. 1; Cash Book, 1923–1929, 144, 178; Directors Minutes, 2:210. The distinction between "wire" and "rod" has never been explicit. Both are usually round or oval in section (unless another shape is specifically noted). Diameters over a half inch or so are almost always "rod"; under an eighth inch, usually "wire"; in between, the terms are often used interchangeably.

40. "Sales Summaries"; Cash Book, 1923–1929, 177, 187, 191; Ledger fragments, 1929–1933, n.p.

41. Directors Minutes, 2:218–19, 223, 228; letter from Waterbury-Farrel, 9 January 1931, PBA, 8, M.

42. Patent Certificate No. 1,931,001, "Processes and Apparatus for Producing Continuous Zinc Wire," 17 October 1933, PBA, 7, P; Smith, "Report," 11.

43. Camp, "Sales Summaries," in Platt Brothers History Notebook No. 1.

44. Ledger fragments, 1929–1933, 1933–1940.

45. Camp interview; "Voting Trust Agreement Between Amy Hart Trafford *et al.*," 26 December 1924, PBA, 10, H.

46. Camp interview; Waterbury *Directory*, 1925; notice of Purinton's finishing equipment in *Metal Industry* 31 (June 1933): 225.

47. Camp interview; "Developments of Recent Years," in *The Waterbury American*, 18 August 1934.

48. Carley quotation in Connecticut Military Census, Industrial Survey Questionnaire, 1918, Connecticut State Library, Record Group 29, Box 65, file no. 1848; Camp interview.

49. Camp interview; interview with Curtiss V. Hart, Secretary-Treasurer (retired), Platt Brothers and Co., 11 April 1989.

50. Camp interview; "Agreement to Terminate Voting Trust Agreement Dated December 26, 1924," 25 April 1946, PBA, 10, J.

51. Ledger, 1909–1914, 86–88; "Securities Account" and "Interest Account" in Ledger fragments, 1914–1933, n.p.

52. Directors Minutes, 2:151–214; "Securities Account" in Ledger fragments, 1914–1933, n.p.

53. Directors Minutes, 2:151–214; "Cash Discounts" and "Securities Account" in Ledger fragments, 1914–1933, n.p.

54. Directors Minutes, 2:223–30; "Labor Account," in Ledger fragments, 1914–1933, n.p.

55. Directors Minutes, 2:231–38; "Labor Account," in Ledger fragments, 1914–1933, n.p.

56. Camp interview.

57. Directors Minutes, 2:246.

58. Camp interview; Grele interview.

59. Directors Minutes, 2:238–46.

60. Howard P. Hart, "Resume of Rolling Experiments," 27 October 1933, type-script, PBA, 8, M; Grele interview; "Notes on Wire Manufacture," Platt Brothers History Notebook No. 1.

61. Directors Minutes, 3:1–35.

62. Ibid., 35–43.

63. Ibid., 35–45, 47–59.

64. Brecher et al., *Brass Valley,* 157–66; "Group Insurance" account in Ledger fragments, 1933–1940, n.p.; Directors Minutes, 3:45, 53; Orton Camp, Jr., interview; Orton Camp, Sr., obituary in *Waterbury Republican,* 13 August 1976.

65. Brecher et al., *Brass Valley,* 158; Camp interview.

66. Directors Minutes, 3:61–83; besides finer increments in diameter, the new wire machine could produce both bright and dull finishes, whereas the Morgan machine only made dull finishes.

67. Ledger fragments, 1941–1948; "Sales Summaries," Platt Brothers History Notebook No. 1; Bruce Clouette and Matthew Roth, *Bristol, Connecticut, 1785–1985* (Canaan, N.H., 1985), 226, 251–53; Camp interview.

68. Directors Minutes, 3:85–105.

69. Ibid., 125–27; Camp interview.

70. Waterbury *Directory,* 1940–1950; *Waterbury Republican,* 25 May 1940 and 13 August 1976 (Camp obituary); Miller interview. The Tax Payers Association was later absorbed into the Chamber of Commerce and had no relation to the Taxpayers Association of the 1970s.

71. Merwin Camp reminiscences, Platt Brothers History Notebook No. 2; Miller interview ("sortie"); "Eyelet Sales" and "Zinc Wire Sales" in Ledger fragments, 1941–1948; Directors Minutes, 3:162.

72. Directors Minutes, 3:154; Hart clipping file in "Zinc Technology" folder, PBA, 8, W; U.S. Bureau of Standards, "Protective Metallic Coatings," Circular No. 80, 1947; "Profit and Loss" account in Ledger fragments, 1941–1948, 1949–1954, n.p.; Directors Minutes, 3:165–93, 4:1–28.

73. "Income" accounts, in Ledger fragments, 1949–1954; Directors Minutes, 3:191, 4:16; Grele interview.

74. Grele interview.

75. Grele interview.

76. Directors Minutes, 4:32–33.

77. Hart interview; Merwin Camp reminiscences; *Waterbury Reublican,* 19 and 23 August 1955.

78. Hart interview; Camp interview; Directors Minutes, 4:34.

79. Camp interview; Directors Minutes, 4:35–38.

80. Grele interview; Directors Minutes, 4:37.

81. Miller interview; Camp interview.

82. Directors Minutes, 4:41–57; General Journal Entries, 1952–1959, n.p.

83. Miller interview.

84. Miller interview; Directors Minutes, 4:57–71; General Journal Entries, 1952–1959, n.p.

85. Grele interview; Miller interview.

86. Miller interview; Directors Minutes, 4:91.

87. Miller interview; Grele interview.

88. Directors Minutes, 4:63, 78, 79–106.

89. Directors Minutes, 4:108–22.

90. Camp interview; "Profit and Loss" account in Ledger fragments, 1941–1948, 1949–1954, n.p.

91. Camp interview; Waterbury *Directory,* 1969, 277.

92. Miller interview; Grele interview; ASARCO purchase order nos. 3934 and 4076, 1975, Platt Brothers History Notebook No. 4; "The Alaska Pipeline Moves Over the Hump," *Iron Age,* 7 July 1975; Directors Minutes, 5:161–68.

93. Grele interview; Miller interview.

94. Grele interview; Miller interview. The method of making the groove is still closely guarded.

95. Grele interview; Miller interview.

96. Directors Minutes, 5:148; Grele interview.

97. Grele interview.

Epilogue (pp. 210–214)

1. Philip Scranton, "Diversity in Diversity: Flexible Production and American Industrialization, 1880–1930," *Business History Review* 65 (Spring 1991): 90.

2. Ibid., 86–88.

3. Charles K. Hyde, *Detroit: An Industrial History Guide* (Detroit, 1980), unpaginated.

4. Matthew Roth, *Connecticut: An Inventory of Historic Engineering and Industrial Sites,* xxv–xxvi, 178–79, 240–46.

5. *Wall Street Journal,* 14 December 1992, 1.

6. Cecelia F. Bucki, *Metal, Minds and Machines: Waterbury at Work* (Waterbury, Conn., 1980), 75–80; Roth, *Connecticut,* xxv, 47, 154–55; Bruce Clouette and Matthew Roth, *Bristol, Connecticut, 1785–1985* (Canaan, N.H., 1985), 251–52, 257.

7. Seymour Melman, "Characteristics of the Industrial Conversion Problem," in Melman, ed., *The Defense Economy: Conversion of Industries and Occupations to Civilian Needs* (New York, 1970), 9–10.

8. Seymour Melman, "Firms without Enterprise," in Melman, ed., *The War Economy of the United States: Readings in Military Industry and Economy* (New York, 1971), 71–76.

Index

Waterbury National Bank, 199–200
Waterbury Savings Bank, 76–77
Waterbury Tax Payers Association, 194
Waterbury Traction Co., 155
Watertown, Conn., 58, 61
Welch, Patrick, 70
Welton, A. W., and Porters Co., 80–82, 86
Welton, Arad W., 36–37, 60, 91, 102
Welton, J. C., 61–66, 72–73, 77, 80, 148
Westinghouse Electric and Manufacturing
 Co., 170
West Stockbridge, Mass., 52, 69, 77
Wheeler, E. S., and Co., 73, 87–88, 139
White, Frank, 149
wire production, 27–28, 42, 53, 180–82, 195–
 98, 202–203
Wolcott, Oliver, Jr., 32
Wooster, David, 27–28

Wooster, Ev, 173–74, 200
Wooster, Jesse, 33
World War I, 18, 166–69
World War II, 167, 185, 193–94, 213

Yale University, 34, 42, 51, 129, 168, 185, 196
Yankee peddlers, 2, 34

zinc, 7, 50, 80, 99, 139, 165–66, 183; buttons,
 58, 90, 92, 99, 114; component of brass,
 36, 56; fuse elements, 168–73; markets, 59,
 96, 121–22, 171; pipe, 74, 80–81, 84; price,
 111, 153–54, 170–71; primary processing, 8,
 57, 71–72, 103, 107, 112, 121–22, 154, 172–73,
 178–80; properties of, 57, 74, 140, 142, 161,
 168–69; quality, 122, 169–72; supply, 103,
 111, 122, 153–54, 170–71; tent buttons, 83,
 99, 106–109; weatherstripping, 74

UNIVERSITY PRESS OF NEW ENGLAND

publishes books under its own imprint and is the publisher for Brandeis University Press, Brown University Press, University of Connecticut, Dartmouth College, Middlebury College Press, University of New Hampshire, University of Rhode Island, Tufts University, University of Vermont, and Wesleyan University Press.

LIBRARY OF CONGRESS CATALOGING-IN-PUBLICATION DATA
Roth, Matthew W.
    Platt Brothers and Company : small business in American manufacturing /
    Matthew W. Roth.
        p.   cm.
    Includes bibliographical references and index.
    ISBN 0-87451-654-4
    1. Platt Brothers and Company—History.   2. United States—
    Manufactures—History.   I. Title.
    HD9729.P58R68   1993
    338.7'671'097467—dc20   93-11001
    ∞